CONFRONTING THE BOMB

CONFRONTING
THE BOMB

A Short History

of the

World Nuclear

Disarmament

Movement

LAWRENCE S. WITTNER

STANFORD UNIVERSITY PRESS

Stanford, California 2009

Stanford University Press
Stanford, California

Library of Congress Cataloging-in-Publication Data

Wittner, Lawrence S.
   Confronting the bomb : a short history of the world nuclear
disarmament movement / Lawrence S. Wittner.
       p.   cm. — (Stanford nuclear age series)
   Includes index.
   ISBN 978-0-8047-5631-0 (cloth : alk. paper) —
   ISBN 978-0-8047-5632-7 (pbk. : alk. paper)
       1. Antinuclear movement—History.   2. Nuclear disarmament—
History.   I. Title.   II. Series: Stanford nuclear age series.
JZ5574.W58   2009
327.1'74706—dc22

                                                                2008055822

Printed in the United States of America on acid-free, archival-quality paper

Typeset at Stanford University Press in 10/14 Minion

To MERLE CURTI, *who*
launched me on this journey long ago

The Stanford Nuclear Age Series

Conceived by scientists, delivered by the military, and adopted by policymakers, nuclear weapons emerged from the ashes of Hiroshima and Nagasaki to dominate our time. The politics, diplomacy, economy, and culture of the Cold War nurtured the nuclear arms race and, in turn have been altered by it. "We have had the bomb on our minds since 1945," E. L. Doctorow observes. "It was first our weaponry and then our diplomacy, and now it's our economy. How can we suppose that something so monstrously powerful would not, after forty years, compose our identity? The great golem we have made against our enemies is our culture, our bomb culture—its logic, its faith, its vision."

The pervasive, transformative potential of nuclear weapons was foreseen by their creators. When Secretary of War Henry L. Stimson assembled a committee in May 1945 to discuss postwar atomic energy planning, he spoke of the atomic bomb as a "revolutionary change in the relations of man to the universe." Believing that it could mean "the doom of civilization," he warned President Truman that this weapon "has placed a certain moral responsibility upon us which we cannot shirk without very serious responsibility for any disaster to civilization."

In the decades since World War II that responsibility has weighed heavily on American civilization. Whether or not we have met it is a matter of heated debate. But that we must meet it, and, moreover, that we must also prepare the next generation of leaders to meet it as well, is beyond question.

Today, over half a century into the nuclear age the pervasive impact of the nuclear arms race has stimulated a fundamental reevaluation of the role of nuclear armaments and strategic policies. But mainstream scholarly work in strategic studies has tended to focus on questions related to the developments, the deployment, and the diplomacy of nuclear arsenals. Such an exclusively managerial focus cannot probe the universal revolutionary changes about which Stimson spoke, and the need to address these changes is urgent. If the academic community is to contribute imaginatively and helpfully to the increasingly complex problems of the nuclear age, then the base of scholarship and pedagogy in the national security–arms control field must be broadened. It is this goal that the Stanford Nuclear Age Series is intended to support, with paperback reissues of important out-of-print works and original publication of new scholarship in the humanities and social sciences.

Martin J. Sherwin
General Editor

Contents

Preface

How should we account for the fact that, since 1945, the world has avoided nuclear war? After all, a nation that has developed weapons generally uses them in its wars. For example, immediately after the U.S. government succeeded in building atomic bombs, it used them to destroy Japanese cities. Furthermore, a nation that has devoted vast resources to developing weapons does not usually get rid of them—at least until it develops more powerful weapons.

But, since August 1945, no nation has used nuclear weapons to attack another, and only a relatively small number of nations have chosen to build them. Also, those nations that have developed nuclear weapons have gravitated toward nuclear arms control and disarmament measures: a Partial Test Ban Treaty; Strategic Arms Limitation Treaties; Strategic Arms Reduction Treaties; and a Comprehensive Test Ban Treaty. Why have they adopted these policies of nuclear restraint?

The conventional explanation is that the danger posed by nuclear weapons has "deterred" nations from waging nuclear war and, overall, has created a situation of nuclear safety. In the words of its proponents, there has been "peace through strength." But this explanation fails to account for some important developments. Since 1945, nuclear powers have not waged nuclear war against non-nuclear powers. Sometimes, in their confrontation with non-nuclear powers, they have suffered military defeat rather than resort to nuclear war. Why? Moreover, if nuclear deterrence works, why bother with nuclear arms control and disarmament treaties? Why worry about nuclear proliferation? Why not simply build, test, and deploy nuclear weapons, free of international constraints?

These unanswered questions alert us to the fact that something is missing from the conventional explanation.

This book argues that the missing ingredient is a massive nuclear disarmament movement—one that has mobilized millions of people in nations around the globe and, thereby, saved the world from nuclear war. It suggests that omitting this nuclear disarmament campaign from explanations of nuclear restraint makes about as much sense as omitting the U.S. civil rights movement from explanations for the collapse of racial segregation and discrimination.

Although the case for this explanation is presented briefly in this book, it is laid out in far greater detail in a scholarly trilogy of mine, *The Struggle Against the Bomb.* The first volume, *One World or None,* carries the story of the movement and its impact through 1953. The second volume, *Resisting the Bomb,* examines these items from 1954 to 1970. And the third volume, *Toward Nuclear Abolition,* chronicles movement activism and response from 1971 to the present. Collectively, these three books run almost 1,800 pages and contain thousands of footnotes. They are based on very extensive research in the files of disarmament organizations and in formerly secret government records, interviews with a broad range of antinuclear activists and government officials, and numerous memoirs, periodicals, and other published materials. Therefore, readers desiring a fuller account of the world nuclear disarmament movement than provided by this book, plus a listing of the many sources upon which it rests, are urged to consult these three hefty volumes.

When I began this project some two decades ago, I believed that the worldwide struggle against nuclear weapons had been ineffectual. After all, I thought, the Bomb has not been banned. But as I plunged into the research—and particularly into the previously secret files of the U.S., British, Soviet, and other governments—I began to realize that government officials were not only deeply worried about popular opposition to nuclear policies (or at least *their* nuclear policies!), but were forced to compromise with this public opposition. Thus, although I do not wish to give the impression that the current campaign for nuclear disarmament is all-powerful or will in all circumstances be able to fend off the nuclear ambitions of government officials, I think it is vital for the public to understand what has saved the world from nuclear war in the past—and may do so again in the future.

Finally, let me express my thanks to the many people who have helped me with the task of putting this study together—and particularly to my wife Dorothy, who has never doubted the necessity of building a new and better world.

L.S.W.

Abbreviations Used

ACDA	Arms Control and Disarmament Agency
AEC	Atomic Energy Commission
AFSC	American Friends Service Committee
AMSA	Action Group Against a Swedish Atomic Weapon
ASA	Atomic Scientists' Association
CND	Campaign for Nuclear Disarmament
CNVA	Committee for Nonviolent Action
CODENE	Committee for Nuclear Disarmament in Europe
CPD	Committee on the Present Danger
CSS	Committee of Soviet Scientists for Peace and Against the Nuclear Threat
CTBT	Comprehensive Test Ban Treaty
END	European Nuclear Disarmament
FAS	Federation of American Scientists
FOR	Fellowship of Reconciliation
Freeze	Nuclear Weapons Freeze Campaign
ICDP	International Confederation for Disarmament and Peace
IKV	Interchurch Peace Council
INF	Intermediate-Range Nuclear Forces
IPB	International Peace Bureau
IPPNW	International Physicians for the Prevention of Nuclear War
KOR	Workers Defense Committee
KOS	Committee for Social Resistance
MAUM	Movement Against Uranium Mining
MCAA	Movement Against Atomic Armaments
NCANWT	National Council for the Abolition of Nuclear Weapon Tests
NMD	National Missile Defense

NPT	Non-Proliferation Treaty
NSC	National Security Council
PSAC	President's Science Advisory Committee
PSR	Physicians for Social Responsibility
SALT	Strategic Arms Limitation Treaty
SANE	Committee for a Sane Nuclear Policy
SDI	Strategic Defense Initiative
SNF	Short-Range Nuclear Forces
SPD	Social Democratic Party
SPU	Student Peace Union
TPA	Turkish Peace Association
USIA	United States Information Agency
VOW	Voice of Women
WAND	Women's Action for Nuclear Disarmament
WILPF	Women's International League for Peace and Freedom
WMWFG	World Movement for World Federal Government
WPC	World Peace Council
WRI	War Resisters' International
WSP	Women Strike for Peace

CONFRONTING THE BOMB

*The great tragedies of history often fascinate people with
approaching horror. Paralyzed, they cannot make up their
minds to do anything but wait. So they wait, and one day
the Gorgon devours them. But I should like to convince
you . . . that strength of heart, intelligence, and courage
are enough to stop fate and sometimes reverse it.*

ALBERT CAMUS, 1956

1   The Secret Struggle

The Bomb had its critics long before it became a reality. During the early years of the twentieth century, scientists warned that radioactive materials, if effectively harnessed, could create enormously powerful explosives. Picking up this theme, H. G. Wells, one of the most popular and influential writers of the era, produced a novel in 1914, *The World Set Free*, featuring a war with "atomic bombs." This war was so devastating that, to avert the world's destruction in a future conflict, its survivors formed a world government which, thereafter, ushered in an unprecedented era of peace and economic progress. Concerned that innovations in science and technology were fast outstripping advances in political institutions, Wells repeatedly argued that an "open conspiracy" of far-sighted, rational people must move beyond the war-making state to build a genuine world community.

This notion of a society of the righteous, committed to saving the world from its own folly, had deep roots in world history. It can be traced back at least to the fourth century, to the Babylonian Talmudic teacher Abbayah. According to this Jewish savant, in each generation there existed at least thirty-six righteous people (*lamed-vav tzaddikim*, in Hebrew) upon whom the survival of the world depended. Jewish fiction and folklore took up the idea of these hidden saints, who played a prominent role in kabbalistic folk legend of the sixteenth and seventeenth centuries and in Hassidic lore after the eighteenth century.

In 1898, with the birth of Leo Szilard, the legend began to acquire a basis in reality. Raised in a Hungarian Jewish family of comfortable circumstances, Szilard was a sensitive, creative, and precocious child. After World War I, he studied in Berlin, where he took his Ph.D. in physics with Albert Einstein. As he watched the rise of fascism in Germany, Szilard hatched an abortive plan to create a small group of wise, unselfish men and women to preserve civilization from the disaster that loomed. Years later, he attributed what he called his "predilection for 'Saving the World'" to the stories told to him by his mother. But the idea may also have been derived from Szilard's reading of novels by H. G. Wells, an author whom he greatly admired. Curiously, Szilard did not read *The World Set Free* until 1932. But thereafter, he noted, "I found it difficult to forget."

Szilard had good reason to remember the book. Having fled from Nazi Germany, he was living in London in 1933 and conducting experiments in nuclear physics. One day that September, when waiting to cross the street, he suddenly conceived the process that could create a nuclear chain reaction and, thus, lead to the construction of atomic bombs. Recognizing what this would mean, Szilard sought to keep the process secret by patenting it and, also, pulling prominent physicists into a conspiracy of silence on the subject. But these efforts had little effect, for Szilard was a relatively unknown, junior scientist and, also, publication of research findings was the norm in his profession. Symptomatically, in late 1938, two German chemists, Otto Hahn and Fritz Strassmann, published the results of their successful experiment with nuclear fission. Receiving news of this experiment in early 1939 in his new home, the United States, Szilard grew alarmed. "All the things which H. G. Wells predicted appeared suddenly real to me," he recalled. Working with an associate at Columbia University, he conducted his own experiments on nuclear fission, from which it became clear that "the large-scale liberation of atomic energy was just around the corner. . . . There was very little doubt in my mind that the world was headed for grief."

Once again, Szilard sought to generate a conspiracy of silence. And this time, given fears of a German breakthrough in this area, Szilard—joined in these efforts by physicists Eugene Wigner and Victor Weisskopf—had greater success. In Britain, the United States, and Denmark, top nuclear scientists agreed to keep their research findings secret. Miraculously, it seemed that they might avert a scramble for nuclear weapons. But a leading French research team balked. Like many scientists, members of the French team considered it unlikely that an atomic bomb would be built for many years, if ever. Furthermore, they detested secrecy in science. As a result, they published their findings in April 1939, thereby precipitating small-scale atomic bomb programs in Germany, Britain, and the Soviet Union.

Much the same thing happened in the United States. In July 1939, Szilard and two of his Hungarian friends met with Einstein, then himself a refugee and vacationing on Long Island. Recognizing Einstein's immense prestige, they hoped to draw upon it to reach President Franklin D. Roosevelt with a warning about the prospect of a German atomic bomb. Einstein agreed, and dispatched a letter, drafted by Szilard, that did catch the attention of the President. With the beginning of World War II, it led to the organization of the Manhattan Project, a vast nuclear weapons development program directed by the U.S., British, and Canadian governments. Szilard, like many other scientists, worked on the project, convinced that they had to produce the atomic bomb—if it could be produced—before the German government did.

A Conflict Emerges

But, even at the start of the Manhattan Project, there was a built-in conflict between the approach of scientists and that of top government officials. Some scientists, like the German refugee Max Born, were horrified by the prospect of an atomic bomb, and refused to work on it at all. Many other scientists, like Szilard, viewed it as no more than a deterrent to a German atomic attack. By contrast, government officials like President Roosevelt and British Prime Minister Winston Churchill were committed to using nuclear weapons—if available—during the war and to retaining them in the postwar years as instruments of national military power.

As the war progressed, this tension between scientists and statesmen grew more acute. In September 1942, Szilard sent a memo to his associates in the Manhattan Project's Chicago Metallurgical Laboratory (Met Lab) that revived his earlier idea for a society of the righteous, a group of intelligent individuals "who can, by repeated discussions, make clear . . . what the existence of atomic bombs will mean from the point of view of the post-war period." In the following years, he expressed ever-greater concern about the fate of humanity in a nuclear-armed world. Meanwhile, the great Danish physicist, Niels Bohr, also began to sound the alarm. Escaping from his German-occupied homeland, Bohr warned British and American statesmen of the unprecedented dangers of a postwar nuclear arms race and urged them to head it off through a U.S.-British-Soviet agreement for postwar nuclear arms control. Churchill, particularly, was furious at Bohr. "I cannot see what you are worrying about," he told the Danish scientist. "This new bomb is just going to be bigger than our present bombs. It involves no difference in the principles of war." Roosevelt, although superficially friendlier to Bohr, secretly lined up with Churchill. Meeting at Hyde Park in September 1944, the British and American leaders agreed to maintain an Anglo-American nuclear monopoly after the war, to reject Bohr's nuclear arms control proposals, to "perhaps" use the atomic bomb against the Japanese, and to place Bohr under investigation.

But new thinking was under way elsewhere, particularly at the Met Lab, where a committee headed by Zay Jeffries solicited the views of scientists on the future of atomic energy. In November 1944, the Jeffries committee produced a report that was submitted to higher authorities. Key sections on atomic energy's social and political implications were written by Eugene Rabinowitch, a biophysicist who had left Russia after the Bolshevik revolution. "No lasting security against a national and international catastrophe can be achieved" through attempts to maintain U.S. atomic supremacy, Rabinowitch warned. "Peace based on uncontrolled . . . development" of atomic weapons "will only be an armistice" that will lead, eventually, to disaster. The conclusion was clear: there was an imperative need for the immediate establishment of "an international administration with police powers" that could control nuclear weapons.

By early 1945, the Met Lab was in ferment, not only over the question of a postwar nuclear arms race, but over the prospective use of the atomic bomb. As the German war effort collapsed, it became clear that the Bomb, far from providing a deterrent to a Nazi atomic assault, might well become an offensive weapon against Japan. Szilard recalled that he began to ask himself: "What is the purpose of continuing the development of the bomb?" That spring, several "seminars" on the social and political implications of atomic energy were held among the restless younger scientists, who discussed international control, use of the Bomb against Japan, and the formation of a scientists' organization. In late April, James Franck, the distinguished refugee scientist who directed the chemistry section of the Met Lab, drew on Rabinowitch for a personal memorandum to higher authorities that stressed two of the themes now agitating the project scientists: the danger of a nuclear arms race and the necessity for international control of atomic energy.

Szilard, who had little patience with following the chain of command, once more moved to alert the President of the United States. On March 25, 1945, at Szilard's request, Einstein gave him an introductory letter to Roosevelt, requesting that the President meet with the emigré physicist on a secret matter. In an accompanying memorandum, Szilard warned that use of atomic bombs would "precipitate a race in the production of these devices between the United States and Russia," with the result that the United States would become increasingly vulnerable to attack and destruction. As alternatives, he recommended delaying use of the Bomb against Japan and working to establish nuclear arms controls. Roosevelt died before he could read the letter. But his successor, Harry Truman, suggested that Szilard meet with James F. Byrnes, an influential South Carolina politician and the new President's designee as secretary of state. Accompanied by Harold Urey (an important Bomb project scientist at Columbia University) and Walter Bartky (the associate director of the Met Lab), Szilard spoke with Byrnes on May 28.

Like the earlier encounter between Bohr and Churchill, this exchange merely highlighted differences of approach. After Szilard made his case against dropping the atomic bomb, Byrnes retorted that the use of the Bomb would help justify the enormous government expenditure on the Manhattan Project and make the Russians "more manageable" in Eastern Europe. There would be no threat to an American nuclear monopoly for some time, Byrnes insisted, for General Leslie Groves, who headed the Manhattan Project, had assured him of that. Byrnes recalled that Szilard's "general demeanor and his desire to participate in policy making made an unfavorable impression on me," and that he was glad that a U.S. intelligence agent "had been following the three gentlemen." Szilard, in turn, later wrote that "I was rarely as depressed as when we left Byrnes' house. . . . I thought to myself how much better off the world might be had I been born in America and become influential in American politics, and had Byrnes been born in Hungary and studied physics. In all probability there would then have been no atomic bomb and no danger of an arms race between America and Russia."

When Szilard returned to Chicago, the project was "in an uproar," as he recalled. Furious at the unauthorized approach to the White House and to Byrnes, General Groves denounced what he claimed was a breach of national security. To bring the issue back within official channels and, at the same time, fulfill a promise he had made earlier to Franck, Arthur Compton, the director of the Met Lab, appointed a Committee on Social and Political Implications of Atomic Energy, with Franck as chair. Meeting in all-night sessions behind locked doors, the committee members—Franck, Szilard, Rabinowitch, Donald Hughes, James Nickson, Glenn Seaborg, and Joyce Stearns—felt their responsibility keenly. "By an accident of history," recalled Seaborg, "we were among a very few who were aware of a new, world-threatening peril, and we felt obligated to express our views." On June 11, the Franck committee produced a report, largely written by Rabinowitch and influenced by Szilard, that argued forcefully against combat use of the Bomb against Japan. "If the United States were to be the first to release this new weapon of indiscriminate destruction upon mankind," warned the committee, "she would sacrifice public support throughout the world, precipitate the race for armaments, and prejudice the possibility of reaching an international agreement on the future control of such weapons." As an alternative, the committee recommended revealing the Bomb to the world "by a demonstration in an appropriately selected uninhabited area."

The Franck Report had little, if any, impact on high-level U.S. government officials. Submitted to the office of U.S. Secretary of War Henry Stimson, it remained there without any response. Rabinowitch recalled that "we waited for some reaction and we waited and waited and we had the feeling we could as well have dropped this report into Lake Michigan." In fact, the decision for the use of the Bomb had already been made. In late April, Stimson had met with the new President and had informed him of "the most terrible weapon ever known in human history" and of his plan to appoint a committee of top government officials to consider its use. Meeting that May, the innocuously named Interim Committee focused on *how* the Bomb should be used, rather than on *whether* it should be used. As Compton recalled, committee members believed that using the Bomb was "a foregone conclusion." Nor was there any interest in international control of atomic energy. Stimson believed that, in the world of international power politics, possession of the Bomb constituted "a royal straight flush." Byrnes, too, argued that "the bomb might well put us in a position to dictate our terms at the end of the war."

Yet criticism of government reliance upon nuclear weapons continued to grow. Arguing in late June that immediate use of the Bomb was unnecessary, Assistant Secretary of War John McCloy suggested to Truman and Stimson that the Japanese should be explicitly warned of its use and offered retention of the emperor on a constitutional basis as a condition of surrender. Assistant Secretary of the Navy Ralph Bard also took this position, telling Truman that, as "a great humanitarian nation," the United States should not initiate a nuclear attack. A group of U.S. military leaders expressed doubts about the need to use the Bomb, particularly as Japan tottered to defeat. Most were top U.S. Navy officers, but they included leading Army officers, as well. General Dwight Eisenhower recalled that he told Stimson in July that he had "grave misgivings, first on the basis of my belief that Japan was already defeated and that dropping the bomb was completely unnecessary, and secondly because I thought that our country should avoid shocking world opinion."

As before, dismay at government plans was strongest among the scientists. At Los Alamos, there was substantial discussion of whether the Bomb should be used, and one scientist, Joseph Rotblat, a physicist, deliberately resigned from the project and returned to his home in Britain. The Met Lab, however, remained the major locus of discontent. "In the summer of 1945," Rabinowitch recalled, he and his colleagues "walked the streets of Chicago vividly imagining the sky suddenly lit up by a giant fireball, the steel skeletons of skyscrapers bending into grotesque shapes." That July, Szilard launched a petition drive, opposing the atomic bombing of Japan and warning that "a nation which sets the precedent" of using atomic bombs "may have to bear the responsibility of opening the door to an era of devastation on an unimaginable scale." Szilard's petitions garnered signatures from 68 scientists at the Met Lab and 67 scientists at Oak Ridge (before further petitioning was halted by the Army) and were banned by U.S. authorities at Los Alamos. Delivered to Groves's office, the petitions languished there until the general finally passed them to Stimson's office, where they were deliberately withheld from the President.

By late July 1945, control over the atomic bomb lay in the hands of the three Allied leaders meeting at Potsdam—Truman, Churchill, and Joseph Stalin—and none showed the least hesitation in using it. After a full description of the first successful Bomb test reached Truman and Churchill on July 18, they met to discuss the future. "Fair and bright indeed it seemed," Churchill recalled. "There was never a moment's discussion as to whether the atomic bomb should be used." Stalin received a brief opportunity to discuss the Bomb with his professed allies on July 24, when, according to Truman's account, he "casually mentioned to Stalin that we had a new weapon of unusual destructive force." Truman recalled that the Soviet leader said "that he was glad to hear it and hoped we would make 'good use of it against the Japanese.'"

This ready acceptance of the Bomb's use in wartime was accompanied by exhilarating visions of postwar national power. Churchill was "completely carried away" by news of the successful U.S. Bomb test, recalled the chief of the Imperial General Staff. "He . . . painted a wonderful picture of himself as the sole possessor of these bombs and . . . thus all-powerful." Truman, too, was dazzled by the vistas opened up by the Bomb. "We were now in possession of a weapon that would not only revolutionize war," he wrote, "but could alter the course of history." Although Stalin was less exhilarated than frightened by the success of the Anglo-American Bomb project, he had a similar remedy at hand for Russia's international problems. Returning from Potsdam, he told Soviet officials to accelerate the pace of the Soviet Bomb program. As the scientists had feared, the nuclear arms race surged forward.

While the leaders of the Big Three laid plans for the future, the atomic bombing of Japan went forward on schedule. On the morning of August 6, without warning, a single American plane, flying unopposed over Hiroshima, loosed its atomic bomb over the city's crowded streets. In the ensuing blast and firestorm, approximately 140,000 people were killed, 95 percent of them civilians. Among those who survived, countless numbers received hideous burns or fatal radiation poisoning. On August 9, the Soviet Union entered the Far East war and the U.S. military unleashed its second atomic bomb over Nagasaki, killing an additional 70,000 people and wounding many others. The following day, the Japanese government—which had desperately sought a peace settlement since the spring of 1945 but had resisted the Allied demand for unconditional surrender—offered to surrender if the emperor and throne were spared. When the U.S. government implicitly accepted this offer, the war came to an end.

Thus, in the final years of World War II, a significant difference of opinion had developed between top government officials, on the one hand, and a circle of scientists and middle-range government officials, on the other. To the official guardians of national security, the Bomb offered a splendid opportunity to bolster national military strength and to humble competing nations. To a growing number of others, however, the Bomb represented a perilous lurch toward unprecedented destruction. Undergirding both perspectives lay the dangers inherent in violent conflict among nations. Although national leaders were too structurally locked into these conflicts to resist the pull toward enhancing national military strength, others were beginning to wonder if, in an age of nuclear weapons, the obsession with national military strength was not the siren song of global annihilation.

2   The Rise of Popular Protest, 1945–1953

Following the atomic bombing of Hiroshima and Nagasaki, a movement against the Bomb rapidly took shape in dozens of countries around the world. Alerted to the existence of nuclear weapons and to their catastrophic effects, hundreds of thousands of people rallied behind a loose, popular crusade to save humanity from nuclear destruction. This movement argued that nations should end the traditional practice of securing their interests by marshaling superior military might—a practice that, with the advent of the Bomb, seemed fraught with new and terrible dangers. At other times, the campaign focused more narrowly on the need to eliminate or control nuclear weapons. In either case, this grass-roots struggle against the Bomb championed an alternative that, for a time, had considerable popular appeal: One World.

Components of the Popular Struggle

At the center of the antinuclear campaign stood the world peace movement. Since the early nineteenth century, citizens' movements for peace had agitated for alternatives to the policies of national aggrandizement and military buildup that so often had led to international conflict and war. But World War II significantly undermined the three major international pacifist organizations—the War Resisters' International (WRI), the Fellowship of Reconciliation (FOR), and the Women's International League for Peace and Freedom (WILPF). In lands under fascist rule, thousands of their supporters were imprisoned or slaughtered, while in non-fascist nations their adherents were marginalized, discredited, and sometimes imprisoned. The once-powerful pacifist influence within religious denominations and within Labor, Social Democratic, and Socialist parties also dwindled.

On the other hand, the world war substantially enhanced the antiwar influence of other groups, especially scientists. Although, traditionally, scientists had been apolitical, this had begun to change in the 1930s, as left-wing currents propelled some scientists toward broader social concerns. World War II accelerated the politicization of the scientific community, for it not only demonstrated the interlocking nature of science and politics, but pulled scientists into nuclear fission research and, thus, into a growing debate over the Bomb.

Furthermore, the devastation wrought by World War II unleashed substantial pressure for world government. The idea of transferring sovereignty from warring nation-states to a global organization went back at least to the Middle Ages and—taken up by peace groups and, finally, politicians—had led to the formation of the League of Nations and the United Nations. But, as the chaos and destruction of World War II brought the international system to the point of collapse, the idea of world government acquired overwhelming momentum. An avalanche of books and pamphlets addressed the issue, among them *One World*, a best-seller by Wendell Willkie, the former Republican candidate for President of the United States. Serialized or printed in an abbreviated form in more than 100 newspapers in the United States and Canada, *One World* sold two million copies in book form within two years of its publication. Even more explicit about the necessity for world government was *The Anatomy of Peace*, a mordant account of the pathology of nations written by Emery Reves, a refugee journalist in the United States. Published in June 1945 and on America's best-seller lists for the next six months, it appeared in 20 languages and in 24 countries by 1950.

Despite Japan's shocking introduction to nuclear weapons, an antinuclear movement in that country took some time to develop—largely because of the control exercised by U.S. occupation authorities. Newspaper stories about the Bomb or about the Japanese peace movement were a favorite target of U.S. censors, and only those articles that portrayed the weapon as shortening the war or leading to peace were printed. The occupation authorities also rode herd on literature and the arts. After spending three nights in Hiroshima surrounded by disfigured bodies and moaning survivors of the atomic bombing, the writer Yoko Ota fled to the countryside, where she drafted her powerful novel, *City of Corpses*. Although completed in November 1945, it could not be published until three years later, and then only in expurgated form. Censorship also limited the impact of two artists, Iri and Toshi Maruki, who had entered Hiroshima three days after the atomic bombing and had begun drawings of the disastrous scene. Although a peace group published the first edition of their drawings in 1950, copies of the book were seized by U.S. occupation officials, who suppressed further editions. Even the American author John Hersey faced severe difficulties having his acclaimed account of the atomic bombing, *Hiroshima*, published in Japan. Only in 1949, after a public protest by the Authors' League of America, did the U.S. authorities permit *Hiroshima*'s publication.

Nevertheless, criticism of the Bomb gradually emerged in Japan, particularly among the *hibakusha* (atomic bomb-affected persons) of Hiroshima and Nagasaki. Immersed in death and suffering, they worked slowly and painfully to give meaning to their terrible experience. In Hiroshima, intellectuals gathered for poetry readings in memory of the dead and, in March 1946, launched *Chugoku Culture*, a magazine whose first issue was devoted to the effects of the atomic bombing. Bringing together some 350 religious and civic groups, a Hiroshima Peace Association was established, sponsoring a citywide Peace Festival in 1947. At the ceremonies, which drew 10,000 people, the city's new mayor, Shinzo Hamai—sensitive to the reaction of U.S. occupation authorities—avoided criticizing the atomic bombing of Japan, but organized prayers against the future employment of nuclear weapons and issued a Peace Declaration, appealing to the world to rid itself of war. By 1948, peace demonstrations memorializing the atomic bombings were regular events in Hiroshima and in Nagasaki.

As the first targets of nuclear war, the two ruined cities became powerful symbols of world peace. In early 1948, the Reverend Kiyoshi Tanimoto, a Methodist minister portrayed in Hersey's *Hiroshima*, began a campaign to have nations around the world set aside August 6 as World Peace Day. Twenty nations responded to the call, holding prayer meetings and other public gatherings on that day. As the idea took hold, Hiroshima's peace leaders forged close ties with their American sympathizers. Sponsored by the Board of Missions of the Methodist church, Tanimoto toured the United States during much of 1948 and 1949, gathering support from religious and pacifist gatherings for a Hiroshima peace center. Thanks to the efforts of Norman Cousins (editor of the *Saturday Review of Literature*), Pearl Buck (novelist), Hersey, and others, the center was established. It arranged for the "moral adoption" of atomic bomb orphans by Americans and provided welfare services for other victims of the atomic attack. Cousins visited Japan in 1949 for the August 6 memorial ceremony and returned with a Hiroshima Peace Petition, signed by 110,000 residents of the city. Although President Truman refused to accept the petition, it was eventually presented to the president of the U.N. General Assembly. Cousins also brought a message from Mayor Hamai, affirming that "the people of Hiroshima ask nothing of the world except that we be allowed to offer ourselves as an exhibit for peace. We ask only that enough peoples know what happened here . . . and that they work hard to see that it never happens anywhere again."

Numerous groups in Japan joined the campaign. Although Japan's pacifist movement had been suppressed under the fascist regime, it experienced a renaissance in the postwar era, when it championed peace and disarmament. Under the leadership of Morikatsu Inagaki, a world government movement also took shape, with the Union for World Federal Government launched, symbolically, on the third anniversary of the Hiroshima bombing. Although these organizations remained rather small, other forces—and particularly the powerful Japanese Socialist party, with strong support from the nation's labor movement—helped provide Japan's peace and disarmament movement with a mass base. In November 1945, at its first postwar congress, the Socialist party declared that it opposed "all militaristic thought and action" and aimed "at the realization of perpetual peace through the co-operation of the peoples of the world." Despite subsequent U.S. government pressure for the rearmament of Japan, the Socialists stuck to these principles. In 1950 and 1951, these groups joined Japanese religious organizations in holding large public rallies for peace and disarmament, with some drawing as many as 20,000 people. Nor were these activities out of line with public opinion. In late 1951, a poll of Japanese students at nineteen colleges reported that only 12 percent favored the rearmament of Japan.

In the United States, the atomic bombing of Hiroshima and Nagasaki created an enormous sensation. Like the war, the bombing was widely supported by the general public, with the major criticism of it coming from pacifists and some religious leaders. But the advent of the nuclear age also inspired a sense of awe and, especially, fear. "Seldom, if ever," reported CBS radio commentator Edward R. Murrow, "has a war ended leaving the victors with such a sense of uncertainty and fear, with such a realization that . . . survival is not assured." The mass media of all persuasions trumpeted the theme that, with the development of nuclear weapons, the destruction of civilization lay at hand. The *Chicago Tribune* warned that a future atomic war would leave the world "a barren waste, in which the survivors . . . will hide in caves or live among the ruins." As America's atomic nightmare grew, the early critics of the Bomb realized that it provided them with an opportunity. "Was there not a chance," Rabinowitch observed, "that the fate of Hiroshima and Nagasaki would cause Man to turn a new leaf? Could we not spur this decision by buttonholing all who would listen and preaching to them . . . our precept for survival: live in peace or perish?"

What Rabinowitch called "the conspiracy to preserve our civilization by scaring men into rationality" was particularly evident among American scientists. In the aftermath of the atomic bombing, atomic scientists' associations sprang up at numerous Manhattan Project work sites. That November, the groups from Chicago, Oak Ridge, Los Alamos, and New York joined together to launch the Federation of Atomic Scientists, which, the following month, reorganized itself as the Federation of American Scientists. Committed to freeing the world from the threat of nuclear war, the new organization claimed seventeen local groups and some 3,000 members by early 1946. Meanwhile, Rabinowitch—together with his colleague Hyman Goldsmith—began editing a new publication that grew into the voice of the scientists' movement: the *Bulletin of the Atomic Scientists*. Bearing its distinctive "doomsday clock," originally set at seven minutes to midnight, the *Bulletin* soon had a circulation of nearly 20,000, including scientists in seventeen countries. In 1946, Szilard launched yet another organization, designed to serve as a fundraiser for the movement: the Emergency Committee of Atomic Scientists. Chaired by Einstein, the Emergency Committee was comprised of a small group of eminent scientists who were determined to place the nuclear issue squarely before the public. Scientists, declared Einstein, "must let the people know that a new type of thinking is essential if mankind is to survive."

Although—like Wells—most of the scientists saw the long-term solution to the nuclear problem in the establishment of a world government, they recognized that developing such an institution would take time. Therefore, in the interim, they rallied behind the idea of international control of atomic energy. Such international control would "buy time" until a world government could be put into place and, in addition, would provide a "first step" along the way. Thus, the scientists' movement lobbied fiercely against Truman's plan for U.S. military control of atomic energy. Then, with the civilian nature of U.S. atomic energy assured, the scientists rallied behind the Acheson-Lilienthal Plan and, later, the Baruch Plan for international atomic energy control. In 1950, when President Truman announced his decision to develop a hydrogen bomb, leaders of the movement sharply protested this addition to the accelerating nuclear arms race. Issuing yet another warning, Einstein proclaimed: "General annihilation beckons."

In addition, following the atomic bombing, other prominent Americans began speaking out against nuclear war, especially world federalists. One of the best-known of them, Norman Cousins, sat down on the evening of the bombing and penned a lengthy editorial, "Modern Man Is Obsolete." The "need for world government was clear long before August 6, 1945," he observed, but the atomic bombing "raised that need to such dimensions that it can no longer be ignored." Becoming a key writer, speaker, and fundraiser for the cause, Cousins turned the editorial into a book that went through fourteen editions, appeared in seven languages, and had an estimated circulation in the United States of seven million. Another key federalist spokesperson was Robert Hutchins, the innovative chancellor of the University of Chicago. Calling repeatedly for world government as the alternative to nuclear annihilation, Hutchins also put university resources behind a faculty committee to draft a world constitution—a document that, by 1949, had secured a worldwide circulation of 200,000 copies. With world government groups springing up all over the United States, six of the largest merged in February 1947 to form United World Federalists. Determined to "strengthen the United Nations into a world government," the new organization had 720 chapters and nearly 50,000 members by mid-1949. Although world federalist leaders emphasized that international control of atomic energy was not sufficient to end the danger of nuclear war, they nevertheless worked closely with the atomic scientists' movement and supported nuclear arms control measures.

American pacifists provided a third key constituency in the U.S. struggle against the Bomb. Although postwar American pacifism was weak in numbers and influence, the U.S. branches of the FOR and the WILPF, as well as the War Resisters League and the Catholic Worker movement, all sharply condemned the postwar development of nuclear weapons and demanded their abolition. As long-term critics of war, they were less inclined than the scientists and the world federalists to focus their energies on a particular kind of weapon or to view its development as a turning point in history. Nevertheless, they recognized its deadly perils and, also, that its unprecedented destructiveness added powerfully to the case against war. As a result, pacifist groups staged small antinuclear demonstrations, developed good relations with other antinuclear organizations, and called upon Americans to respond appropriately to the unprecedented challenge of nuclear weapons. In *Gandhi and the H-Bomb*, a pamphlet produced for the FOR, A. J. Muste—perhaps the best-known American pacifist leader—argued: "If the A-bomb and the H-bomb do not move us to achievements in the social and political realm as revolutionary as those that have taken place in the material, there is no hope left for civilization."

Criticism of the Bomb also emerged within the broader society. A few prominent Democrats, democratic socialists like Norman Thomas, and some influential religious leaders expressed their grave concern about the terrible destructiveness of the new weaponry. Although the Federal Council of Churches and the Catholic Church did not challenge the building of U.S. nuclear weapons, they did begin to champion the idea of nuclear arms control and disarmament. Furthermore, soundings of American public opinion also indicated significant misgivings about the Bomb. In September 1946, 67 percent of Americans polled said that they wanted the United Nations strengthened "to prevent all countries, including the United States, from making atomic bombs." In March 1950, only weeks after Truman's announcement that the U.S. government would build an H-bomb, Americans supported new efforts toward a nuclear arms control agreement with the Soviet Union by 68 to 23 percent.

In Britain, the antinuclear campaign leaned heavily upon similar constituencies to those in the United States. Although the pacifist Peace Pledge Union had lost the mass membership it had attained in the 1930s, together with the British FOR and the Friends Peace Committee it condemned the atomic bombing of Hiroshima and Nagasaki, assailed the growing nuclear arms race, held Hiroshima Day demonstrations, and promoted plans for nuclear arms control and disarmament. Meanwhile, working among Britain's scientists, Joseph Rotblat helped organize the Atomic Scientists' Association (ASA). Formally launched in the spring of 1946, the ASA served as the British counterpart to the Federation of American Scientists. It published a small journal (*Atomic Scientists' News*), sponsored an Atomic Train exhibition (a major attempt at popular education on the dangers of nuclear weapons that was visited by 146,000 people), and promoted international control of atomic energy. In addition, fear of the Bomb went hand-in-hand with the idea of world government, which was championed by such prominent figures as Bertrand Russell and Sir John Boyd Orr (the director of the U.N. Food and Agriculture Organization) and drew crowds of thousands to public meetings at which it was discussed.

The most effective leader of British federalism was Henry Usborne, a Labour member of parliament. Stunned by the atomic bombing of Hiroshima, Usborne organized a Parliamentary Group for World Government and introduced a world federalist resolution that secured the backing of nearly 100 M.P.s. He also launched a Crusade for World Government which organized "World Government Week" in assorted cities, held mass meetings, secured favorable coverage in the press, published a newsletter and other literature, and attracted some 15,000 registered supporters. In an age of nuclear weapons, Usborne declared, "the choice is indeed between one world or none."

These ideas resonated with other elements of British society. In the immediate aftermath of the atomic bombing, both major political parties adopted an unusually somber tone about the future, and even the London *Times*, voice of the British establishment, editorialized that "it must be made impossible for war to begin, or else mankind perishes." Although the British churches—particularly the Anglican Church—were cautious about criticizing nuclear weapons, greater opposition emerged within the Labour Party. Issuing a "Peace Letter" to the British Foreign Secretary in 1948, 34 Labour party backbenchers called for Britain's repudiation of atomic weapons and broad disarmament measures. In May 1946, a poll found that only 28 percent of British respondents thought that, in the long run, the release of atomic energy would do more good than harm, while 46 percent thought it would do more harm than good. That same year, 74 percent of British respondents approved (and only 9 percent disapproved) a proposal "to put the control of atomic energy under the United Nations Security Council." When the prospect emerged that the U.S. government might use the Bomb in the Korean War, most Britons sharply repudiated the idea.

Although opposition to the Bomb was less prevalent in Canada, it was nevertheless on the rise. The small Canadian FOR branch circulated literature stressing the dangers of the Bomb, and appealed to the Canadian government to ban it, work to halt global production of nuclear weapons, and place an embargo on Canada's export of uranium to the United States. In November 1945, 122 members of the Canadian and British scientific staff engaged in atomic research at the laboratories of Canada's National Research Council sent a message to the political leaders of Canada and Great Britain, warning that the atomic bomb was "the most destructive force known to mankind, against which there is no military defense and in the production of which no single nation can have an enduring monopoly." Under the impetus of the Bomb, world government groups sprang up in Canada's major cities and, in 1951, merged to form the World Federalists of Canada. The general public, as well, seemed ready to relinquish traditional aspects of national sovereignty for the purpose of securing effective international disarmament. According to the Canadian Institute of Public Opinion, in July 1946 59 percent of Canadian respondents approved having Canada "turn over control of all her armed forces and munitions, including atomic bomb materials, to a world parliament, providing other nations did the same."

Similar developments occurred in another British Commonwealth nation, Australia. The newsletter of the Federal Pacifist Council, published in the aftermath of the atomic bombing of Hiroshima, reported optimistically: "Overnight, people have awakened to the truth of what pacifists have been crying in the wilderness for decades ... MANKIND CANNOT AFFORD ANOTHER WAR." World government became a lively issue, particularly in pacifist ranks, with Eleanor Moore, a WILPF leader, championing it fervently. Scientists' organizations devoted considerable attention to the social implications of atomic energy, and frequently quoted appeals from American scientists calling for its international control. Indeed, Australia's best-known scientist, Marc Oliphant, insisting that "atomic weapons ... render wars of the future suicidal and utterly indefensible," became a sharp critic of nuclear weapons and renounced work on any projects with military significance. Australians also organized local antinuclear events on World Peace Day. In early 1949, 55 percent of Australians polled favored (and only 29 percent opposed) giving control of all national armed forces to a world government. Polled in September 1950 about possible U.S. employment of the atomic bomb in the Korean War, 73 percent of Australian respondents opposed it.

Although the antinuclear movement was weaker in New Zealand, it appeared there, as well. New Zealand's pacifists—having been not only discredited but imprisoned during World War II—were a small, isolated, and exhausted lot in the war's aftermath. Nevertheless, they sharply condemned the atomic bombing of Japanese cities, distributed literature produced by the Federation of American Scientists, and took the lead in organizing Hiroshima Day marches in urban centers. Appraising the new weaponry, both newspapers and politicians warned darkly of catastrophe. "I have felt disturbed about the consequences of this bomb and its effects in the future if war breaks out," stated one legislator; "the atomic bomb is a frightful instrument against humanity." In these circumstances, the idea of world government grew in popularity and, by 1950, two small branches of the World Movement for World Federal Government had emerged in New Zealand.

The advent of nuclear weapons also stirred a wave of public concern in France. Commenting on the destruction of Hiroshima, the former resistance leader Albert Camus argued that modern civilization had "reached the last degree of savagery," in which nations were faced with the prospect of "collective suicide." According to the French Socialist party, the development of the atomic bomb left the world's nations with the choice: "Perish or unite." Although the bitter experience of France under the wartime fascist occupation undermined the appeal of pacifism, atomic scientists came out of the war with greater credibility, and they used it to promote the international control of atomic energy. Meanwhile, world government organizations sprang up quickly and, by 1950, the seven French branches of the World Movement for World Federal Government claimed over 38,000 members.

Curiously, the activities of a young American war veteran, Garry Davis, provided the most important catalyst for France's postwar rejection of nationalism. Having served as a bomber pilot during World War II, he watched in horror what he termed the "march of nations toward World War Three." He recalled: "A curious phrase beat faintly inside my mind, a phrase which seemed to echo from nation to nation and . . . around the globe. 'One world or none,' wrote Wendell Willkie; 'One world or none,' reaffirmed Bertrand Russell . . . ; 'One world or none,' repeated Gandhi and Einstein." In September 1948, deciding that it was time to "secede from the old and declare the new," Davis traveled to Paris, pitched his pup tent on a small strip of United Nations territory, and proclaimed himself a citizen of the world. With this gesture, he became the toast of Paris. Endorsements of Davis and of the world citizenship flowed in from Camus, André Gide, Jean-Paul Sartre, André Breton, and numerous other French intellectuals, many of whom appeared with him at press conferences or other public gatherings. An estimated 15,000 enthusiasts flocked to one of these meetings, at which Davis, wearing his old air corps flight jacket, talked of the need to abolish the "narrow nationalism which has always resulted in war and death." By January 1950, Davis's World Citizens registry, with signers from all over the globe, neared the half-million mark. By mid-1951, some 400 French communities had proclaimed themselves "mundialized," or world territory.

In war-weary France, threatened by a new—and perhaps nuclear—conflict among the great powers, Davis had tapped a deep vein of public concern. Another former resistance fighter, Claude Bourdet, the editor of *Combat,* turned over a column in that newspaper to the World Citizens movement and, soon, another one to French pacifists. The influential *Le Monde* began to champion nonalignment in the growing Cold War, and reprinted an article along these lines, written by Szilard, that had appeared in the *Bulletin of the Atomic Scientists.* Joining *Le Monde* in advocacy of nonalignment was the influential Catholic left-wing magazine, *L'Esprit.* In late 1949, when the Soviet Union conducted its first nuclear test, the reaction was acute. "Everyone is asking," noted a *New York Times* correspondent, "where is the exit?" After Truman spoke loosely about the possibility of using the atomic bomb in Korea, an enormous furor developed. A U.S. intelligence analysis concluded that, in France, there existed "a general public repugnance to the use of this weapon under any but the most dire circumstances."

The antinuclear campaign was more subdued in postwar Germany. During twelve years of fascist rule, the Nazi regime had outlawed pacifist groups and arrested their leaders, many of whom died in concentration camps or were executed. Nevertheless, pacifism underwent a small revival after the war. Attracting some 12,000 members in the three Western zones by 1950, the venerable German Peace Society worked to uproot Prussian militarism, educate youth for reconciliation between nations, and to ban nuclear weapons. Its small monthly publications reported on the warnings of scientists in other lands, with Einstein prominently featured. "Every bullet does not strike," declared one of its leaflets, "but every atom bomb does." Other small pacifist groups also sounded the nuclear alarm. The world government movement burgeoned, with more than 5,000 Germans joining world federalist groups and 125,000 signing up with the World Citizens registry of Garry Davis. For most peace-minded West Germans, the issue of German rearmament was paramount, and—together with the Social Democratic Party (SPD) and the Evangelical (Protestant) Church—they threw themselves into the campaign against it.

Although the issue of nuclear weapons sometimes took a back seat to more immediate concerns, Germany's peace groups did work, successfully, to keep it alive. On August 6, 1948, now World Peace Day, peace groups in Hamburg (including the German Peace Society and the League for World Government), the SPD youth group, and cultural organizations sponsored a meeting at the university under the title "Never Again Hiroshima." Early the following year, the German branch of the WILPF organized a women's meeting around the theme: "We want peace, not atomic war." In August 1949, World Peace Day was again celebrated in numerous localities. In Berlin, where eleven peace groups sponsored a large demonstration in the French sector, an "eternal fire" was lit in a large bronze lamp bearing the inscription: "Above all nations—humanity." Meanwhile, on August 5, the eve of the anniversary of the Hiroshima bombing, some 800 persons filled the University of Hamburg auditorium for a memorial meeting sponsored by the WRI branch and supported by 31 local groups, including the German Peace Society, the WILPF, the World Citizens, and the Crusade for World Government. Reports of the meeting were carried on the radio and in the press. A poll in June 1950 found that only 18 percent of West German respondents considered the U.S. atomic bombing of Japan justified and that 53 percent disapproved use of the atomic bomb in any future war.

The Italian peace movement, like its German counterpart, recovered slowly after the many years of fascist repression. Pacifists gradually regrouped around Professor Aldo Capitini of the University of Perugia and his friend Ferdinando Tartaglia, a Catholic priest. Together, they founded the Movement of Religion and, later, an Italian Association for Resistance to War. Much larger numbers of Italians flocked to the world federalist movement—especially to the Italian Movement for European Federation and World Federation, which claimed some 137,000 members by June 1949. In these ranks—and among Italians in general—antinuclear sentiment was widespread. The Italian press cited the well-known philosopher, Benedetto Croce, who remarked that, without humanity's moral and intellectual progress, the development of the Bomb would prove a catastrophe. According to a U.S. intelligence report on Italy, the U.S. government's decision to build the hydrogen bomb "brought forth the cry that this development was a 'last tragic warning to humanity' to find a path to peace or face complete destruction." Polling Italians in late 1950, one opinion survey found that, of those who thought that the United States might use the Bomb in a new war, six out of ten opposed such action.

Within Scandinavia, Denmark fielded the strongest antinuclear campaign. Preparing for the WILPF's international conference in 1946, the large Danish section proposed that the parent organization take on the nuclear issue, for "the end of civilization will be the result if atomic energy is not subjected to international control." World government activism provided another important element. Founded in 1946, the organization One World conducted hundreds of meetings, established local chapters, and by the summer of 1950, had some 13,000 supporters, including members of parliament. In a 1949 newspaper feature on One World, one of its leaders explained: "After the atom bomb, One World is the only defense." That same year, One World sponsored "The Atomic Age," an exhibit presented throughout Scandinavia that was designed to "show the devastating powers of the atomic bomb." Its organizers ordered 3,000 copies of pamphlets from America's Emergency Committee of Atomic Scientists and secured permission to translate them into Danish, Swedish, and Norwegian. In fact, the atomic scientists had considerable prestige in postwar Denmark, and Niels Bohr emerged as the nation's most influential critic of the nuclear arms race. The "whole scientific community," Bohr predicted, would "join in a vigorous effort . . . to appeal to humanity at large to heed the warning which has been sounded."

Distaste for nuclear war also grew rapidly in Sweden. Here, as elsewhere, pacifist groups were keen critics of nuclear weapons, but had only a small following. The new world government organizations were bigger and more dynamic. Visits by Henry Usborne, Bertrand Russell, Edith Wynner and other overseas luminaries sparked large public meetings and membership campaigns by world government organizations, such as the Swedish Group for World Federation. Interviewed on Swedish National Radio in December 1947 in a broadcast entitled "One World—or None," U.S. scientist Harold Urey argued that there was no conceivable military defense against nuclear weapons. The only safety, he said, lay in world government. Reported in detail by the Swedish press, the program created a substantial stir and was twice rebroadcast. The pacifist-oriented Swedish Peace and Arbitration Society, eager to promote the idea, published and distributed 50,000 copies of Urey's remarks. Much the same message was delivered in 1951, when federalist activists, flying in helicopters over Sweden's major cities, scattered leaflets calling for the creation of a popular movement for "world government and world peace," and concluding: "One World or none."

Although pacifism was also rather weak in Norway, newer peace currents were stirring here, as well. Spurred on by the nuclear arms race and by visits from British federalists, sentiment for world government gathered momentum and coalesced with the formation of a new organization, One World. Pacifists cooperated closely with the world federalists, as well as with the atomic scientists, to promote an awareness of the dangers of nuclear weapons. In 1947, the Norwegian WILPF branch printed and distributed a translation of Urey's antinuclear article, "I'm a Frightened Man," and also organized a very large public meeting in Oslo on the nuclear issue. The pacifist group also distributed an article by Hutchins ("The Secret of the Atomic Bomb Does Not Exist") and an antinuclear pamphlet by a Norwegian physicist, Leiv Kreyberg. Responding to pressure from pacifists, the Norwegian state radio station aired a broadcast, on August 6, 1949, on peace events in Hiroshima. It included a talk by a physicist at Trondheim Technical College who warned of the horrors of nuclear war. By 1950–51, antinuclear sentiment was rife in Norway.

In the Netherlands, too, nuclear resistance gradually took shape. Church and Peace, a small pacifist group affiliated with the FOR, claimed that, in a new war, "Europe will be completely lost. Preparation for this war means deliberate suicide for Europe." Meanwhile, inspired by the efforts of their U.S. counterparts, thirty Dutch scientists formed a team to lecture to civic leaders and public gatherings on the need for international control of atomic energy. World government activists organized public meetings, many addressed by Usborne, Russell, and other federalist proponents, and by 1950, nearly 29,000 people had joined the six Dutch branches of the World Movement for World Federal Government. As in France, the independent Left also turned to peace and disarmament activism, and a new movement it inspired, the Third Way, critiqued the nuclear arms race. Not surprisingly, Dutch revulsion at nuclear weapons grew. In November 1948, a Gallup poll reported that 52 percent of Dutch respondents thought that, in the long run, atomic energy would do more harm than good—more than twice the number adopting the positive interpretation.

Elsewhere in Western Europe, the situation was much the same. In Belgium, pacifism was weak and often preoccupied with other issues, but a rising world government movement vowed to work "against the atomic danger and the advent of a third war." In Austria, leading pacifists like Johannes Ude and scientists like Hans Thirring condemned the nuclear arms race, with Ude serving as a sponsor of World Peace Day. In Ireland, where pacifist groups consistently condemned nuclear weapons, even the mainstream press cast a baleful eye on the arms race. The time had come, observed the *Irish Times*, "to bring the Americans and the Russians together in order to call a halt to this insane race for armed supremacy."

By contrast, there was little overt resistance to nuclear weapons in the Soviet Union and Eastern Europe. To be sure, Soviet scientists did receive antinuclear literature mailed to them by their Western counterparts, and some expressed guarded signs of dismay at the Soviet Bomb project. Furthermore, scientists in Bulgaria and Czechoslovakia held meetings to discuss the international control of atomic energy. Moreover, small groups of Hungarians, Poles, Yugoslavs, Czechs, and East Germans showed an interest in world government. In Czechoslovakia, *The Anatomy of Peace* had a wide circulation, and reviews of it appeared in almost all Prague newspapers during 1947. Nevertheless, in the Soviet Union, pacifist organizations, like other antimilitary groups, had long ago been banned and effectively destroyed. Furthermore, Soviet scientists, motivated by patriotism and fear of antagonizing their brutal government, worked tamely to develop nuclear weapons. In Eastern Europe, too, the advent of Communist dictatorships snuffed out independent peace activism—as in Czechoslovakia, where the Communist coup of February 1948 brought an end to a growing world federalist organization.

The picture was somewhat brighter in the nations of the Third World. In Mexico, the small FOR group published a pacifist periodical and antimilitary pamphlets, among them a translation of Urey's "I'm a Frightened Man." In China, scientists' organizations, warning of "the total extermination of the human race," demanded international action to control nuclear weapons. In Argentina, the FOR journal featured a story by Einstein entitled "World Government or War of Extermination?" In India, where Gandhi repeatedly condemned nuclear weapons, pacifists held ceremonies in New Delhi on August 6, 1949, to mark World Peace Day. Small world government organizations emerged in Brazil, India, Turkey, Pakistan, Mexico, the Philippines, and elsewhere. Often these diverse groups had overlapping concerns. Joining the world federalist movement, the Argentina Pacifist Association publicized world federalism in its journal and displayed photos of Britain's Atomic Train exhibition. Although issues of poverty and national independence frequently eclipsed concerns about nuclear weaponry among people in the Third World, an August 1947 survey found that 66 percent of Mexican respondents favored an international agreement to prohibit the manufacture of atomic bombs.

This worldwide upsurge of concern about the Bomb prompted the major international pacifist organizations to make the nuclear issue a key item on their agendas. In 1948, the WRI circulated the Declaration of Peace that had been read at the foot of the Memorial Tower of Peace in Hiroshima by the mayor of that city. The International FOR organized its 1950 world conference around the theme of "Reconciliation in an 'Atomic World'— The Task of the Christian Pacifist." That year and the following one, the WILPF championed the idea of an armaments "truce," in which nations would halt production and use of weapons while a world disarmament conference convened to consider the replacement of national armed forces by a U.N. international police force. In December 1949, when leaders of these organizations and others met at a World Pacifist Meeting, in India, they voted "to cooperate with all genuine attempts to bring about disarmament, general or unilateral." Arguing that "the Atomic Age is proving the futility of military protection," they laid plans for the development of a worldwide nonviolent resistance movement.

Although antinuclear scientists failed in their attempts to build a formal international organization, they did manage to develop an informal network of concerned scientists. Determined to "promote an interchange of information and ideas" leading to "international atomic energy control," the Federation of American Scientists (FAS) mailed over 10,000 pamphlets on the nuclear issue to scientists in more than 60 nations. Among these publications were the Acheson-Lilienthal proposal, the Baruch proposal, and an FAS best-seller, *One World or None*. The American FAS and the British ASA remained particularly close, printing each other's statements in their publications and holding occasional joint meetings. In 1950, when Niels Bohr, in an *Open Letter to the United Nations*, argued that "a radical adjustment of international relationships is . . . indispensable if civilization shall survive," it received not only widespread support in Denmark, but from the growing scientists' movement. Both the ASA and the FAS distributed the *Open Letter* to their members and defended it against press criticism. It also provided a major topic of discussion at an international meeting they held that September.

Of the leading antinuclear groups, the most effective in developing a significant international organization were the world federalists. In September 1946, delegates from 37 organizations convened in Luxembourg and voted to establish the World Movement for World Federal Government. By the summer of 1950, the World Movement had some 156,000 members, located in 56 groups around the world. Millions of other people, although not members, had been converted to the idea of world government, including an estimated one million from 78 countries who had registered as World Citizens. UNESCO opinion polls in nine nations during 1948 and 1949 found that world government was favored by a majority or plurality of respondents in six of them (Britain, France, Italy, the Netherlands, Norway, and West Germany) and rejected in only three (Australia, Mexico, and the United States). Although the Bomb was not the only issue discussed by world federalists, their rhetoric and concerns were clearly linked to their sense of nuclear menace. Addressing the 1949 conference of the World Movement for World Federal Government, its president, Lord Boyd Orr, warned the delegates of "a third world war with atomic bombs" that would "put an end to our civilization."

The Communist-Led Movement

During these years, there also developed another kind of nuclear disarmament movement—one aligned with Soviet foreign policy. As the

Cold War heightened to the point of military confrontation, Communist leaders organized a mass movement to condemn Western foreign and military policy. A key component of this campaign was an effort to stigmatize nuclear weapons and, thereby, undermine the military advantage of the United States in this area. Furthermore, by directing their own peace movement, Communist leaders hoped to project the image of the Soviet Union as a peace-loving nation, attract new recruits to their parties, and overshadow nonaligned nuclear disarmament campaigns, which raised embarrassing questions about the Soviet Union's role in the Cold War and the arms race. Thus, although world Communist leaders initially applauded the atomic bombing of Japan, they eventually came around to denouncing nuclear weapons—or at least those weapons not in the hands of the Soviet Union.

Thanks to the antifascist role of the Soviet Union and Communist parties in World War II, Communism grew rapidly in the immediate postwar era and gained influence in many nations, especially among scientists and intellectuals. Drawing upon this influence, Communist leaders began to organize a "peace" campaign under their direction through the convening of a World Congress of Intellectuals for Peace in August 1948, in Wroclaw, Poland. Here, amid a vitriolic denunciation of the United States and other Western nations, they laid the groundwork for a World Peace Congress that met the following April, in Paris. According to the eminent French scientist (and Communist) Frédéric Joliot-Curie, who chaired the conclave, the Paris meeting and an allied gathering in Prague represented 600 million people in 72 countries—a figure apparently derived by counting the entire populations of Communist nations and adding on the memberships of Communist parties and Communist-controlled groups elsewhere. More denunciations of the West followed, as did wild applause for Communist ventures. Lauding Communist military advances, the head of the Chinese Communist delegation proclaimed: "Led by the Soviet Union, the camp of peace and democracy . . . is capable of sending the warmongers to the grave." The assemblage also established a new organization to conduct a Communist-led peace and disarmament campaign, the Partisans of Peace.

One of the key ventures of the new organization focused on nuclear weapons. In March 1950, at an international conference in Stockholm, the Partisans of Peace adopted an ingenious resolution, drafted by Soviet writer Ilya Ehrenburg, that became known as the Stockholm Peace Appeal.

It demanded "the unconditional prohibition of the atomic weapon," the branding of the government that first used the weapon as "a war criminal," and signatures on the appeal by "all people of good-will." Despite the moderate tone of the Stockholm Peace Appeal, it stigmatized a weapon in which the West enjoyed a military advantage, sidestepped the complexities of how to ban the Bomb, and was the exclusive property of a Communist-directed peace campaign. Therefore, the petition process, although immense, remained confined largely to Communists and Communist sympathizers. Drawing upon the substantial apparatus of the Peace Partisans—and behind them the staunch support of governments in Communist nations and of Communist parties in other nations—the Stockholm petition campaign claimed 500 million signatures from 79 countries by the end of 1950. But more than 400 million of the alleged signers came from Communist nations, including what were purportedly the entire populations of the Soviet Union and its East European satellites.

In November 1950, after the outbreak of the Korean War, the Peace Partisans met again and reorganized their movement into the World Peace Council (WPC). Headed by Joliot-Curie, the WPC claimed that it was comprised of more than 75 national peace committees and 150,000 local groups. Labeling itself "the genuine voice of peace-loving mankind," the WPC condemned the United Nations and launched blistering attacks on the U.S. government, which it charged with everything from waging "germ warfare" in Korea to fomenting a third world war. Characteristically, the WPC never expressed any doubts about the peace-loving nature of Communist governments.

With this peace campaign almost entirely dependent upon Communist parties for support, its strength in different nations reflected the size and influence of these parties. In the United States, the small, unpopular, and besieged Communist Party organized a number of controversial peace conferences in 1949 and 1950, as well as a tiny Peace Information Center, which distributed the Stockholm Peace petition. By contrast, in France, where the Communist Party had a substantial membership and popular support, the Communist-led Movement for Peace grew into a mass organization, garnering some 14 million signatures on the Stockholm petition. In these and other non-Communist nations, the Communist-led movement stridently denounced the governments of Western nations as "warmongers," lauded the governments of Communist nations as paragons of peace, and sneered derisively at nonaligned peace organizations. In Communist nations, governments used the full apparatus of state power to whip up public support for (or at least acquiescence in) the Communist-led peace campaign. When some church leaders refused to play a role in it, the authorities had them arrested. Meanwhile, the Soviet press churned out stories about Soviet citizens eagerly lining up to sign the Stockholm petition and about allegedly happy Soviet workers who were overfulfilling their production quotas to build up the strength of the Soviet Union and, thus, bolster peace. In contrast to the American heirs to "fascist slavery and annihilation," reported the head of the Soviet Peace Committee, the Soviet Union was "marching boldly along the path of peace because the immortal genius of the great fighter for peace and the happiness of peoples—the great Stalin—lights our way."

Not surprisingly, the leading organizations and personalities in the nonaligned movement gave the Communist-led peace campaign a chilly reception. Although individual pacifists sometimes participated in Communist-led ventures, the pacifist internationals refused to send delegates to the world conferences organized by the Communist-led movement or to support them in other ways. As two WILPF leaders recalled, "it was difficult, and sometimes painful, to cast doubts on expressions of solidarity in the cause of peace ... that claimed a mass following" through the WPC and its affiliates, "but impossible not to do so when these movements were so at variance with the real conditions of life behind the Iron Curtain and so lacking in criticism of provocative actions by Communist governments." The nonaligned scientists' movement also kept its distance. Asked to send a message to the 1949 World Peace Congress in Paris, Einstein replied that he did not believe this kind of gathering would "really serve the cause of international understanding," for "it is more or less a Soviet enterprise and everything is managed accordingly." According to a report on the September 1950 meeting of delegates from the British ASA and the American FAS, the Stockholm Peace Appeal was considered no more than "a piece of propaganda." Similarly, in 1951, when the WPC seemed on the verge of sending several observers to a conference of the World Meeting for World Federal Government, in Rome, both the executive committee and the delegates voted to bar their admission.

Thus, by the early 1950s, the worldwide struggle against the Bomb had two divergent components. The Communist-led component was massive and well-funded but, at the same time, politically isolated outside of Communist nations thanks to its pro-Soviet orientation. The nonaligned movement, though smaller and much less tightly structured, had a greater impact, particularly upon public opinion. Indeed, by emphasizing the prospect of nuclear holocaust, peace and disarmament groups helped generate a shift in popular thinking toward the approval of limits set on national sovereignty, ranging from the international control of atomic energy to outright world government. Admittedly, pacifists, atomic scientists, and world government advocates, sometimes joined by religious leaders, played the leading role in voicing such ideas, but poll after poll showed that such concepts were taking root in the broader society. Confronted by the unprecedented danger of nuclear war, people showed a remarkable willingness to accept new thinking about international relations.

3   Government Response, 1945–1953

Well aware of the rising public concern about nuclear weapons, government officials sought some means of accommodation with the movement against the Bomb. The leaders of the great powers consulted with nuclear critics, warned of nuclear dangers, and backed plans for international control of atomic energy. But, as the Cold War gathered momentum, they began to show less interest in fostering nuclear arms controls than in winning a nuclear arms race. Ultimately, then, they commenced a steady retreat from the new thinking to the old. Nevertheless, the retreat was only partial. In nations further from the centers of power, government officials remained committed to nuclear arms control and disarmament. And even in the nuclear and would-be nuclear nations, government leaders continued at least their rhetorical support for nuclear arms controls and showed a newfound hesitation at the launching of nuclear war.

The United States

In the United States, government leaders were shaken by the enormous destructiveness of the Hiroshima bombing and by the sharp criticism that it generated. At President Truman's cabinet meeting of August 8, 1945, according to one record of the gathering, he "expressed concern" about apparent papal condemnation of the Bomb and "pointed out that the cooperation of the Vatican is needed in days to come, particularly in dealing with the Catholic countries of Europe." To the President's dismay, on August 9 he received word from the Federal Council of Churches that it, too, was about to issue a public condemnation of the atomic bombing. When top U.S. officials gathered in the White House the following morning, Stimson suggested that the bombing be halted. According to one of those present, "he cited the growing feeling of apprehension and misgiving as to the effect of the atomic bomb even in our own country." Taking

Stimson's advice, Truman told his cabinet later that day that he had ordered a halt to the use of atomic bombs in the war.

As debate grew over the wisdom and morality of the bombing, the Truman administration became increasingly embarrassed and defensive. When Szilard sought to publish his anti-bombing petition of July 17, 1945, the U.S. Army threatened to have him fired from his job at the University of Chicago and prosecuted under the Espionage Act. In November 1945, attempting to counter disturbing reports about deaths in Japan from radioactivity, General Groves informed a congressional committee that doctors had assured him that radiation poisoning was "a very pleasant way to die." Shortly afterward, Robert Oppenheimer accompanied Undersecretary of State Dean Acheson to the White House and remarked that some atomic scientists felt they had blood on their hands. Incensed by the incident, Truman told Acheson: "I don't want to see that son of a bitch in this office ever again." Oppenheimer, he claimed, had "turned into a crybaby. I don't want anything to do with people like that."

At the same time, the widespread public uneasiness about nuclear weapons pushed U.S. officials toward a new approach. On September 11, 1945, Stimson warned Truman that the Bomb constituted "a first step in a new control by man over the forces of nature too revolutionary and dangerous to fit into the old concepts." Two weeks later, Acheson wrote Truman that "international controls" over nuclear weapons "should be sought to prevent a race toward mutual destruction." Barraged by the public and by his advisors, Truman launched a dramatic reversal of U.S. policy. On October 3, in a message drafted by Acheson that he delivered to Congress, the President declared: "The release of atomic energy constitutes a new force too revolutionary to consider in the framework of old ideas." Therefore, "the hope of civilization lies in international arrangements looking, if possible, to the renunciation of the use and development of the atomic bomb." In November 1945, when the leaders of the United States, Britain, and Canada met to consider nuclear issues, they adopted a joint statement—the Truman-Attlee-King Declaration—that brought the new thinking into focus. It called for the establishment of a U.N. commission to prepare recommendations "for the elimination from national armaments of atomic weapons and of all other major weapons adaptable to mass destruction."

The Truman administration's first concrete proposal along these lines was the Acheson-Lilienthal Plan. Meeting in early 1946, a government committee—headed by Acheson and with important input from TVA director David Lilienthal and from Oppenheimer—crafted an ingenious formula for the international control of atomic energy. Announced in March 1946 and soon known as the Acheson-Lilienthal Plan, it provided for the creation of an Atomic Development Authority, an international body that would maintain a monopoly of fissionable material and distribute it only in "denatured" form for peaceful purposes. Meanwhile, existing nuclear weapons would be destroyed and a system of international inspection would alert nations to any violations of the agreement.

The Acheson-Lilienthal Plan was a direct result of the new climate of thinking fostered by critics of the Bomb. Referring to the plan, Lilienthal observed that he had received his first "acquaintance with . . . the atomic energy problem" from a conference at the University of Chicago organized by Szilard and the scientists' movement. Oppenheimer, particularly, had been deeply influenced by the scientists' movement and especially by Bohr, whereas Acheson felt the public pressure for nuclear disarmament keenly. Drawing on the ideas of the Franck report, Bohr, and the postwar campaign against nuclear weapons, the Acheson-Lilienthal report emphasized not only the immense danger posed by the Bomb but the hopelessness of military defense against the new weapon and the futility of national attempts to maintain a nuclear monopoly. Shortly after the report appeared, Oppenheimer wrote privately that it "proposes that in the field of atomic energy there be set up a world government" and "that in this field there be a renunciation of national sovereignty."

However, the Acheson-Lilienthal Plan represented the zenith of the movement's influence upon American public policy for, starting in March 1946, the U.S. government began moving toward a more traditional approach. In part, this shift resulted from Truman's appointment that month of Bernard Baruch, a crusty, aged South Carolina financier, to serve as the U.S. representative to the new U.N. Atomic Energy Commission. Deeply suspicious of the Soviet Union, Baruch was determined to craft a U.S. atomic energy proposal that better served what he considered U.S. national interests than did the Acheson-Lilienthal Plan. He remarked: "I think Messrs. Truman, Attlee and King got stampeded into making their original proposals." Eventually, then, the Baruch Plan called for elimination of the Security Council veto in enforcement actions, punishment of offending nations (presumably by war), and retention of the U.S. nuclear monopoly until the final stage of international control. Nevertheless, the Baruch Plan did constitute a serious nuclear arms control proposal, which, if adopted, would have strengthened world authority through unprecedented limitations on national sovereignty. Presented at the United Nations in June 1946, it was rejected by the Soviet Union.

If the Baruch Plan represented an unproductive compromise between the new thinking and the old, subsequent U.S. policy signaled a substantial reversion to traditional norms of international behavior. Even as diplomatic negotiations continued over the international control of atomic energy, the U.S. government substantially upgraded its nuclear arsenal until, by late 1949, it contained approximately 200 atomic bombs. That July, Truman secretly told a group of diplomats from friendly countries that "we'll never obtain international control" and, therefore, "we must be strongest in atomic weapons." Although U.S. officials kept up a public pretense of desiring to control nuclear weapons, the reality was that they had lost interest in the idea. Uncomfortable with U.S. hypocrisy, Acheson—now secretary of state—complained to Lilienthal at the end of the year that "we keep saying we want the control policy when we don't."

Indeed, in the context of a growing Cold War, the nuclear arms race rapidly accelerated. On October 5, 1949, shortly after Truman announced the first successful test of a Soviet atomic bomb, Lewis Strauss, a member of the U.S. Atomic Energy Commission (AEC), sent a letter to his fellow commissioners that called for "an intensive effort" to build a hydrogen bomb, a weapon with a thousand times the power of the bomb that had destroyed Hiroshima. "That is the way to stay ahead," he insisted. A self-made businessman, Strauss believed that "the only thing that retires a weapon is a superior weapon." And the H-bomb "may be critically useful against a large enemy force both as a weapon of offense and as a defensive measure."

Unexpectedly, though, substantial resistance to producing an H-bomb developed within the AEC. The General Advisory Committee, chaired by Oppenheimer and composed of scientists, unanimously opposed such a policy. Six members declared their belief that "the extreme dangers to mankind inherent in the proposal wholly outweigh any military advantage that could come from this development." Given its unlimited destructive power, the H-bomb could "become a weapon of genocide." Conversely, by refusing to develop the weapon, the United States could provide "by example some limitations on the totality of war"; at the same time, it would remain protected by its large stock of atomic bombs. Responding to this report, the AEC split three to two in its November 9 recommendation to the President. The minority, led by Strauss, championed a crash program to build the new weapon, but the majority, led by Lilienthal, opposed it. "To launch upon a program of Superbombs," Lilienthal declared, "would set us upon still another costly cycle of misconception and illusion about the value to us of weapons of mass destruction."

Despite the stand of the AEC majority and of the General Advisory Committee, the outcome was heavily weighted toward building the new weapon. As Truman recalled: "I believed that anything that would assure us the lead in the field of atomic energy development for defense had to be tried out." On January 31, 1950, in the penultimate meeting on the issue, the President conferred with three top officials from the National Security Council, who presented him with differing views. Lilienthal, who was one of them, tried to make the case for a new disarmament initiative, but the President interrupted him and insisted that he hadn't "any alternative but to go ahead and that was what he was going to do." Recalling that he had stood up to "a steamroller," Lilienthal felt that Truman was "clearly set on what he was going to do before we set foot inside the door." The entire meeting lasted seven minutes.

Thereafter, the administration rebuffed calls for disarmament initiatives, secured the resignation of key opponents of the H-bomb from the General Advisory Committee, and developed immense nuclear construction projects. Within a few years, the U.S. nuclear construction program absorbed approximately one-tenth the electricity produced in the United States. On November 1, 1952, the U.S. government set off its first thermonuclear device in the Pacific. Vastly more powerful than the bomb that had devastated Hiroshima, the weapon obliterated an entire island, one mile in diameter, and left a huge crater on the ocean floor.

And yet, despite this lurch forward in the nuclear arms race, the Truman administration remained uneasy about using nuclear weapons. During the Korean War, for example, there seemed good military reasons to use them. For one thing, U.S. forces were close to military defeat at the hands of non-nuclear powers. Furthermore, there was no prospect of a nuclear counterattack by the Soviet Union—a nation that was not participating in the conflict, had only recently developed an atomic bomb, and lacked an effective delivery system for it. But, thanks to the worldwide antinuclear campaign, employing the Bomb in war had become politically difficult. U.S. intelligence reported that, in Great Britain, there existed "widespread popular alarm concerning the possible use of the A-bomb." Similarly, the State Department's Far East specialist warned that use of the Bomb on an Asian population would cause a "revulsion of feeling" to "spread throughout Asia. . . . Our efforts to win the Asiatics to our side would be cancelled and our influence in non-Communist nations of Asia would deteriorate to an almost non-existent quantity." In military terms, the Bomb probably would be effective, observed Paul Nitze, head of the State Department's policy planning staff. But using it would "arouse the peoples of Asia against us." In these circumstances, political considerations overwhelmed military ones, and Truman rejected calls by top U.S. military officers to win the Korean War with nuclear weapons.

Even so, given their commitment to maintaining U.S. military superiority, U.S. officials reacted with great hostility toward nuclear critics, particularly the Communists. In March 1949, when one of the Communist-led peace conferences convened in New York City, the FBI spied on its leaders and the State Department denied visas to all foreign delegates from non-Communist countries who it believed held Communist views. The following month, as the Peace Partisans met in Paris, the State Department sought to discredit them by disseminating hostile material in labor, intellectual, and religious circles. Thereafter, it barred a Peace Partisans delegation from visiting the United States, pressed friendly governments to block the holding of Communist-organized peace congresses in their countries, and launched its own peace propaganda campaign. Denouncing "the Trojan dove from the Communist movement," Acheson charged that the Stockholm petition was no more than "a propaganda trick in the spurious 'peace offensive' of the Soviet Union."

Leading spokespersons for the Communist-led campaign came in for rough treatment. In the summer of 1950, the State Department barred Paul Robeson, a prominent figure at Communist-led peace congresses, from overseas travel. Early the following year, the U.S. government indicted five leaders of the Peace Information Center for failing to register as agents of the Partisans of Peace and its successor, the WPC. Among those indicted, fingerprinted, and handcuffed was its 83-year-old chair, W. E. B. Du Bois, who faced five years' imprisonment, a $10,000 fine, and loss of civil and political rights. Although a federal court dismissed the charges against the Peace Information Center in late 1951, the following year the State Department denied an application by Du Bois and his wife to travel to a peace conference in Brazil.

U.S. officials also attacked nonaligned activists. In 1946, General Groves vetoed the award of a proposed Certificate of Appreciation to Szilard. "It was quite evident" that Szilard "showed a lack of support, even approaching disloyalty, to his superiors," the general charged. When Szilard and other leaders of the scientists' movement proposed a meeting of American and Soviet scientists to discuss nuclear arms control, Secretary of State Byrnes blocked the venture. Highly critical of the atomic scientists, Baruch complained to Lilienthal: "The only thing the scientist does is to frighten the public about atomic energy, and [this] may force something foolish to be done." On another occasion, he argued that "the scientists should keep to their field and not go into ethics or politics." Not surprisingly, Baruch decided to "drop the scientists" from the planning process for international control of nuclear weapons. Although the scientists' movement had a good relationship with the AEC during its early years, this changed after Lilienthal was succeeded as AEC chair by Gordon Dean, one of the two AEC commissioners who had supported building the H-bomb. In late 1950, the AEC seized and burned 3,000 copies of the *Scientific American* for publishing an article on the H-bomb by one of the weapon's leading scientific critics, Hans Bethe.

The U.S. government took a particularly hard line toward politically active scientists in other nations. Based on a study he did for the FAS, Victor Weisskopf estimated in April 1952 that "at least 50% of all the foreign scientists who want to enter the U.S. meet some difficulties." These difficulties included lengthy delays in obtaining visas or outright denials of them. Although the State Department usually failed to provide explanations, scientists in the field of nuclear physics or whose political activity was "suspected of being unorthodox by U.S. standards" were the most frequently rejected group. Among them were Rudolph Peierls and H. S. W. Massey of Britain, the president and the executive vice-president of Britain's ASA. Discussing the ban on his travel to the United States, Marc Oliphant, the distinguished Australian physicist, recalled that the U.S. consul general "assured me that I was not accused of having any Communist affiliations or of subversive activity. But my public speeches . . . and my campaigning for peace 'were providing bullets for the Russians and other enemies to fire back at the U.S.'"

America's own atomic scientists became the subjects of intense loyalty-security investigations and experienced repeated attacks upon their patriotism. In September 1946, as part of its plans for emergency detention of alleged subversives, the FBI told the Justice Department that "existing scientific groups have been infiltrated by Communists with the view in mind of propagandizing the relinquishment of the secret of the atomic bomb." Four years later, Senator Joseph McCarthy charged that the FAS was "heavily infiltrated with communist fellow-travelers." As one historian has observed, "no group was more closely inspected or forced so often to prove their loyalty" than American scientists. "Because of this special attention, physicists and mathematicians made up more than half of the people who were identified as Communists in congressional hearings. Hundreds of scientists were mercilessly pursued, often losing their jobs, some of them ending in exile or suicide."

Given his repeated calls for peace and nuclear disarmament, Einstein became an important target of government suspicion and surveillance. Although Einstein had never shown any signs of being a Soviet agent or a Communist, in 1950 the FBI launched an investigation of the famed scientist to explore both possibilities. In part, this action resulted from a request by the Immigration and Naturalization Service, which suggested the appealing prospect of canceling his citizenship. Eventually, J. Edgar Hoover's minions gathered some 1,500 pages of evidence on Einstein's allegedly subversive activities, including articles he had written for the *Bulletin of the Atomic Scientists* and other publications calling for nuclear arms controls and world government. Only in 1955, after the famed scientist's death, did the FBI close the Einstein case.

Other nonaligned nuclear critics also received a sharp rebuff. When the chair of Britain's Peace Pledge Union arrived in the United States to embark on a speaking tour arranged by American pacifists, he was seized by U.S. agents and held for two weeks before being allowed to continue. Excoriating "the 'One Worlders,'" Baruch charged that they were undermining plans for nuclear arms controls. On October 18, 1948, in a public address, Truman warned about the dangers of atomic weapons, but cautioned that it would "be a long while before the great powers constitute the friendly family of nations which is often described as 'One World.'"

Other components of the federal government also assailed nuclear critics. Conducting an investigation of United World Federalists in 1948, the House Committee on Un-American Activities charged that sixteen persons whose names appeared in its literature were affiliated with other groups cited as "Communist-front and/or subversive." In 1952, a rider tacked onto federal legislation barred the distribution of funds to federal agencies that promoted, directly or indirectly, "one-world government or one-world citizenship." In accordance with its provisions, the federal government removed numerous books from its overseas information centers. Meanwhile, Senator McCarthy and his cohorts repeatedly attacked the "one-worlders."

Naturally, providing the public with a positive view of U.S. nuclear weapons was very important. Concerned about the furor that had erupted over the U.S. atomic bombing of Hiroshima and Nagasaki, Truman and other officials arranged for Stimson to write an article that would make the case for it. Stimson hoped the article, published in 1947, would offset the critique of the bombing by scientists and "satisfy the doubts of that rather difficult class of the community which will have charge of the education of the next generation, namely educators and historians." In February 1950, worried about public reaction to the latest U.S. entry in the arms race, Truman told Acheson that "the least said about the so-called hydrogen bomb by officials . . . the better it will be for all concerned." In 1952, the President approved the recommendation of the government's Psychological Strategy Board that "we must be extremely careful in our public statements about atomic weapons." Before issuing such statements, officials should ask themselves if this information would "strengthen the morale of the free world" or "create the fear that the U.S. may act recklessly in the use of these weapons."

Britain

During the fall of 1945, under what the U.S. State Department called "heavy public pressure," numerous officials in the British government championed the new thinking. Referring to the atomic bomb, Stafford Cripps, a member of the new Labour Party cabinet, declared that it was "absolutely vital and essential that we should not allow this new form of destruction to be let loose on the world. . . . War has become certain national and international suicide." Addressing parliament, Foreign Secretary Ernest Bevin declared that, with "the coming of the atomic bomb," the world was "driven relentlessly" toward "a greater sovereignty." There would have to be "a world law with a world judiciary to interpret it, with a world police to enforce it," and with "a world assembly" to enact it. Britain's new prime minister, Clement Attlee, too, called for "a bold course [that] can save civilization." Writing to Truman on September 25, he argued: "If mankind continues to make the atomic bomb without changing the political relationships of States, sooner or later these bombs will be used for mutual annihilation." Thus, there needed to be "a fresh review of world policy and a new valuation of what are called national interests." These views fed into the dramatic Truman-Attlee-King Declaration that November.

But as the Cold War advanced and as it became clear that Washington, despite earlier assurances, planned to maintain a U.S. nuclear monopoly, pressures mounted within the British government to build Britain's own nuclear weapons. The chiefs of staff argued that "to delay production pending the outcome of negotiations regarding international control might well prove fatal." Others, such as Bevin and Attlee, believed that Britain, as a great power, required the most advanced weapons available. Speaking at a meeting of the Defence Sub-committee of the British cabinet in October 1946, Bevin sharply criticized those who said that Britain could not afford the Bomb and expostulated: "We've got to have this thing over here whatever it costs. . . . We've got to have the bloody Union Jack flying on top of it." In January 1947, at a meeting of the subcommittee that gave the go-ahead for the Bomb project, he once again argued forcefully that Britain, as a great power, "could not afford to acquiesce in an American monopoly of this new development."

Within official ranks, the only substantial dissent came from P. M. S. Blackett, a physicist serving on the government's Advisory Committee on Atomic Energy. In a lengthy memo submitted in late 1945, he contended that an atomic weapons program would be both costly and of limited value to Britain's defense. Accordingly, Blackett recommended that Britain proclaim that it would not manufacture them, that it welcomed inspection by the United Nations, and that it invited other countries to do the same. About a year later, in another memo and in meetings with Attlee, he championed Britain's continued abstention from production of nuclear weapons.

But these arguments met with a brusque rejection by the British government. Dismissing Blackett as a "layman" on political and military problems, the prime minister referred his first memorandum to the chiefs of staff, who expressed their "complete disagreement" with its assumptions and conclusions. Attlee concurred. Blackett's later proposals encountered even fiercer resistance. The Foreign Office called them "dangerous and misleading rubbish." Commenting on the same matter, the minister of state opined that the only issue requiring action was Blackett's continued presence on the government's advisory committee. The British nuclear weapons program moved forward steadily, with no interruption. In late 1951, when the opposition Conservatives returned to power, they gave it their eager support. As a result, Britain's first atomic bomb was exploded over Australia's Monte Bello Islands in October 1952.

As in the United States, this commitment to building a nuclear arsenal prompted efforts to contain the critics. A key way to accomplish this was to limit public knowledge of the British nuclear weapons program. Consequently, until 1952, it was concealed not only from the public, but from parliament and most of the cabinet. The Attlee government also looked askance at the nuclear disarmament activities of some of the leading British atomic scientists. Commenting on ASA leaders, one of Attlee's top aides warned: "It is a curious, but none-the-less important fact, that extreme brilliance in scientific research is very frequently coupled with immaturity of outlook. . . . Many of the young men engaged on atomic research, who are hand-picked for their brilliance, are adolescent in their approach to political and similar questions." Naturally, government officials cooperated as little as possible with the Atomic Train exhibition, the ASA's most important attempt at popular education on atomic energy. Senior government officials deliberately declined invitations to the exhibit's opening. Later, when Rotblat invited Attlee to visit the Atomic Train during its stay in London, both the defense minister and the foreign secretary advised him to reject the offer, which he did.

The British government also adopted a very hostile approach to the Communist-led peace movement. In October 1950, with a Communist-initiated peace conference looming at Sheffield, Bevin denounced the Communist-led peace campaign as "a fraud." The BBC, especially in its foreign broadcasts, also began a steady campaign against Communist-organized peace meetings. Following up, Attlee used a well-publicized speech that November to condemn plans to hold "a bogus peace conference at Sheffield." Through "the precious Stockholm Peace Appeal" and other measures, he charged, the Communist organizers sought "to paralyze the efforts of the democracies to arm themselves." To counter this, he declared, the British government would "refuse admittance to those whose intention one knows is to burn the house down." Consequently, the government denied admittance to approximately half the conference delegates. Giving up the struggle, the conference organizers moved the gathering to the far more welcoming environs of Warsaw.

British public opinion remained more of a problem. Although the government managed to avoid agitating the public by keeping the existence of the British Bomb program a secret, other Bomb-related issues sometimes caused serious difficulties. The most significant of these erupted when Truman, at his press conference of November 30, 1950, implied that the U.S. government was considering the use of the Bomb in Korea. According to the record of a British cabinet meeting later that day, in the context of "great alarm in the House of Commons," Attlee proposed to announce his intention to go to Washington to consult with Truman. Although he remarked that "the responsibility for deciding on the use of the atom bomb would have to be defined," the prime minister seemed more concerned about how to deal with public opinion, for he "said that urgent action was necessary in order to allay popular anxiety." This point was later reiterated by Acheson, who recalled that the British ambassador told him that "the principal pressure was from the British domestic political situation and increasing public anxiety over present developments." In Britain, as in the United States, government officials had to reckon with the fact that waging nuclear war had become extremely unpopular.

The Soviet Union

Although the Soviet nuclear project was well under way by August 1945, the U.S. atomic attacks on Hiroshima and Nagasaki convinced the Soviet leadership to initiate a crash program to obtain the Bomb. In the middle of that month, shortly after Stalin's return from Potsdam, he called together the people's commissar of munitions, his deputies, and Igor Kurchatov (the physicist who directed the Soviet nuclear project) for a meeting at the Kremlin. "A single demand of you, comrades," Stalin said. "Provide us with atomic weapons in the shortest possible time. You know that Hiroshima has shaken the whole world. The balance has been destroyed. Provide the bomb—it will remove a great danger from us." Long profoundly suspicious of the capitalist West, Stalin was concerned not only that the Bomb's vast power lay in hands other than his own but that the U.S. government seemed perfectly willing to use it as a weapon of war and diplomacy. Soviet leaders trusted American leaders no more than the latter trusted them.

Indeed, in his memoirs, Nikita Khrushchev claimed that Stalin was not merely suspicious of Anglo-American leaders, but "frightened to the point of cowardice." According to Khrushchev, Stalin knew "that we faced the possibility of still another war—one which would be fought with modern weapons. ... And he also knew that in this sphere we lagged behind the West." Consequently, "Stalin trembled with fear," Khrushchev recalled; "how he quivered!" Terrified that "the capitalist countries would attack the Soviet Union," Stalin "ordered that the whole country be put on military alert.... Guns were set up around Moscow, loaded with shells, and manned around the clock by artillery crews, ready to open fire at a moment's notice." Obsessed with Soviet vulnerability, Stalin "completely monopolized all decisions about our defenses, including—I'd even say *especially*—involving nuclear weapons and delivery systems."

Spurred on by Stalin, the Soviet Union made great efforts to match America's nuclear achievements. Under the direction of Lavrenti Beria—the chief of the secret police, to whom Stalin had entrusted the venture—the atomic bomb project recruited leading Soviet scientists, engineers, and industrial managers; large numbers of others came from the ranks of political prisoners, who performed approximately half the nuclear research. Prison laborers carried out most of the widespread mining and construction work. Disturbed that the Bomb was not ready by 1947, Stalin initiated a purge of the nuclear scientists. This scientific purge, aimed especially at Jews, probably delayed progress on the project. Finally, on August 29, 1949, the Soviet Union tested its first atomic bomb, thereby performing the feat in only a little more time than the United States had taken.

Although Soviet scientists began work on the theoretical possibilities of a hydrogen bomb in 1948, this project, like the race to develop an atomic bomb, was stimulated—at least in part—by American efforts. Klaus Fuchs—who spied for the Soviet Union during his nuclear research in the United States and in Britain—had told his Soviet contact about wartime studies of the H-bomb at Los Alamos, and Truman had announced the American decision to build an H-bomb in January 1950. Furthermore, the first American thermonuclear test, in 1952, apparently played a role in accelerating Soviet research and suggesting technical breakthroughs. Consequently, just as the production of the first Soviet atomic bomb encouraged the U.S. government to develop a hydrogen bomb, so U.S. efforts to build a hydrogen bomb encouraged Soviet leaders to proceed with the development of their own. It was tested less than a year later, in 1953.

Given the Soviet regime's sharp fear of America's nuclear monopoly, it is not entirely clear why the Soviet Union did not react more favorably to the Baruch Plan. Some observers have speculated that the Soviet government could not tolerate the abolition of the veto—and thus dominance of the control process by a Western majority—entailed in the U.S. proposal. Others, such as Baruch, claimed that Soviet leaders feared "permitting their country to be subjected to inspection from without." Both objections seem implicit in the Soviet counterproposal, which called for destroying U.S. atomic stockpiles without inspection or enforcement. The key to understanding Soviet policy might be that Soviet leaders, like their American and British counterparts, had decided to head off what they perceived as threats to their national security by the traditional method of amassing military strength. Because they expected to possess nuclear weapons in the near future, the Baruch Plan, which would terminate their nuclear development program while leaving the United States in possession of its atomic bombs for an indefinite period, had little appeal. Indeed, to overcome the U.S. nuclear monopoly, all they had to do at the U.N. atomic energy talks was to stall, making deferential gestures to international control of nuclear weapons, until the Soviet Bomb was ready.

Meanwhile, the Soviet government, recognizing the growing public fear of world destruction, sought to capitalize upon it by mobilizing the Communist-led peace campaign. Initiated and lavishly funded by the Kremlin, the Partisans of Peace movement and its successor, the WPC, became part of a massive Soviet propaganda effort to channel popular discontent with nuclear weapons into opposition to U.S. foreign policy and backing for its Soviet counterpart. In November 1949, at the behest of Mikhail Suslov, the Soviet official responsible for international Communist affairs, the Cominform adopted a resolution heaping praise on the "mighty movement of the partisans of peace" and directing Communist parties and other Communist-controlled groups to make the Communist-led peace campaign their top priority. According to the Suslov resolution, that campaign "should now become the pivot of the entire activity" of Communist parties and organizations.

Naturally, the Soviet press produced a flood of adoring stories about the Partisans of Peace and, later, the WPC. The Paris Peace Congress "has stirred the hearts of millions and millions," the Soviet *New Times* reported, and "the might of the Soviet Union infuses them with new strength for a successful struggle against the warmongers." In these circumstances, noted *Pravda*, anyone in any country who refused to sign the Stockholm petition automatically proved himself "an accomplice and henchman of the warmongers." Such resistance was no more than "a vain effort to turn back the wheel of history," argued the *New Times*, for "the front of peace is invincible." Indeed, "the warmongers are suffering defeat after defeat in their struggle against the mighty movement of the partisans of peace."

Soviet support for the worldwide Communist peace campaign was displayed in other ways, as well. Mounting an enormous effort, Soviet officials encouraged or coerced what they claimed was "the entire adult population of the country" into signing the Stockholm petition. They also mobilized substantial numbers of Soviet agricultural and industrial workers to put in additional shifts or to overfulfill their production quotas. To encourage the population further, the Soviet government installed large, brightly painted "peace" signs along the highways outside Moscow bearing such inspirational slogans as "U.S.S.R. pillar of peace." The Soviet government also began awarding Stalin Peace Prizes for "outstanding services in combating the warmongers and promoting peace." According to the *New Times*, this was perfectly appropriate, for "the international peace front" drew its "inspiration" from "the genius of the great Stalin," the "man who heads the world front of struggle for peace." Not surprisingly, the prizes went to the luminaries of the Communist-led peace campaign.

Kremlin officials took a considerably less favorable view of pacifists. "Pacifist ideology," declared Soviet leader Georgi Malenkov in 1949, "usually combines a verbal condemnation of war with total inaction." In similar fashion, an article in *Pravda* the following year argued that "well meant pacifist wishes cannot curb the subversive policy against peace." Apparently hostile to the WILPF, the Soviet government worked to deny that international pacifist group nongovernmental organization status at the United Nations. Furthermore, like their American counterparts, Soviet officials were dismayed by the activities of pacifists within their own Cold War camp. When dozens of members of Jehovah's Witnesses, a pacifist religious sect, were arrested by the Polish government for their refusal to sign the Stockholm petition, *Izvestia* headlined a story on the event: "Warmongers' Accomplices Are Caught Red-Handed." The Soviet newspaper reported proudly that "this band of American spies and diversionists has been liquidated." *Pravda* insisted: "With the fighters for peace or with the warmongers—there is no third way!"

The atomic scientists also came in for sharp criticism. Writing in *New Times* in June 1946, a Soviet military affairs specialist produced a slashing attack on the FAS book, *One World or None*. The atomic scientists' "florid talk about a 'world state,'" he charged, "is actually a frank plea for American imperialism." In June 1947, Andrei Zhdanov, a member of the Politburo and reputedly second in command to Stalin, publicly condemned "the Kantian vagaries of modern bourgeois atomic physicists," thereby launching a heated ideological campaign against Western and Soviet scholars. Over the next few years, Soviet newspaper or magazine articles attacked Einstein (a proponent of "world domination"), Bohr (a "western bourgeois idealist"), and other leaders of the scientists' movement. Meanwhile, Soviet films warned

Soviet scientists against becoming "homeless cosmopolitans" or "passport-less wanderers in humanity." In 1948, when the Emergency Committee of Atomic Scientists sought to arrange a conference of leading scientists from East and West to discuss the failure to secure nuclear arms controls, the Soviet government shut the door firmly on the proposal.

At least some of this resistance by the Soviet regime to scientific "cosmo-politanism" was based on a growing fear of the concept of world government. Apparently connecting the world federalist idea to the more modest Baruch Plan, the Soviet government launched a shrill attack. In October 1946, Molotov warned of "world domination by way of . . . world government," and the following year Zhdanov devoted considerable attention to the subject in his address to the founding meeting of the Cominform. The purpose of the campaign for world government "is to mask the unbridled expansion of American imperialism," he charged. "The idea of world government has been taken up by bourgeois intellectual cranks and pacifists, and is being exploited not only as a means of . . . ideologically disarming the nations that defend their independence against . . . American imperialism, but also as a slogan especially directed against the Soviet Union."

This became the official Soviet position. *Pravda* claimed that United World Federalists wanted "disarmed nations throughout the world under the surveillance of armed American police," a plan "copied from the filthy utopian sketch of Hitler's 'New Order.'" In the Soviet press, Garry Davis was denigrated as a "debauched American maniac," while Bertrand Russell was dismissed as "the English fascist Malthusian philosopher." Fortunately, asserted a Soviet commentator, humanity was not compelled to take "the path of degeneration along which fascist creatures like Bertrand Russell are leading it."

And yet, the Kremlin's preoccupation with mobilizing a Communist-led peace campaign and with discrediting that campaign's competitor indicated that the nonaligned path had become an important one in world affairs. Like its American and British counterparts, the Soviet government was feeling the pressure of the nonaligned peace movement—and responding to it. Furthermore, in the context of the nonaligned antinuclear campaign and of the U.S. proposals for international control of atomic energy, the Kremlin had given rhetorical support to the idea of nuclear arms control and rhetorical opposition to the idea of nuclear war. Although such positions could certainly be reversed, their proclamation did help to establish an international norm and, thereby, make a reversal more difficult.

Elsewhere

Although, in response to public pressure, America's postwar allies adopted public positions that exhibited some degree of nuclear restraint, they certainly did not reject nuclear weapons outright. Thus, the French government, while proclaiming that its atomic energy program was solely for peaceful purposes, moved slowly but steadily toward acquiring a nuclear weapons capability. Similarly, the Canadian government, although announcing a decision not to manufacture atomic bombs and playing a high-profile role in nuclear arms control negotiations, leaned heavily upon the United States for its military defense and sold plutonium and uranium to the U.S. and British governments for the production of nuclear weapons. France's ambassador to the U.N. Atomic Energy Commission remarked privately to American officials that the French, British, and Canadians had "followed the American lead" during the nuclear arms control debate and that "this had been, and remained, necessary." Even though the French public was developing a "great nervousness" about nuclear weapons, France "would, of course, continue to follow the lead" of the United States.

Nevertheless, policymakers from America's NATO allies did grow jittery at the prospect that the U.S. government might move precipitously to use nuclear weapons. In late 1950, shortly after Truman's loose talk about employing the atomic bomb in the Korean War, the Canadian government publicly warned against escalation of that conflict. Reacting to the same incident, the French Foreign Office released a statement declaring bluntly that "the Korean objectives are not important enough to justify the use of the atomic bomb." A U.S. official at the United Nations secretly reported that "many European and Commonwealth delegations" had expressed "great apprehension with respect to the President's statement and hope that it didn't mean what it seemed to mean." Although Truman's clarifying message eased the situation, it did not entirely remove the "great shock" that his original remarks had caused.

Attitudes toward nonaligned peace groups varied widely within the ranks of America's allies. In Scandinavia, where peace groups had long been accorded some measure of respect, governments appointed pacifists to important posts and assisted their organizations in small ways. In Denmark, the prime minister issued a public statement of support for Bohr's *Open Letter* and the government informed the U.S. State Department that it attached "very great importance" to the thoughts expressed in it. Elsewhere—

and particularly in countries with more militaristic traditions—U.S. allies reacted with greater hostility. In late 1950, police raided the offices of the Argentina Pacifist Association, confiscating its records and seizing the latest issue of its journal. Suspicious of groups refusing military service, the right-wing Greek government arrested large numbers of Jehovah's Witnesses, sentencing some to long jail terms and executing others. Numerous other Western nations imprisoned conscientious objectors, and Spain provided death without trial for open rejection of military training. In West Germany, the government not only banned Hiroshima Day events, but arrested leading pacifists. Western governments reacted with even greater animosity to the Communist-led peace campaign.

Among the Soviet Union's Cold War allies, there was less dissent on the issue of nuclear weapons. Overjoyed by the Soviet Union's atomic breakthrough of 1949, they depicted it—in line with East bloc peace propaganda—as a blow against war. "In the past," noted the Chinese newspaper *Ta Kung Pao*, "the atomic bomb used to be the secret weapon of imperialism, monopolized by war-lovers to cow peoples of other nations." But "the Soviet Union is a veritable home of world peace, and . . . once a dangerous weapon is mastered by the Soviet Union, it is forthwith turned into an instrument of peace." In East Germany, the press greeted the news of Soviet nuclear weapons gleefully, and the Czech, Romanian, Bulgarian, and Polish governments shared this enthusiasm. The Polish foreign affairs ministry formally announced that Soviet possession of the Bomb would greatly facilitate a solution to the problem of international control of atomic energy.

Those who challenged this benign vision of Communist military might incurred the wrath of Communist governments. "We are not, we cannot be pacifists," declared General George Palffy at the Hungarian Communist party conference of June 1948. According to Palffy and party leader Matyas Rakosi, the "danger of pacifism" was serious. Reporting to the WRI in the summer of 1950 on events in East Germany, the pacifist Heinz Kraschutzki noted that "recently, pacifism and the idea of a neutralized Germany have been put on the list of those movements that are officially considered as dangerous." The idea of world government also came under fire, with *Free Bulgaria* charging that its impetus came from "the most power-hungry imperialists."

When they considered it necessary, Communist officials supplemented this verbal attack with direct repression. In Bulgaria, the government imprisoned one WRI leader and barred others from traveling to international meetings. In Hungary and Czechoslovakia, WILPF groups were officially disbanded and outspoken Christian pacifists were forced to resign their ministries. In East Germany, the authorities disbanded the German Peace Society and also prevented the FOR from operating. Throughout Eastern Europe, world federalist organizing efforts were blocked by government action.

By contrast, nations on the periphery of the Cold War camps and beyond it assumed a stance more critical of nuclear weapons. After the Tito-Stalin split of 1948, Yugoslavia shifted rapidly to a position of Cold War neutrality and, in this new role, promoted nuclear disarmament. Another neutral, Sweden, developed a civilian atomic energy program, but called for nuclear abolition. Although Finland had signed a Treaty of Friendship, Cooperation, and Mutual Assistance with the Soviet Union, it, too, avoided entanglement in the Cold War and became a sharp critic of nuclear weapons. Like Finland, Japan also had its postwar role shaped, at least in part, by one of the great powers. Under the U.S. occupation regime, Japan adopted a new constitution that, in Article 9, renounced "war . . . and the threat or use of force as a means of setting international disputes." American authorities soon changed their minds about the desirability of this provision. But, together with the strength of the Japanese peace movement, Article 9 remained an important barrier against government action to remilitarize Japan and to acquire nuclear weapons.

Although these governments reacted to the peace movement in differing ways, they all recognized its importance. Pursuing a policy of good relations with the Soviet Union, Finland responded quite favorably to the Communist-led peace campaign. By contrast, the Swedish government found it repugnant. Expressing his "considerable disgust" at the use of the word "Stockholm" in the Stockholm peace petition, Sweden's Social Democratic prime minister publicly denounced the petition as "international Communist propaganda." The Swedish government remained on much better terms with nonaligned peace groups and, in fact, granted small financial subsidies to some of them. In Japan, apparently at the behest of U.S. occupation officials, the authorities abruptly canceled the Hiroshima peace memorial ceremony of August 1950 and all other events linked to the atomic bombing, but relented the following year. In Yugoslavia, Tito's government initially dissolved independent pacifist groups but, after its break with the Soviet Union, not only established its own nonaligned peace organization (the Yugoslav National Committee for the Defense of Peace) but brought prominent pacifists and other peace activists to Yugoslavia for conferences on peace and disarmament.

Some of the sharpest condemnations of nuclear weapons came from the leaders of Third World nations. In November 1949, Carlos Romulo of the Philippines, then U.N. General Assembly president, called for the temporary suspension of atomic bomb production and for the prohibition of the use of existing bombs. Perhaps the most eloquent and persistent critic of nuclear weapons, however, was India's first prime minister, Jawaharlal Nehru. As early as 1946, he expressed his hope that "India, in common with other countries," would "prevent the use of atomic bombs." Speaking before a New York City audience in 1949, Nehru declared that India rejoiced at not having the Bomb. A fear complex governed the world, he lamented, and "when nations become afraid, others get afraid," leading to "deplorable consequences." Later that year, shortly after Truman broached the subject of using nuclear weapons in the Korean War, Nehru publicly condemned the use "anywhere at any time" of the Bomb, which he characterized as the "symbol of incarnate evil."

In addressing the issues of the nuclear arms race, these Third World leaders clearly adopted the prescriptions and rhetoric of the nonaligned nuclear disarmament movement. Starting in 1946, Romulo delivered direct pleas for "world government" to the United Nations. He also championed a favorite idea of the atomic scientists' movement: the convocation of a world conference of scientists to develop a new approach to the international control of atomic energy. Nehru, too, became a champion of world federation. "The world . . . moves inevitably towards closer cooperation and the building up of a world commonwealth," he declared in 1946 in an important policy address. "It is for this One World that free India will work." Despite the disinterest of the great powers, he continued to articulate this position. "We talk of world government and One World and millions yearn for it," he told a radio audience in 1948. "World government must and will come."

Although peace and disarmament groups remained weak in the Philippines and India, other factors magnified the world peace movement's influence upon these nations. Both countries gained their independence in the aftermath of World War II and, consequently, their leaders sometimes viewed themselves as natural spokespersons for the emerging Third World. Furthermore, India's independence struggle had employed nonviolent resistance, an approach that had a substantial impact on the politics of the postcolonial era. In addition, Western peace activists had close ties with both Romulo and Nehru. Romulo's 1946 speech, for example, was written by two world federalist leaders from the United States. Norman Cousins also cultivated his contacts with Romulo—among other means, by publishing his poetry in the *Saturday Review*. Cousins enjoyed excellent relations with Nehru, as well, and interviewed him at length for his book *Talks with Nehru*. Feeling a natural kinship with the Indian leader, numerous Western peace activists sought to mobilize him, sometimes successfully, on behalf of peace and disarmament.

Crisis and Decline of the Movement, 1950–1953

Despite the influence that the antinuclear campaign had upon public policy, it went into a sharp decline during the early 1950s. In Britain, the ASA became largely moribund, while in the United States the FAS dwindled and the Emergency Committee of Atomic Scientists collapsed entirely. Although the *Bulletin of the Atomic Scientists* continued to provide a vital resource for the scientists' movement and for the public, it faced serious difficulties securing adequate funding and constituency. The World Movement for World Federal Government (WMWFG) was also in trouble, with the largest branch, the American, losing more than half of its membership by mid-1951. So difficult did it become to support the WMWFG's activities that the small staff at its Paris headquarters sought private loans to purchase office supplies, and leaders of its student affiliate auctioned off their personal belongings. Meanwhile, the World Citizens movement of Garry Davis virtually disappeared. Nor was the situation any better among the pacifists. In Scandinavian nations and in Switzerland, the WILPF lost approximately half its membership. In the Netherlands the Third Way deteriorated rapidly, while in the United States the membership of pacifist organizations declined substantially, leading to cutbacks in staff and office space. Even in Japan, the annual Hiroshima commemoration ceremonies were thrown into disarray.

What had undermined this once-thriving movement? A key factor was the escalating Cold War, which left little room for ideas of disarmament and One World. With the advance of international conflict, newspapers, political parties, religious bodies, and the general public grew increasingly committed to employing nuclear weapons for national defense. In France, the Socialists joined more conservative parties in supporting the maintenance of the American nuclear arsenal. In Canada, reported the FOR secretary, people "cling to the old patterns of violence in their attempts to protect themselves" from the Soviet Union; and, "although people admit you can't destroy an ideology with bombs, they seem to feel they have no other recourse." Asked about the development of the British atomic bomb in early 1952, shortly after it was announced by the government, Britons expressed approval of the weapon by 60 to 22 percent. Such attitudes not only severely limited popular support for the antinuclear campaign, but in some cases cut into its ranks as well—particularly after the inception of the Korean War.

Nonaligned proponents of disarmament also labored under the heavy burden of being identified with Communism. Traditionally, fierce nationalists had accused advocates of peace of siding with the enemy. And, in the case of the early Cold War, as British pacifist Vera Brittain recalled, "international Communism chose that moment to wave a banner called 'Peace,'" thus making the charge appear to stick. The results were devastating. On crowded streets in New York City, pacifists found people so afraid to accept their leaflets that sometimes twenty minutes would elapse before they could distribute one. In New Zealand, "the word 'Peace' has become suspect—to use the word is to be branded a dupe of Moscow," complained an editorial in the *New Zealand Christian Pacifist*. "The Peace Partisans have made it more difficult to work for peace," reported the Swedish WILPF section; "people think that everything with the word peace in it is communistic." World federalist groups encountered a barrage of anti-Communist abuse, particularly in the United States. The *Chicago Tribune* charged that "veteran followers of the Communist party line" lurked "quietly in the background" of the world federalist movement. Even in Communist nations, the official Communist support for "peace" discredited nonaligned peace activism, for increasing numbers of people viewed their Communist rulers less as liberators than as jailers.

In addition, the movement was undermined by exhaustion, a sense of futility, and escapism. It is difficult to maintain social movements at a high level of mobilization over lengthy periods of time, for activists grow tired and long to return to their private lives. This was particularly true of activists in the postwar antinuclear campaign, for—as nations armed themselves for nuclear war—it seemed that their efforts had gone for naught. Furthermore, it was very hard to sustain a movement that directly confronted the issue of mass annihilation. Admittedly, fear of a nuclear holocaust had played a key part in the struggle against the Bomb. But could this intense fear be maintained? To judge from numerous barometers of public sentiment, it could not. According to a British government-sponsored survey in 1951, "the immediate reaction" of "a large part of the population to the very idea of a possible war" was "to wish not to hear about it."

Mixed Results

Despite the decline of the popular movement against the Bomb, it did produce important results. Admittedly, the leaders of the great powers—brushing aside the movement's efforts to secure nuclear arms control and disarmament—commenced a nuclear arms race that, ultimately, produced additional and far more devastating nuclear weapons. And certainly the movement failed to create One World. But it did play a vital role in establishing nuclear arms controls and disarmament as official national objectives and in preventing a recurrence of nuclear war. In 1945, the Truman administration had launched the atomic bombing of Japanese cities without moral qualms or worries about the public reaction. Receiving news of the Hiroshima bombing, the President jubilantly proclaimed it "the greatest thing in history." Five years later, however, thanks in large part to the movement, the use of nuclear weapons to annihilate cities had become politically unacceptable, and government officials, including Truman, resisted it. From the standpoint of human survival, this was a very significant shift in policy.

4   Movement Renaissance, 1954–1958

Beginning in 1954, a second wave of uneasiness about nuclear weapons swept around the world. The rapid development of the hydrogen bomb—a weapon with a thousand times the power of the bomb that had destroyed Hiroshima—revived the idea that humanity was teetering on the brink of disaster. Atmospheric nuclear weapons tests, particularly, stimulated public concern. They scattered clouds of radioactive debris around the globe and, furthermore, symbolized the looming horror of a U.S.-Soviet nuclear war. Deeply disturbed by the nuclear arms race, prominent individuals issued eloquent warnings, ban-the-bomb organizations waged nuclear disarmament campaigns, and public opinion turned in an antinuclear direction. And these developments had important consequences.

Ominous Events

Not until 1954 did nuclear testing deeply impress itself on public consciousness. The turning point was the first U.S. H-bomb test, conducted by the AEC on March 1, 1954. It occurred on Bikini atoll, located in the Marshall Islands. The AEC had staked out a danger zone roughly the size of New England around the test site. But the blast proved to be more than twice as powerful as planned and generated vast quantities of highly radioactive debris. Within a short time, heavy doses of this nuclear fallout descended on four inhabited islands of the Marshall grouping—all outside the danger zone—prompting U.S. officials to evacuate 28 Americans working at a U.S. weather station and, days later, 236 Marshallese. The Americans went relatively unscathed, but the Marshall Islanders soon developed low blood counts, skin lesions, and hemorrhages under the skin and ultimately suffered a heavy incidence of radiation-linked illnesses, including thyroid cancer and leukemia.

Much of this might have gone unnoticed by the outside world had there not been a further incident. About eighty-five miles from the test site—and also beyond the official danger zone—radioactive ash from the H-bomb explosion showered a small Japanese fishing boat, the *Lucky Dragon*. By the time the ship had reached its home port two weeks later, the twenty-three crew members were in an advanced stage of radiation sickness. The Japanese government promptly hospitalized the ailing fishermen and destroyed their radioactive cargo. But as the disturbing news spread across Japan, a panic swept that nation. Although most of the crew recovered, the ship's radio operator died during hospital treatment.

In the midst of growing international turmoil, U.S. officials sought to reassure the public. On March 31, in a statement read at President Dwight Eisenhower's press conference, Lewis Strauss, the AEC chair, maintained that the testing was not out of control and that the Marshall islanders were "well and happy." The Japanese fishermen seemed to be experiencing some problems, but these, Strauss insisted, were minor, with their skin lesions caused not by radioactivity but by "chemical activity" in the coral. In any case, he implied, the Japanese alone bore the responsibility for their ailments, for the *Lucky Dragon*, he stated falsely, "must have been well within the danger area." The only discomforting observation came during the question period, when Strauss remarked that an H-bomb could be made "as large as you wish"—large enough to destroy "any city."

Despite the ominous portents, the drift continued toward nuclear catastrophe. The United States conducted more nuclear test explosions, while military experts predicted that, in a future war, the new weaponry would kill hundreds of millions of people. Brushing aside the earlier caution of the Truman administration, the U.S. National Security Council (NSC) resolved in late October 1953 that, in the event of hostilities with the Soviet Union or China, "the United States will consider nuclear weapons to be as available for use as other munitions." Early the following year, Secretary of State John Foster Dulles publicly unveiled the administration's new military policy, based on "massive retaliation." Addressing a press conference on March 16, 1955, Eisenhower stated that, in a battlefield situation, the U.S. government would employ tactical nuclear weapons "just exactly as you would use a bullet or anything else." Moreover, if a "big war" occurred, the United States would "push its whole stack of chips into the pot." According to NSC 5707/8, signed by the President on June 3, 1957: "It is the policy of the United States to place main . . . reliance on nuclear weapons;

to . . . consider them as conventional weapons from a military point of view; and to use them when required to achieve national objectives."

Other Western nations also turned to nuclear weapons as the solution to their national security dilemmas. Insisting that developing the hydrogen bomb was the only way to "maintain our influence as a world power," Churchill initiated the British H-bomb program in July 1954. The French government began a nuclear weapons development program later that year. Elements in the West German government also seemed ready to secure a nuclear weapons capability. In the meantime, Western governments leaned heavily upon NATO to meet their nuclear needs. According to the minutes of a NATO foreign ministers meeting on December 13, 1956, the British argued that the Western alliance had to have "tactical atomic weapons." The West Germans wanted "tactical atomic weapons . . . available down to [the] divisional level." For their part, the Dutch, the Italians, and the Greeks expressed approval of the new weapons, with the French observing that "everyone [is] aware that nuclear weapons are required." Although the leaders of other Western nations did not encourage the deployment of nuclear weapons on their territory, most seemed happy enough to be sheltered under the U.S. nuclear umbrella, despite the risk of nuclear attack that that implied.

Communist nations, too, showed a keen appetite for nuclear weapons. Despite Mao Zedong's earlier dismissal of the atom bomb as "a paper tiger which the U.S. reactionaries use to scare people," the Chinese government began its own nuclear weapons program in January 1955. In the Soviet Union, a period of indecision followed Stalin's death in 1953. Initially, Malenkov and, later, the new Soviet party secretary, Nikita Khrushchev, pointed to the enormous destructiveness of nuclear war. Nevertheless, like his Western counterparts, Khrushchev was fascinated by nuclear weapons and missiles, which he felt would enable the Soviet Union to deter foreign aggression and exercise substantial influence in world affairs. Consequently, the Soviet nuclear weapons program surged forward. Speaking at the Twentieth Soviet Party Congress of February 1956, Khrushchev warned that, if "the imperialists" unleashed a war, the Soviet Union would give them "a smashing rebuff." That November, during the Suez crisis, he threatened the British and French governments with nuclear annihilation.

In these circumstances, although Nehru and other Third World leaders sharply criticized the nuclear arms race and the heightened prospect of nuclear war, nuclear arms control and disarmament were simply not on the agenda of the Cold War competitors. According to the record of a meeting of top U.S. national security officials in 1954, there was general agreement that the U.S. government "would not be drawn into any negotiations" for "the control or abolition of nuclear weapons." Speaking to Japanese officials in the summer of 1955, Dulles contended that nuclear weapons "are here to stay," and "even if it were possible to abolish them . . . it is doubtful whether abolition would be desirable." Nor, despite a desire for nuclear stability and restraint, did the Soviet Union show much genuine interest in nuclear arms reductions. As the Soviet ambassador to the United States, Anatoly Dobrynin, later recalled, at this point his government's talk of disarmament was "nothing more than a good piece of propaganda."

Some Important Signs of Dismay

Even so, many people found these developments deeply disturbing. As might be expected, worldwide pacifist organizations renewed their earlier de-mands for nuclear arms control and disarmament, as did the remnants of the world federalist movement. Meeting in September 1954, the World Association of Parliamentarians for World Government warned that "rival nations are now engaged in the most dangerous arms race of all time," one that threatened the continued "existence of human life." In his 1954 Easter message, Pope Pius XII assailed the "new, destructive armaments, unheard of in their capacity of vio-lence." The World Council of Churches called for an international agreement to end nuclear testing, a pledge by nations to refrain from use of the Bomb, and the elimination of nuclear weapons.

Prominent intellectuals, particularly, raised an outcry against the nuclear menace, and none was more zealous than Bertrand Russell. As he recalled: "I felt I *must* find some way of making the world understand the dangers into which it was running blindly, head-on." Eventually, he hit upon the idea of is-suing a public statement, signed by a small group of the world's most eminent scientists, warning of the gathering crisis. Securing Einstein's backing, Russell then approached other esteemed figures. In July 1955, speaking before represen-tatives of the communications media at a meeting in London, chaired by Rot-blat, Russell summarized the background of the statement and of its impressive signatories. In the shadow of the Bomb, it declared, "we have to learn to think in a new way. We have to learn to ask ourselves, not what steps can be taken to give military victory to whatever group we prefer" but, rather: "What steps can be taken to prevent a military contest of which the issue must be disastrous to all parties?" Thanks to the statement's dramatic phrasing, the eminence of its signers, and Einstein's signature upon it only moments before his death, this Russell-Einstein Manifesto—as it became known—received very widespread and favorable coverage.

Russell's efforts served as key ingredients in the revival of the international scientists' movement. During the previous year, concerned by the development of thermonuclear weapons, the leaders of the American FAS and the British ASA had begun discussing the possibility of organizing an International Conference on Science and World Affairs. Now, with the appearance of the Russell-Einstein Manifesto, the event began to take shape. Thanks to an offer from Cyrus Eaton, a wealthy Cleveland industrialist, to cover the transportation and living costs for a meeting of scientists at a conference center he had built in Pugwash, Nova Scotia, the first Pugwash Conference on Science and World Affairs met in July 1957, with twenty-two participants from ten Western, Eastern, and nonaligned countries. The previously forbidden contact among leading scientists of "enemy" nations imparted to the meeting an atmosphere of excitement and even danger. Nevertheless, the Pugwash gathering was infused by a general sense of respect, goodwill, and common purpose that united participants across Cold War barriers. "We are all convinced that mankind must abolish war or suffer catastrophe," they declared, "and that the dilemma of opposing power groups and the arms race must be broken." Thereafter, Russell became the titular head of an ongoing Pugwash movement and Rotblat served as its secretary-general. Although the mass media gave this new movement little attention, it became well-known and highly respected among the scientists of East and West.

Scientists were mobilized against the arms race with greater public fanfare by Linus Pauling. A longtime critic of the Bomb, Pauling was an eminent chemist at the California Institute of Technology. His best-known crusade began in 1957, when he traveled to St. Louis to address a Washington University honors convocation on the subject of science and the modern world. On the day before his speech, Pauling discussed it with Barry Commoner—a biologist at the university and a key figure in local nuclear disarmament activities—and hatched the idea of a plea by American scientists for an international agreement to end nuclear testing. Addressing the convocation, Pauling declared movingly that "no human being should be sacrificed to the project of perfecting nuclear weapons that could kill hundreds of millions of human beings" and "could devastate this beautiful world in which we live." The enthusiastic response from the audience convinced Pauling to move ahead with an anti-testing petition, which he distributed to scientists at more than a hundred U.S. colleges and universities. Within ten days, it had been signed by about two thousand scientists. That June, Pauling released this "Appeal by American Scientists" to the press. Pauling also began circulating the petition overseas, and—within a year—secured signatures on it by 11,038 scientists from forty-nine nations. They included 37 Nobel laureates, as well as more than a fifth of the members of the U.S. National Academy of Sciences, 95 Fellows of the Royal Society of London, and 216 members of the Soviet Academy of Sciences.

Probably the most influential international appeals were issued by Albert Schweitzer. Born in 1875 in Alsace, then part of Germany, Schweitzer had carved out careers as a distinguished musician and philosopher before settling down in the jungles outside Lambaréné, in French Equatorial Africa, to work selflessly as a medical missionary. Well-known as a proponent of reverence for life, he was awarded the 1952 Nobel Peace Prize. In January 1957, Cousins, determined to draw upon Schweitzer's immense prestige, visited him in Africa with the goal of having him speak out against the nuclear arms race. Although Schweitzer disliked taking stands on political issues, Cousins convinced him to confront this one. That April, speaking on Radio Oslo, Schweitzer delivered his "Declaration of Conscience." Nuclear test explosions, he said, were "a catastrophe for the human race, a catastrophe that must be prevented." Humanity "must muster the insight, the seriousness, and the courage to leave folly and to face reality." Broadcast in some fifty nations and covered in countless newspapers, Schweitzer's message had an enormous impact on public opinion throughout the world. Moreover, he became a relentless crusader against the Bomb. The following April, he delivered another three antinuclear radio addresses over Radio Oslo. Writing to Cousins in May 1958, the 83-year-old Schweitzer remarked that he was exhausted by these efforts, but "more important is that the appeals catch the attention of people and awake them."

National Protest

In fact, people were awakening, all over the world and, as befit the first victims of nuclear war, the Japanese were in the vanguard. In May 1954, shortly after the *Lucky Dragon* incident, middle-class housewives in Tokyo's Suganami ward, determined "to protect the lives and the happiness of all mankind," began a petition campaign against H-bombs. By the following year, this "Suganami

Appeal" had attracted the signatures of 32 million people—about a third of the Japanese population. Meanwhile, the municipal councils of most Japanese cities, towns, and villages passed resolutions urging the United States to ban atomic and hydrogen bombs. *Hibakusha* associations emerged in Hiroshima, Nagasaki, and nationwide, agitating not only for medical treatment and other relief measures, but for an end to the nuclear arms race. In August 1955, thousands of delegates, mostly Japanese, convened in Hiroshima for the First World Conference against Atomic and Hydrogen Bombs, an event sponsored by many of the nation's political, religious, and scientific luminaries. Its first evening session drew 30,000 people. The following month, building on this success, organizers of the event established the Japan Council against Atomic and Hydrogen Bombs (Gensuikyo), which developed affiliates all across the country.

Japanese antinuclear sentiment heightened in the following years. In February 1957, more than 350 Japanese scientists issued a public appeal to their British colleagues, asking them to help convince the British government to cancel plans for forthcoming nuclear tests. Nuclear testing, they argued, was "the worst sort of crime against all human beings." That May, the Zengakuren—the radical Japanese student organization—launched boycotts of classes and massive public rallies against nuclear weapons, with the participation of an estimated 350,000 students at more than 200 universities. Gensuikyo, now the most broadly based and powerful peace group in Japanese history, staged peace walks, organized petition campaigns, and sponsored numerous local and national rallies against nuclear testing. In July 1957, 87 percent of the Japanese surveyed told pollsters that they favored a complete ban on atomic and hydrogen bombs.

In Britain, as well, the H-bomb caused an enormous stir. Pacifist groups condemned nuclear weapons and nuclear testing, as did the more broadly based National Peace Council. Abandoning its traditional silence on nuclear issues, the British Council of Churches expressed dismay at the radioactive fallout generated by U.S. nuclear tests in the Pacific. Meanwhile, Britain's trade unions and a growing number of Labour M.P.s began to criticize nuclear weapons. Indeed, in the aftermath of the Bikini Bomb tests of 1954, the Labour Party introduced a parliamentary resolution calling on the Conservative government to work for an end to nuclear testing. Antinuclear organizations sprang up, including a Hydrogen Bomb National Campaign. With the Rev. Donald Soper as chair and other clergy and Labour M.P.s in leading roles, the campaign held poster demonstrations in Whitehall, addressed public meetings, and circulated a petition—eventually signed by half a million Britons—calling for internationally negotiated nuclear disarmament. Polls found that, although most Britons supported their nation's manufacture of the H-bomb, most were very wary about using it and, furthermore, favored international agreements banning nuclear tests and abolishing nuclear weapons.

Against this backdrop, ban-the-bomb activity began to take more specific shape in Britain. In February 1957, a National Council for the Abolition of Nuclear Weapon Tests (NCANWT) was launched, and by the end of the year it had established more than a hundred local chapters. Meanwhile, advocates of civil disobedience organized a Direct Action Committee Against Nuclear War, which planned a protest march, in the spring of 1958, to the Atomic Weapons Research Establishment, at Aldermaston. Thanks to rising antinuclear sentiment in the Labour Party, hopes were bright that it would repudiate nuclear weapons at its fall 1957 conference. But, when it failed to do so, J. B. Priestley, one of Britain's best-known playwrights, published a stinging rejoinder in the *New Statesman*, calling upon Britons to rise to the occasion and "defy this nuclear madness." The British people seemed to waiting for "something great and noble," he said, "and this might well be a declaration to the world that . . . one power able to engage in nuclear warfare will reject the evil thing forever." When Priestley's article drew an enormous favorable response, leaders of the NCANWT met with intellectual and cultural luminaries and fashioned a new disarmament organization with a broader mandate, the Campaign for Nuclear Disarmament (CND). It was agreed that Russell would serve as president, Canon L. John Collins as chair, and Peggy Duff of the now-defunct NCANWT as organizing secretary.

CND quickly became the major force in the British antinuclear campaign. In February 1958, taking over the NCANWT's arrangements for a large public meeting in London, CND attracted thousands of people to hear impassioned speeches on behalf of nuclear disarmament by Russell, Collins, Priestley, Michael Foot (a leader of the Labour left), and A. J. P. Taylor (a prominent historian). Priestley and Taylor, particularly, emphasized the need for Britain's renunciation of nuclear weapons, an idea that inspired great enthusiasm among the audience and became CND's central demand. In the wake of the London gathering, more than 250 other CND meetings were held up and down the country, with many drawing large crowds and raising substantial sums of money. CND created special subgroups to enlist students, women, faith groups, and Labour Party activists, distributed vast quantities of antinuclear literature, and put together 270 local chapters around the nation. Joining the planned Aldermaston march, CND contributed large numbers of participants, as well as a new and rather eerie symbol: a circle encompassing a broken cross. Containing the semaphore signals for the *n* and *d* of "nuclear disarmament," the emblem was also designed to symbolize human despair in a world facing the threat of nuclear catastrophe. As the four-day march by thousands of well-dressed, earnest citizens—many bearing the nuclear disarmament symbol, in its stark funereal black and white—proceeded through the chilling rain, it provided a powerful demonstration of the growing public resolve to halt the nuclear arms race. Although surveys found that only a minority of Britons favored their country's unilateral renunciation of nuclear weapons, they also reported that Britons favored internationally enforced nuclear disarmament by a ratio of seven to one.

Antinuclear activism was also on the upswing in West Germany. With the arrival of the first U.S. nuclear weapons stationed in that country and the beginning of related NATO military exercises, the opposition Social Democratic Party (SPD) warned that the nation would become a nuclear battlefield in a war that would end in "collective suicide." In 1957, as the conservative government's plans moved forward for arming the Bundeswehr with U.S. tactical nuclear weapons and officials talked vaguely of developing West Germany's own nuclear arsenal, eighteen of the nation's most eminent physicists issued a public statement, warning of the dangers and stating that none of them would participate "in the production, the tests, or the application of atomic weapons." Although sharply denounced by the ruling Christian Democrats, this Göttingen Manifesto drew strong support from the opposition parties. Indeed, the SPD and the Free Democrats—with an eye on polls showing broad public opposition to West Germany's acquisition of nuclear weapons—now made that a central issue in the hotly contested 1957 parliamentary campaign. Although the Christian Democrats emerged with a resounding victory, largely based on domestic issues, the SPD also increased its share of the vote.

For this reason, and also because polls still indicated widespread West German dismay at providing the Bundeswehr with nuclear weapons, the SPD and its labor union supporters launched a dramatic, extra-parliamentary campaign, the Struggle Against Atomic Death. Begun in March 1958, it erupted into a mass movement after the West German parliament approved deployment of atomic armaments later that month. As it spread across the nation, over half a million West Germans took part in more than a hundred antinuclear rallies. Groups of faculty and physicians issued antinuclear appeals. Writers and artists signed resolutions against government policy. Students demonstrated at the universities. Antinuclear strikes broke out at twenty factories. Even after public policy became irreversible and the SPD abandoned the campaign, nuclear weapons remained remarkably unpopular in West Germany. In July 1958, according to polls, 92 percent of the population favored (and only 1 percent opposed) an international ban on the manufacture of nuclear weapons. That November, 64 percent of poll respondents indicated that they considered nuclear tests harmful to future generations.

The Netherlands also experienced an upsurge of antinuclear protest. In 1955, a Dutch Committee for the Abolition of Atom Bomb Experiments issued a petition, signed by more than a hundred scientists and other prominent figures, highlighting the dangers of radioactive contamination and calling on the Dutch government to work for the abolition of nuclear testing. In February 1957, the Dutch Reformed Church appealed to the government to work toward the end of nuclear tests. Later that year, another committee, Stop Atom Bomb Tests, issued a petition along similar lines, signed by some 650 doctors. Anxious to unite previously disparate groups and individuals around resistance to the nuclear menace, peace activists established Anti-Atom Bomb Action that same year. It advocated an end to nuclear tests, a ban on the manufacture of nuclear weapons, and the destruction of existing stockpiles. Such attitudes were widespread. According to one poll, in late 1957 the Dutch population, by a ratio of five to one, thought H-bomb explosions endangered the health of future generations.

Similarly, concern about nuclear weapons acquired new momentum in Scandinavia. Reporting from the region in May 1957, a *New York Times* correspondent declared that "just about everybody" wanted to see an end to nuclear weapons tests. Responding to Schweitzer's appeal to halt nuclear testing, 225,000 Norwegians—out of a population of only 3.5 million—signed a petition along these lines. Pacifists joined other groups in holding large anti-testing demonstrations. In 1957, the governing Labor Party's general congress unanimously resolved that nuclear weapons tests should be immediately halted and—in a clear challenge to NATO policy—"that atomic weapons should not be placed on Norwegian territory." In Denmark, No More War, the Danish WRI group, passed a resolution appealing to Danes to "refuse the offer of American guided missiles." One antinuclear protest, in May 1958, drew a crowd of from eight to ten thousand people, who filled Copenhagen's Town Hall. Secretly, the

U.S. embassy warned the State Department against pressuring the Danes to accept NATO nuclear weapons, for "public opinion here is not yet prepared for this step."

In Sweden, opposition to nuclear weapons was heightened by proposals from the military to make that country a nuclear power. A fierce debate ensued, particularly within the governing Social Democratic Party, with the powerful Social Democratic Women's Organization, led by Inga Thorsson, arguing strongly against nuclear weapons. Portions of the Social Democratic and labor press also adopted a sharply critical stance. Pacifists, religious leaders, and prominent intellectuals assailed nuclear weapons in public meetings, in newspapers, and on the radio, and a citizens' petition against Swedish nuclear weapons garnered 95,000 signatures. In June 1958, a group of twenty-one intellectuals launched the Action Group Against a Swedish Atomic Weapon (AMSA). Arranging meetings, rallies, and discussions on the subject of the Bomb, AMSA reached a broad audience and had a particular appeal among young people. Although the Social Democratic Party distanced itself from AMSA's purely pacifist approach, the overall antinuclear campaign led to a remarkable turnabout in public opinion. Between June 1957 and October 1959, support for building a Swedish atomic bomb fell from 40 to 29 percent, and opposition grew from 36 to 51 percent.

Swiss activists also developed a vigorous antinuclear campaign. In May 1958, responding to press reports of enthusiastic support among Swiss military officers and some government leaders for the arming of the country's military forces with atomic weapons and inspired by the Struggle Against Atomic Death in neighboring West Germany, a gathering of some 120 individuals associated with churches, unions, cultural institutions, and the sciences convened in Bern. Here they organized the Swiss Movement Against Atomic Armaments, with the goal of launching a popular referendum that would add a ban on atomic weapons to the Swiss constitution. Although pro-nuclear forces launched a powerful counterattack, the Swiss Movement drew substantial support among pacifists, intellectuals, the Protestant clergy, and Social Democrats. It distributed Schweitzer's call for nuclear disarmament, engaged in a heated public debate with pronuclear forces, and began a petition drive to gather the 50,000 signatures necessary to place the antinuclear referendum on the ballot.

Elsewhere in Western Europe, the mood was much the same. In France, more than a third of the scientists, engineers, and technicians employed by the French AEC petitioned to keep their nation's atomic energy program limited to peaceful purposes. A French nuclear armament program also drew the fire of the Socialist Party. Surveyed in March 1958, 85 percent of French respondents favored an international ban on nuclear weapons. In Italy, the leadership of the governing Christian Democratic Party, anxious to deflect criticism of nuclear weapons by the powerful Communist and Socialist parties, unanimously adopted a resolution lauding nuclear disarmament and calling for the employment of atomic energy solely for peaceful purposes. In Belgium, a National Committee against the Nuclear Peril emerged in early 1958, and some 150,000 Belgians signed a petition calling for a ban on nuclear tests. Between 1957 and 1958, the percentage of Belgians viewing nuclear tests as harmful rose from 60 to 71 percent. In Ireland, activists formed an Irish Campaign for Nuclear Disarmament (CND) in 1958. The aim of the new group, they announced, was "to press for the immediate suspension of nuclear tests" and to back "policies which may further the ultimate aim of nuclear disarmament." Attracting the support of many prominent figures in the sciences, arts, and literature, Irish CND distributed leaflets on the effects of nuclear weapons, picketed the embassies of the nuclear powers, and in December held its first large public meeting, chaired by the mayor of Dublin.

Across the Atlantic, in the United States, there was also an upsurge of concern. Liberal and scientific publications issued dire warnings, novels and films focusing on the Bomb proliferated, the FAS called for a nuclear test ban, and pacifists leafleted, placed antinuclear ads in newspapers, and refused to take shelter during civil defense drills. "Against the weapons of modern war," insisted the FOR, "there is no defense!" In public pronouncements, liberal religious denominations began to call for a ban on nuclear testing and for the renunciation of nuclear war. Meanwhile, Cousins joined with the Rev. Tanimoto in 1955 to bring Japanese girls disfigured and crippled by the Hiroshima bombing to New York City's Mount Sinai Hospital for plastic and reconstructive surgery. Although the widely publicized visit of the "Hiroshima Maidens" focused on benevolent action, it certainly had antinuclear implications. By 1955, according to the polls, 67 percent of Americans favored an arms reduction agreement among the major powers. Recognizing the growing public uneasiness and influenced by Cousins, Adlai Stevenson—the Democratic presidential candidate—made halting nuclear testing a key issue in his 1956 campaign.

Sensing that the moment was ripe for a breakthrough on the nuclear testing issue, U.S. activists began a concerted campaign of their own. In June 1957, Cousins and Clarence Pickett of the American Friends Service Committee

(AFSC) convened a meeting of twenty-seven prominent Americans, at New York City's Overseas Press Club, to consider appropriate measures. Although the participants rejected the idea of establishing a new organization, they decided to support the launching of an ad hoc effort to focus American opinion on the dangers of nuclear testing. "The normal drive for survival has been put out of action by present propaganda," observed Erich Fromm, an eminent psychoanalyst and supporter of the new venture. "We must ... try to bring the voice of sanity to the people." Adopting the idea, the planning group called itself the National Committee for a Sane Nuclear Policy.

The new organization—soon known as SANE—made its debut on November 15, 1957, with an advertisement in the *New York Times*. Written by Cousins and signed by forty-eight prominent Americans, the ad contended that "we are facing a danger unlike any danger that has ever existed. In our possession and in the possession of the Russians are more than enough nuclear explosives to put an end to the life of man on earth." In this context, "the slogans and arguments that belong to the world of competitive national sovereignties ... no longer fit the world of today or tomorrow." Calling for the immediate suspension of nuclear testing by all countries, SANE argued that this action would both halt radioactive contamination and provide "a place to begin on the larger question of armaments control." The great "challenge of the age," it maintained, is to move beyond the national interest to "a higher loyalty"—loyalty "to the human community."

SANE's advertisement, as its newsletter recalled, "started a movement." By the end of 1957, thousands of enthusiasts had written to SANE's overwhelmed national office, and citizens in various parts of the country had reprinted the ad in twenty-three newspapers. Given the "electrifying" response at the grassroots, a SANE leader recalled, a new membership group "came spontaneously into being." Thus, despite the initial caution of its founders, by the summer of 1958 SANE had become a national organization, with some 130 chapters and 25,000 members. Later that year, SANE broadened its goal from halting nuclear testing to securing internationally enforced nuclear disarmament. Holding press conferences, arranging television interviews, and churning out literature on nuclear dangers, SANE had become America's largest, most visible, and most influential peace organization.

As in Britain, some advocates of nuclear disarmament turned to nonviolent civil disobedience. Organizing Non-Violent Action Against Nuclear Weapons, they held an illegal protest by entering the U.S. nuclear testing site in Nevada in 1957. The following year, a pacifist crew, led by former U.S. naval captain

Albert Bigelow, sought to sail a thirty-foot vessel, the *Golden Rule*, into the U.S. nuclear testing zone in the Pacific. Although they were arrested and imprisoned for this action, their journey was continued by two other Americans, Earle and Barbara Reynolds, who succeeded in sailing their ship, the *Phoenix*, into the U.S. test zone. Although these and other civil disobedience actions did little to halt nuclear tests directly, they did draw substantial publicity and focus public attention on preparations for nuclear war. Pacifist groups found these ventures particularly attractive, and in September 1958 formed a more tightly structured organization to promote nonviolent civil disobedience: the Committee for Nonviolent Action.

The critique of the nuclear arms race resonated strongly in American society. Nevil Shute's somber novel of nuclear death, *On the Beach*, became a bestseller in 1957, and some forty U.S. newspapers serialized it. Democratic congressional leaders began holding hearings on nuclear dangers. Polls reported that U.S. public backing for a multilateral nuclear test ban ranged from 49 percent (a plurality) to a hefty majority. In March 1958, a Gallup poll found that 70 percent of the American public favored international action to "make sure—by regular inspections—that no nation, including Russia and the United States, makes atom bombs, hydrogen bombs, and missiles."

In Australia and New Zealand, as well, antinuclear sentiment was on the rise. Australian pacifist groups organized meetings condemning nuclear weapons, while nationwide exhibits of the Marukis' "Hiroshima Panels" drew large crowds and sympathetic editorials in major newspapers. In 1958, some 360 Australian scientists signed the Pauling petition calling for an end to nuclear testing—a position also backed by the Australian Council of Trade Unions and the Australian Labor Party. Polls found that, between late 1957 and late 1958, the percentage of Australians who thought that H-bomb tests endangered future generations rose from 46 to 57 percent. Similarly, New Zealand's pacifists threw themselves into the antinuclear campaign, holding a public meeting that drew 1,600 people and circulating a petition against nuclear testing that secured the signatures of some 11,000. Meanwhile, New Zealand's Labour Party, impressed by the upsurge of antinuclear sentiment, announced its opposition to all future tests of nuclear weapons. Encouraged by these events, as well as by the formation of CND in Britain, groups focusing on the nuclear weapons issue appeared in Auckland, Dunedin, Christchurch, and Wellington. In 1958, they joined to establish the Movement against Further Testing, Manufacture, and Use of Nuclear Weapons.

Although ban-the-bomb groups were less common in the Third World, public opinion in the nations of this region was quite similar. Polls in Latin American cities found most residents hostile to nuclear testing and wary of atomic energy. In India, a poll of New Delhi residents in the spring of 1958 found that 90 percent thought the United States should halt its nuclear tests. That July, a Gallup poll concluded that 78 percent of its Indian respondents favored—and only 1 percent opposed—the establishment of a worldwide organization to ensure that no nation could make atomic or hydrogen bombs. Sometimes, Third World opposition to the nuclear arms race represented an extension of the strong anti-imperialist sentiments of the region. When the French government began to discuss its plan for nuclear testing in the Sahara, protest against the idea grew dramatically in French West Africa. "We do not want our continent to be a second Hiroshima," declared an African labor leader. The proposed French tests were "the criminal initiative of the imperialists who believe they are the masters of African soil."

Even in the Soviet Union, where political repression limited the possibilities for overt agitation, negative attitudes about nuclear weapons began to emerge, particularly among the scientists. Igor Kurchatov, the physicist directing the Soviet Bomb project, recalled that he was profoundly shaken by the first Soviet H-bomb test. "That was such a terrible, monstrous sight!" he told a friend. "That weapon must not be allowed ever to be used." Andrei Sakharov, another Bomb project scientist, dared to suggest just that to the commander of the Soviet Union's missile forces—advice that this military officer did not appreciate at all. After Stalin's death, some scientists resigned from the Bomb project. Others, like Peter Kapitza, perhaps the nation's best-known physicist, refused Khrushchev's pleas to work on it and, instead, carried on a friendly dialogue with Bertrand Russell about the necessity for halting the production and testing of nuclear weapons. In 1954, a group of four senior scientists from the Soviet Bomb project, including Kurchatov, secretly warned Soviet officials that nuclear war would lead to "the termination of all life on Earth." The concern of "the world community" was "entirely understandable," they reported, and there was no alternative to "a complete ban on the military utilization of atomic energy."

In subsequent years, Soviet antinuclear efforts intensified. Sakharov and other scientists published articles condemning nuclear testing, while hundreds of Soviet scientists signed Pauling's anti-testing petition. Alarmed by what Sakharov had told him about the effects of nuclear tests in the Semipalatinsk region, the physicist Zhores Takibayev sent a petition to Khrushchev protesting Soviet explosions there—a venture that earned him an official reprimand. When the Soviet government made plans to resume nuclear testing in the fall of 1958, Sakharov approached Kurchatov with a proposal to cancel the planned tests, and Kurchatov, who agreed with it, traveled to Yalta in an effort to convince Khrushchev, as well. Although Khrushchev refused to halt the Soviet testing program, Sakharov followed up by personally approaching Khrushchev and appealing for an end to Soviet tests. Sakharov "was obviously guided by moral and humanistic considerations," Khrushchev recalled; he "hated the thought that science might be used to destroy life, to contaminate the atmosphere, to kill people slowly by radioactive poisoning." Consequently, "my arguments didn't change his mind, and his didn't change mine."

What accounts for these daring—and potentially dangerous—attempts by Soviet scientists to block Soviet nuclear testing and prevent nuclear war? Ironically, the Soviet regime's need for top scientists to work on building the Bomb meant that they escaped from the worst abuses of the totalitarian state and lived in an atmosphere of relative freedom. Soviet scientists read about the Russell-Einstein manifesto and other critiques of nuclear weapons in the *Bulletin of the Atomic Scientists*, available at their library, and were deeply influenced by them. They also attended the Pugwash conferences, where they developed a strong sense of affinity with their Western colleagues. Recalling his own growing concern about the nuclear menace, Sakharov attributed it to "the influence of statements on this subject made throughout the world by such people as Albert Schweitzer, Linus Pauling, and others." On another occasion, he declared his indebtedness to Einstein, Russell, and others concerned about "the fate of mankind." The worldwide movement had been effective at propagating its message, even within the relatively closed confines of the Soviet Union.

Aligned and Nonaligned Movements

The Communist-led peace movement—operating through the WPC and its affiliates—also stepped up a critique of nuclear weapons. As in the past, its massive conferences and other ventures were partisan affairs, stressing Western villainy and Communist bloc virtue. In 1955, Kuo Mo-jo, chair of the China Peace Committee, helped launch the latest Communist-organized petition drive in his country with a sizzling attack on the "atom-maniacs in the United States." By contrast, he argued, the Soviet government was working to abolish nuclear weapons and the Chinese government would be "using atomic energy for peaceful purposes." In fact, the Chinese nuclear weapons project began two months before, and neither he nor other leaders of the China Peace Committee ever questioned it. Similarly, in 1956, the WPC avoided issuing any rebuke to the Soviet Union's bloody military conquest of Hungary. The major conflict within WPC ranks was over which official Communist policy to follow: the Soviet (which stressed nuclear disarmament) or the Chinese (which increasingly emphasized support of Third World "liberation struggles"). As the Soviet government funded and controlled the WPC, the antinuclear cause prevailed. Both sides in this intramural rift, however, agreed that the nonaligned peace movement was dangerously independent. As a result, they either spurned it, criticized it, or sought to control it.

For their part, nonaligned peace groups, suspicious of the Communist-led movement and appalled by its double standard, kept their distance from it. In 1956, the German section of the WRI released a statement condemning the failure of the WPC and its local affiliate to respond to Soviet H-bomb tests. "Are Russian atomic and hydrogen bombs less dangerous than the American variety?" it asked tartly. In Sweden, AMSA discouraged its members from participating in the Communist-led peace movement. Responding in 1958 to two of its local branches which inquired about sending delegates to a forthcoming WPC conference, Britain's CND urged them to stay clear of it. In the United States, pacifist groups studiously avoided coalition ventures with Communist-controlled organizations, and SANE repeatedly rebuffed the WPC's appeals for cooperative activity. Writing in October 1958, SANE's Homer Jack told pacifist leader A. J. Muste that American peace activists "should not cooperate with the World Council for Peace," but should themselves help organize a world peace conference on nonaligned principles. Thus, the Communist-led peace campaign remained rather isolated—in sharp contrast to the nonaligned movement, which burgeoned considerably during these years.

Policymakers and Protest

Around the world, governments watched the upsurge of nuclear disarmament activism with considerable interest. For the leaders of neutral and nonaligned nations, the movement held considerable promise for buttressing their case against the nuclear arms race and nuclear war. In May 1958, Yugoslavia's president, Josip Broz Tito, congratulated Russell on the second Pugwash conference, observing that he was "confident" that such efforts would help responsible statesmen achieve their goal of "eliminating the danger of use of weapons of mass destruction." That September, the Austrian government hosted a Pugwash gathering in Vienna, addressed by the nation's president, Russell, and other luminaries. Nehru also applauded the Pugwash conferences, as well as the antinuclear ventures of Cousins and Schweitzer. In June 1957, after Schweitzer's first radio broadcast, Nehru told Cousins that he was "sure that Schweitzer's statement has helped" create "a far greater realization all over the world of the effect of these test explosions." Calling for follow-up efforts by the medical missionary, Nehru maintained that "pressure must come from awakened and, where possible, organized public opinion."

The leaders of Communist bloc nations were considerably less enthusiastic, at least when the movement impinged on their own priorities. Determined to maintain the Soviet public's Cold War militancy, Kremlin officials blocked writers from publishing books with a mordant view of war. Similarly, Soviet authorities vetoed publication of the grim analysis of nuclear war by Kurchatov and his colleagues. The government-controlled mass media ridiculed pacifism, depicting it as bizarre and crankish. "Soviet military ideology has nothing in common with pacifism," *Red Star* told readers in 1957; instead, it relies on "constant vigilance and preparedness for victorious defense of the socialist countries against the attacks of imperialism." As indicated by the continued Soviet support of the WPC, Soviet leaders found the Communist-led movement considerably more appealing than its nonaligned competitor.

In East Germany, too, where the authorities billed Marxism-Leninism as "the peace concept par excellence," the ruling Communist party denounced pacifism for undermining the resistance of the masses to Western imperialism. Although the East German communications media devoted considerable attention to the Göttingen appeal by West German scientists, the population did not get a chance to read it, for the press published a bowdlerized version that omitted phrases that might embarrass the regime. Similarly, the East German press lauded a West Berlin "march against atomic death" in April 1958, but distorted its character by exaggerating Communist participation and by making it appear that the demonstrators shared the East German government's policy positions.

Nevertheless, as Soviet officials observed the rise of the nonaligned antinuclear movement in non-Communist nations, they developed respect for it as a factor that could restrain Western belligerence and bring the dangerous nuclear arms race under control. Khrushchev, particularly, began to stress the importance of what he called "peace forces" to bolster his 1956 contention that war with the West was not inevitable. That year, in an unusual move, he allowed Kurchatov to travel to Britain "to establish useful contacts with the Western scientific community." In 1958, he personally authorized the publication of Sakharov's articles assailing nuclear testing. That May, in a meeting with the WPC's Joliot-Curie, Khrushchev emphasized the importance of public opinion and stated his belief that a peace movement did not necessarily have to identify fully with Soviet foreign policy.

Reversing the venomously hostile behavior characteristic of the Stalin years, the Soviet government began to court leaders of the nonaligned peace movement. Russell, once condemned as a fascist warmonger, found his messages on nuclear disarmament and world government printed in Soviet publications, accompanied by favorable editorial comments. In the past, Cousins had applied repeatedly for a visa to visit the Soviet Union, but without success—or even a response. In 1958, however, he was suddenly admitted for a lecture tour. Although, initially, Soviet officials felt uneasy about the Pugwash conferences, they did facilitate the participation of top Soviet scientists in the 1957 and 1958 meetings, as well as a warm letter of thanks by Khrushchev to the conference host, stressing "the great importance" he attached to "the efforts of scientists of countries of the world to remove the terrible threat of nuclear war hanging over humanity."

Western bloc officials, too, could not ignore the growing antinuclear campaign. "Our Allies are seriously concerned about the impact of the slogan 'Ban the Bomb,'" reported Harold Stassen, Eisenhower's advisor on arms control issues. "Public opinion in Europe has been enamoured with the slogan." In West Germany, Chancellor Konrad Adenauer felt alarmed at the opposition to his pro-nuclear position by the bulk of public opinion and great concern at the issuance of the Göttingen and Schweitzer appeals. Schweitzer's prestige was "very great in Germany," the chancellor remarked ruefully, for he spoke "almost with the authority of the Bible." In Italy, a U.S. government report warned, the government was "under considerable pressure from Italian public opinion to support moves in the direction of banning nuclear bomb production and tests." In Norway, the prime minister conceded that the Schweitzer appeal had "tremendous significance." Thanks to "the public fear of the effects of radiation," an Australian diplomat acknowledged, his government, too, faced difficulties justifying nuclear weapons tests. In Japan, the government felt thoroughly intimidated by antinuclear sentiment.

The British government considered itself besieged. Shortly after the *Lucky Dragon* incident, Churchill told Eisenhower that "there is widespread anxiety here about the H-bomb and I am facing a barrage of questions." Although the prime minister loyally defended U.S. nuclear testing and U.S. possession of the Bomb, the situation continued to worsen. In January 1956, at a meeting of top British and U.S. officials, the British foreign secretary warned that there was "a considerable and growing body of public opinion in the U.K. in favor of some form of regulation" of nuclear testing. "The government had to decide whether to be dragged along behind or to take an initiative themselves." In 1957, the prime minister complained to the Americans that "nuclear test limitation" had become "an important domestic political issue."

Viewing the emergence of the nuclear disarmament movement with alarm, Western bloc leaders groped for means to resist it. Under enormous pressure from its antinuclear public, the Japanese government remained the most accommodating, treating pacifists with courtesy and even sending greetings to the first World Conference Against Atomic and Hydrogen Bombs. Other governments, though, were more combative. Determined to discredit the Pauling petition, the French proposed that the participants in the North Atlantic Council gather derogatory information on petition signers in their respective countries. In Canada, the government pressured Eaton to cancel the 1958 Pugwash conference. In Germany, Adenauer and other government officials sought to intimidate antinuclear scientists and badgered Strauss "to obtain a retraction from Schweitzer." Assailing the SPD's proposal for maintaining a nuclear-free Germany, Adenauer charged that it would "result in the communization of Europe."

British policy toward nuclear disarmament activism was quite hostile. After the ASA produced reports emphasizing the radiation dangers of the H-bomb and strontium-90, the government brought so much pressure to bear on the organization that it abandoned such activities and, then, collapsed. Convinced that "the Communists" wanted to use the 1958 Pugwash conference "to secure support for the Soviet demand for the banning of nuclear weapons," the British Foreign Office initially sought to encourage an attitude of skepticism toward it. When, despite these efforts, preparations for the conference moved forward, the Foreign Office turned to conspiring with key scientists on how best to influence it. As plans for the third Pugwash conference emerged, the Foreign Office warned of the possibility "that this will be more dangerous from our point of view than its predecessors," for it might result in "a major propaganda drive against nuclear weapons." Among the dangerous participants it cited were Russell, Rotblat, and Rabinowitch.

The British government found the rise of CND particularly disturbing. In a March 1958 memo on the "Anti H-Bomb Campaign," the undersecretary of state warned that it "could prove most damaging to the foreign and defense policies of Her Majesty's Government." As this was a matter "of great urgency," it was necessary "to discuss the appropriate measures for dealing with this development at the highest level." In fact, such discussions were already under way. Only four days after CND's inaugural meeting, the home secretary suggested the need for "some counter-propaganda" to Prime Minister Harold Macmillan. Later that month, he brought together Macmillan and other top officials to discuss "how we can better organize the anti-antinuclear campaign." In the aftermath of this gathering, Macmillan not only approved measures to undermine the first Aldermaston March, but on March 24 sent a memo to the cabinet's public relations director, declaring: "It is most important that we should find some way of organizing and directing an effective campaign to counter the current agitation against this country's possession of nuclear weapons." Macmillan outlined plans for securing useful television coverage, and also suggested that he approach "influential publicists," "reliable scientists," and "Church of England Bishops." In response, the Cabinet officer launched an ambitious campaign that mobilized luminaries behind the government's nuclear weapons program. The press proved quite cooperative, he assured Macmillan, and "we are more than usually busy 'killing' stories."

Indeed, numerous governments sought to counter the influence of antinuclear groups through the management of public opinion. In Japan, this meant issuing declarations publicly favoring nuclear arms control and disarmament while privately reassuring U.S. officials that such statements were merely sops to antinuclear sentiment. With some embarrassment, the Japanese foreign minister secretly explained to Dulles: "The psychological situation in Japan compels the government to stand for disarmament." In the aftermath of the controversial Bikini H-bomb tests, the New Zealand government told the press that it was studying their radioactive effects. But, privately, the minister of external affairs assured the U.S. ambassador that his government's action "stemmed more from political necessity than from any actual apprehension about the after-effects of the explosion." "With so much talk going on," he explained, "the government politically was not in a position to ignore the matter." Another method of staving off popular criticism was to tightly control the release of information. In 1954, recognizing that its decision to proceed with an H-bomb program would offend the consciences of "substantial" numbers of Britons, the British Cabinet opted to keep its plans secret. Later that year, it began pressuring the BBC to keep a full discussion of the H-bomb off the air. In 1956, the Cabinet decided to avoid an early announcement of British nuclear test plans, lest it "stimulate political controversy."

Criticism of nuclear weapons deeply irritated the U.S. government. In 1956, when Adlai Stevenson called for an end to nuclear testing, Vice President Richard Nixon denounced the Democratic Party candidate for propounding "catastrophic nonsense." Regarding Schweitzer's 1957 radio broadcast as what Strauss called "a body blow to the testing program," the AEC played a key role in blocking television coverage of his talk and the CIA began distributing his private correspondence to U.S. government agencies. After Schweitzer's 1958 radio address, the FBI launched an investigation of the Schweitzer Fellowship, the U.S.-based organization that funded the missionary's hospital at Lambaréné. For his part, the secretary of state warned the nearest U.S. diplomatic official that Schweitzer's articles and speeches had been "highly critical" of nuclear testing and, thus, had been "closely adhering [to the] Communist line."

The U.S. government regarded scientists as especially dangerous. When a paper written for a U.N. conference by Hermann Muller, a Nobel Prize-winning geneticist, raised the issue of the genetic effects of radiation, the AEC had it withdrawn from the conference agenda. In an effort to undermine the influence of two other nuclear critics, the AEC worked to destroy the career of the physicist Ralph Lapp and withdrew the security clearance of the physicist Robert Oppenheimer—the latter a decision that led to his administrative "trial" and the termination of his government service. Convinced that Linus Pauling followed "the Communist Party line," the State Department denied him a passport for overseas travel on three occasions, only to retreat in embarrassment after late 1954, when Pauling received the Nobel Prize for Chemistry.

The appearance of Pauling's 1957 petition against nuclear testing was the final straw. At a press conference, Eisenhower implied that Pauling was part of a Communist conspiracy—a charge that triggered numerous attacks along these lines, plus plans for an investigation of Pauling by the Senate Internal Security Subcommittee. In early 1958, Edward Teller—the key figure in the U.S. government's H-bomb program—assailed Pauling's worldwide petition in a

Life magazine article. Nuclear test radiation, Teller argued, "need not necessarily be harmful," but "may conceivably be helpful."

The Eisenhower administration also confronted the perils of pacifism. Viewing the nation's small pacifist groups as a major threat to national security, government officials kept close tabs on them. The FBI had long been hot on the trail of pacifist troublemakers—planting informers at their meetings, gathering antinuclear literature, leaking derogatory information about them, and making occasional attempts to have them prosecuted. Alerted in November 1957 to plans by the WILPF, the FOR, and the War Resisters League to hold a "Prayer and Conscience Vigil" of five to fifteen people in Washington, DC to protest the development and use of nuclear weapons, J. Edgar Hoover fired off a memo on this to the attorney general, the State Department, the AEC, the Secret Service, the intelligence agencies of the armed forces, and the special assistant to the President for national security affairs. When Bigelow and other pacifists announced their plan to sail the *Golden Rule* into the U.S. nuclear testing zone in the Pacific, the U.S. secretary of state, the AEC, and U.S. Navy officers carried on lengthy discussions as to what should be done about it, while U.S. intelligence agencies swapped data on Bigelow, including information on his private telephone conversations and legal plans. Arrests followed in this case and those of a similar nature, along with charges by Strauss and other government officials that these ventures were part of a devious Communist conspiracy.

Similarly, the administration took a mordant view of Norman Cousins and SANE. Although Cousins and Eisenhower had exchanged warm letters in 1951–52, Strauss and his friends on the White House staff saw to it that Cousins' subsequent letters and requests for a meeting with the President were sidetracked and, sometimes, not even acknowledged. After the establishment of SANE, Cousins and Norman Thomas made another try, sending Eisenhower information about the new organization and proposing that he meet with SANE's leaders. Rejected on this score, they met with Strauss, who lectured Thomas about "the impossibility" of effectively monitoring nuclear tests and the allegedly small health risks from nuclear fallout. Following up, the FBI began extensive investigations of SANE's national organization and local chapters in 1958. Although the investigations never concluded that SANE was anything other than a citizens' organization promoting international agreements for nuclear disarmament, the FBI emphasized the potential dangers of the group, for Communists, it charged, were attempting to infiltrate it.

From the administration's standpoint, overseas developments were just as dangerous. In West Germany, where the U.S. ambassador reported that a 1957 election victory by the antinuclear Social Democrats and Free Democrats could "only be regarded with horror," Dulles and Eisenhower worked behind the scenes to strengthen Adenauer's grip on power. The situation was even worse in Japan, where, according to the U.S. ambassador, the *Lucky Dragon* incident had led the nation "to revel in [its] fancied martyrdom" and the "position of neutralists, pacifists, feminists, and professional anti-Americans . . . has been strengthened." Characteristically, Strauss argued that the irradiated Japanese fishing boat was really a "Red spy outfit," part of a "Russian espionage system." Although the CIA, after conducting an investigation of this charge, rejected it as utterly without foundation, Strauss continued to repeat it for more than a decade. Meanwhile, the AEC brushed off Japanese complaints about U.S. radioactive contamination of their country by stressing its "pride" in "the high degree of safety with which the American nuclear tests have been conducted."

The administration also worked diligently to control public opinion. Conferring with the AEC chair in 1953, Eisenhower suggested that "thermonuclear" be left out of AEC press releases and speeches. "Keep them confused as to 'fission' and 'fusion,'" the President advised. Discussing a proposed policy of nuclear candor at an NSC meeting, Secretary of Defense Charles Wilson argued that this was not "the right moment to acquaint the American people with the facts" about nuclear weapons, for such facts were "more likely to frighten people than to reassure them." Naturally, then, the government sought to hide its nuclear operations—as in the spring of 1958, when it kept secret its nuclear test series in the Pacific. Furthermore, public statements by administration officials deliberately minimized the dangers of nuclear fallout, thereby leading Americans downwind of U.S. nuclear tests in Nevada to pay little attention to their irradiation—until, of course, the ensuing epidemic of cancer, leukemia, genetic deformities, and death swept over their lives and the lives of their children. Disturbed by the findings on foreign opinion secured through its secret polls, the administration dramatically expanded U.S. overseas propaganda operations. Appealing for support of the new U.S. Information Agency in 1955, Eisenhower explained: "We are trying to convince the people in the world that we are working for peace and not trying to blow them to kingdom come with our atom and thermonuclear bombs."

Governments Change Policies

Although numerous governments perceived the nuclear disarmament movement as a threat to their national security policies, only two of them—France and China—dared to flout it openly and, even then, not completely. Determined to ensure France's national defense and its independence in world affairs, the French government announced its nuclear weapons program in 1958. At the same time, it maintained its rhetorical support for nuclear disarmament. Similarly, the Chinese government—keenly aware of U.S. nuclear threats and uncertain to what degree it could trust the defense guarantees of its Soviet ally—accelerated work on Chinese nuclear weapons. Sometimes, Mao displayed a remarkable equanimity about the consequences of nuclear war. "We shouldn't be afraid of atomic bombs and missiles," he told a November 1957 conference of world Communist leaders. "No matter what kind of war breaks out . . . we'll win. As for China, if the imperialists unleash war on us, we may lose more than three hundred million people. So what? War is war." Nevertheless, China's Central Military Commission, chaired by Mao, resolved in mid-1958 that China was "developing nuclear weapons in order to warn our enemies against making war on us, not in order to use nuclear weapons to attack them." Furthermore, China's government desired to "reach agreement on nuclear disarmament."

British policy shifted more substantially. Although the Macmillan government made nuclear weapons the center of its defense strategy and succeeded in testing Britain's first H-bomb, by 1958—as a British disarmament official recalled—"the pressure of public opinion against nuclear testing had . . . become a serious factor; no British government could afford to appear to drag its feet." According to the record of a meeting with U.S. government officials that June, Macmillan argued that the contents of a forthcoming U.N. report "would help the agitators and critics to make a strong case against continued tests" and, therefore, the British and the Americans would have to decide "whether we could continue testing." In July, he warned the British foreign secretary that, after the appearance of the U.N. report, "we will not be able to stand up against the pressure in the [U.N. General] Assembly and public opinion here."

Other U.S. allies, too, were beginning to call for change. Japanese officials—pressed by unanimous parliamentary resolutions calling for a nuclear test ban—commenced efforts to secure it. Meeting with U.S. State Department officials in June 1957, Prime Minister Nobusuke Kishi told Dulles that "the

Japanese are very serious about this matter" and that it was his "fervent hope" that "some arrangement could be arrived at to prohibit all nuclear tests." That same year, when a storm of domestic opposition arose over Kishi's remark that the Japanese constitution did not bar the maintenance of nuclear weapons for defense, he quickly retreated, claiming that he had no intention of providing Japanese forces with nuclear arms or allowing the Americans to station them in Japan. Conferring with U.S. officials, the Japanese foreign minister warned them that introducing nuclear weapons into his country was a political "hot potato."

The governments of Australia and New Zealand also showed signs of straying from the fold. In the aftermath of the disastrous Bikini H-bomb experiments and the resulting furor, the Australian government told the British that it would no longer allow thermonuclear tests on Australian soil. Although New Zealand's government assisted the British with the ensuing tests at Christmas Island, Prime Minister Keith Holyoke informed London that his country did not want to acquire nuclear weapons or to serve as "a storage base for them." When the opposition Labour Party swept to power in 1957, it continued this policy and took another step in an antinuclear direction by issuing the New Zealand government's first clear call for a ban on nuclear testing.

Within the NATO alliance, too, there were increasing signs of uneasiness about nuclear weapons programs. In December 1957, as the U.S. government laid plans to provide its NATO allies with intermediate-range ballistic missiles, the Danish and Norwegian governments—chastened by domestic controversy over the weapons—sharply rejected peacetime deployment of the missiles in their countries. Furthermore, Canada's prime minister stressed that the new missile placement went "beyond" past NATO agreements and "requires careful study." Ultimately, only Italy and Turkey accepted the new missiles. In addition, according to the record of a NATO meeting in February 1958, there was a "general recognition" of the "public anxiety over nuclear tests," and both Belgium and Canada requested their short-term suspension. In the following months, Canada and Norway called for a reappraisal of NATO's support for continued nuclear testing, with the Norwegians citing their "great concern over public reaction."

The sharpest criticism of the nuclear arms race continued to come from nonaligned nations. In the spring of 1957, the Bandung conference of Afro-Asian nations argued that nuclear disarmament was "imperative to save mankind and civilization from the fear and prospect of wholesale destruction." The governments of India, Indonesia, and Ceylon sharply condemned nuclear testing, with the Indian repeatedly raising objections to the U.S. government's use of the Marshall Islands, a U.N. trust territory, for its nuclear tests. Although Sweden's armed forces and opposition parties championed the development of nuclear weapons, the Social Democratic government began gravitating toward rejecting them. Behind the emerging non-nuclear policy, recalled Prime Minister Tage Erlander, lay the influence of nuclear critics, his determination to avoid a split in his party's ranks, his conclusion that Swedish nuclear weapons entailed risks for Sweden's neutrality, and his belief that "we ought to support the efforts going on to prohibit nuclear weapons." In the fall of 1958, Sweden's foreign minister, addressing the U.N. General Assembly, called for a treaty to ban nuclear testing.

Even the Soviet government was beginning to change its policy. At the Soviet Party Congress of February 1956, Khrushchev drew upon the nuclear issue to argue that there was no reasonable alternative to peace. "Either peaceful coexistence or the most destructive war in history," he stated; "there is no third way." Officially endorsed by the party gathering, "peaceful coexistence" seemed likely to provide the Soviet Union with at least two substantial benefits. First, as Khrushchev had stated, it would help to avert a disastrous war with the West. In addition, by bolstering the contention of Soviet propaganda that Moscow followed a "peace-loving policy," it would appeal strongly to the many people around the world horrified by the nuclear arms race. The following year, alarmed by Mao's cavalier attitude toward nuclear war, Khrushchev canceled plans to provide the Chinese government with nuclear assistance. He also began to grow more serious about negotiating a test ban treaty—a measure that seemed likely to improve relations between Washington and Moscow, inhibit U.S. advances in nuclear weapons technology, prevent the acquisition of nuclear weapons by West Germany and China, and evoke a favorable response from world opinion.

With foreign policy and propaganda goals pointing in the same direction, the Soviet government made a daring move: a unilateral suspension of nuclear tests, which it announced publicly on March 31, 1958. Although Soviet military experts opposed this initiative on the grounds of national defense, it was a clever gambit on the chessboard of world politics. It presented the U.S. and British governments with the choice of either following the Soviet example or suffering worldwide public condemnation.

In fact, even before confronting this dilemma, the U.S. government had begun to shift course, particularly with respect to the employment of nuclear weapons. In January 1956, Henry Cabot Lodge Jr., U.S. ambassador to the United Nations, complained that the atomic bomb had acquired "'a bad name,' and to such an extent that it seriously inhibits us from using it." He was correct. According to the record of an NSC meeting later that year, when the joint chiefs of staff and other administration officials called for greater flexibility in the employment of nuclear weapons, Eisenhower responded: "The use of nuclear weapons would raise serious political problems in view of the current state of world opinion." In May 1957, countering ambitious proposals by Strauss and the Defense Department for nuclear war-fighting, Dulles told an NSC meeting, according to the minutes, that "world opinion was not yet ready to accept the general use of nuclear weapons. . . . If we resort to such a use of nuclear weapons we will, in the eyes of the world, be cast as a ruthless military power, as was Germany." Dulles predicted, hopefully, "that all this would change at some point in the future, but the time had not yet come." Brushing off renewed pleas from the secretary of defense to use nuclear weapons, the secretary of state remained adamant that the United States must not "get out of step with world opinion."

Popular pressure also underlay the administration's growing interest in arms control and disarmament. In the spring of 1954, shocked at the worldwide protest unleashed by the *Lucky Dragon* incident, Dulles convinced Eisenhower to launch a study to determine if the U.S. government should agree to Nehru's proposal for a moratorium on nuclear testing. Although the study opposed backing a testing moratorium, continued public uneasiness led Eisenhower, in 1955, to appoint Stassen as his special assistant on disarmament. That fall, Stassen met with the President to discuss what his notes called "the Ban-the-Bomb Psychological Problem," which included both the "position of our allies" and "United States public opinion." Meanwhile, Dulles argued that the U.S. government must "make some positive move in the direction of disarmament," for the "popular and diplomatic pressure for limitation of armament . . . cannot be resisted by the United States without our forfeiting the good will of our allies and the support of a large part of our own people." Although Dulles did not favor a test ban, the growing popular clamor, including Stevenson's support for a ban, led Eisenhower to order a new study of the matter in September 1956. The President cited "the rising concern of people everywhere over the effect of radiation from tests, their reaction each time a test was reported, and their extreme nervousness over the prospective consequences of any nuclear war."

Despite vigorous opposition to a test ban by Strauss, the secretary of defense, and the joint chiefs of staff, other forces in the administration began to succumb to public pressure. Meeting with Teller and other top scientists in the U.S. nuclear weapons program in June 1957, Eisenhower warned them that "we are ... up against an extremely difficult world opinion situation" and that he did not believe "that the United States could permit itself to be 'crucified on a cross of atoms.'" Later that year, Eisenhower appointed a President's Science Advisory Committee (PSAC), a group of experts who often shared the views of the FAS. According to the PSAC chair, "the growing worldwide criticism of nuclear testing ... provided an atmosphere of urgency" for its early meetings. Not surprisingly, it recommended that a test ban was both feasible and desirable. Meanwhile, Dulles, informed by the CIA that the Soviet Union stood on the verge of announcing a unilateral suspension of nuclear tests, called together crisis meetings of U.S. government officials in late March 1958. At the first of them, he proposed that Eisenhower announce that, after the U.S. nuclear test series later that year, the U.S. government would not authorize any further nuclear testing. If this statement were released before the Soviet announcement, declared Dulles, "it would make a great diplomatic and propaganda sensation to the advantage of the United States." The secretary of state explained: "I feel desperately the need for some important gesture in order to gain an effect on world opinion."

The March 31 Soviet announcement of its testing moratorium—which produced an enormous propaganda success for that nation and embarrassment for the United States—decided the matter. As one U.S. arms control official recalled: "The Russians boxed us in." Dulles told the President that, if U.S. nuclear testing continued, "the slight military gains" would "be outweighed by the political losses." Conferring with the President that summer, he declared that "the opinion of peoples throughout the world is sharply opposed to the continuance of nuclear testing." Consequently, "if the United States did not announce its readiness to cease nuclear testing ... world opinion would ascribe aggressive intent to the United States, which would be definitely harmful to this country." That August, Eisenhower told a group of U.S. officials, enthusiastic about nuclear weapons, that "the new nuclear weapons are tremendously powerful," but "they are not ... as powerful as is world opinion today in obliging the United States to follow certain lines of policy." Six days later, he overruled the objections of Defense Department and AEC officials to his plans for the suspension of nuclear testing, pointing to "the political benefits of this action."

On August 22, he announced that, as of the end of October 1958, the United States would suspend nuclear testing for the following year and was willing to enter negotiations with other nations for a full-fledged nuclear test ban.

As a result, on October 31, 1958, for the first time since the grim inaugural of the nuclear era, nuclear explosions ceased around the globe.

5   Victories and Retreats, 1958–1970

Despite the 1958 moratorium on nuclear weapons testing, the nuclear disarmament movement continued its dramatic advance. Roused from politics as usual by the spiraling nuclear arms race, millions of people were determined to ban the Bomb. Their determination was reinforced by the disastrous Paris "summit" conference of 1960, by the fruitless nuclear arms control negotiations among the great powers at Geneva, and by the 1962 Cuban missile crisis, during which the world teetered eerily on the brink of nuclear war. Furthermore, even the 1958 testing moratorium proved evanescent. France began atmospheric nuclear testing in 1960, the Soviet Union resumed atmospheric nuclear testing in 1961, the United States and Britain reverted to underground testing in 1961 and to atmospheric testing in 1962, and China began its first nuclear tests in 1964. As the great powers made nuclear testing, intercontinental ballistic missiles, and preparations for nuclear war ever more prominent features of their "national security" programs, popular resistance to the Bomb grew to unprecedented proportions.

The Movement at High Tide, 1958–1965

In Britain, as Canon Collins noted, "CND prospered beyond our wildest dreams." Its nuclear disarmament symbol "became as well known as the Union Jack . . . and to thousands the world over it became a sign of sanity and hope." Membership surged, as tens of thousands of supporters flocked to the antinuclear campaign. By 1961, CND could point to more than 800 local groups and twenty-six full-time staff members. Marches and demonstrations erupted throughout the British Isles. In 1960, when CND reversed the course of its annual Aldermaston march, 40,000 antinuclear demonstrators, in a column six miles long, swept into the nation's capital. At their final destination, Trafalgar

Square, a crowd estimated at from 60,000 to 100,000 people gathered behind nuclear disarmament banners from unions, churches, political parties, universities, and regions throughout Britain. Observers agreed that it was the largest and most significant popular rally held in Britain since the Chartist demonstrations of 1848.

This upsurge of antinuclear action had a powerful impact on the British Labour Party. In 1959, that party explicitly committed itself to immediately halting all British nuclear tests and to working for an agreement among nations other than the United States and the Soviet Union to renounce nuclear weapons. In October 1960, as the Labour Party's annual conference convened at Scarborough, nuclear disarmament demonstrators flooded the streets of the town, adorned by CND banners, and key unions lined up behind CND's demand for Britain's unilateral nuclear disarmament. Rejecting pleas by the party leadership, the delegates adopted a resolution calling for "the unilateral renunciation of the testing, manufacture, stockpiling and basing of all nuclear weapons in Great Britain." Although party leaders managed to reverse this position at Labour's fall 1961 conference, they continued to criticize Britain's role as an independent nuclear power.

Despite these inroads into mainstream politics, many British activists were growing impatient. The young militants of the Direct Action Committee, convinced that time was limited for the profound changes necessary to save the world from annihilation, conducted small-scale, daring civil disobedience projects and sought, unsuccessfully, to pull CND into them. Meanwhile, the CND rank and file and even Russell were becoming dissatisfied with the pace of change. Into this explosive situation came an American graduate student, Ralph Schoenman, who convinced the CND president that the time had come to organize a massive campaign of civil disobedience that would galvanize public opinion and compel the beleaguered British government to abandon the Bomb. In September 1960, Russell began dispatching letters to prominent personalities, urging them to join a Committee of 100 that would direct the campaign.

Launched at a meeting in October 1960, the Committee of 100 secured the backing of some of Britain's most outstanding cultural luminaries. In its first action, on February 18, 1961, an estimated 5,000 people, led by Russell, staged a sit-down outside the Ministry of Defense, in downtown London. Although no arrests took place on that occasion, that April, at another Committee venture, the police arrested 826 participants. Following up in July, the Committee announced a new wave of civil disobedience to occur in September, with large-scale action in London and at the U.S. nuclear submarine base at Holy Loch. On September 17, the day of the planned sit-down at Parliament Square—an event now officially banned by the government—upwards of 12,000 people arrived. Barred by the police from entering the area, they eventually occupied Trafalgar Square. The police arrested 1,314 demonstrators in London and another 351 at Holy Loch.

Yet, after delivering this rebuke to the government's authority, the Committee lost momentum. In December, it sought to hold massive demonstrations at seven widely scattered military bases. But lacking mass backing outside of London, it drew only some 7,000 people. Meanwhile, arrests and government persecution began to take their toll. Furthermore, within the Committee's ranks, a disdain for authority caused growing confusion and chaos. Rebuffed by the Committee leadership on a proposal to support civil disobedience at the conclusion of the Aldermaston march, activists went ahead and organized it anyway. Even Russell lost patience with his creation, and resigned the Committee of 100's presidency in early 1963.

By contrast, CND continued to serve as a powerful source of pressure for nuclear disarmament. In 1962, CND's Aldermaston march drew a record 150,000 people to its culminating rally. Drawing disproportionately upon the middle class, CND proved especially popular with its socially concerned, organizationally active, and politically avant-garde elements, usually located in the human welfare and creative professions. On university campuses, the 150 CND chapters became some of the largest, most powerful student groups. Newspapers and magazines carried stories and cartoons on nuclear dangers. Although polls revealed that most Britons did not support civil disobedience and unilateral disarmament, they also showed that overwhelming majorities favored halting nuclear tests and securing nuclear disarmament treaties. As a new British musical group, the Beatles, toured the United States in March 1964, young Paul McCartney, appearing on television, blithely stated the view of most Britons: "Ban the Bomb."

A comparable movement took shape in Canada. In 1959, after preliminary correspondence with Norman Cousins and SANE, Mary Van Stolk of Edmonton founded a community group, the Committee on the Control of Radiation Hazards. Determined to end nuclear testing, Van Stolk traveled across Canada, speaking to concerned citizens and convincing them to form the Canadian Committee for the Control of Radiation Hazards. After the Canadian government announced that it planned to purchase Bomarc missiles from the United States, presumably to be fitted with nuclear warheads, the new group turned into a full-fledged ban-the-bomb organization. The following spring, it began circulating a petition calling on the government to reject nuclear weapons for Canada. The petition soon had some very eminent endorsers—including prominent educators, well-known authors, powerful newspapers, provincial legislators, and the Canadian Labor Congress—and eventually drew 200,000 signers. As thousands of members poured into the new organization, delegates to its February 1962 national convention voted to rename it the Canadian Campaign for Nuclear Disarmament.

The Canadian movement was burgeoning. In July 1960, advocates of women's peace activism organized the Voice of Women, which plunged into petitioning, letter-writing, staging press conferences, and collecting baby teeth to test for strontium-90. In addition, a student antinuclear organization, Combined Universities CND—with twenty-one chapters and a lively journal, *Our Generation Against Nuclear War*—became the youth group of Canadian CND. Much like their British counterparts, Canada's peace and disarmament organizations held Easter marches and agitated zealously against nuclear weapons. Addressing a campaign rally in late May 1962, Prime Minister John Diefenbaker was startled to find the meeting hall "filled with cries of 'Ban-Ban-Ban the Bomb.'" In 1963, activists made the deployment of U.S. nuclear weapons in Canada a heated issue in the nationwide election campaign, helping to turn public sentiment against it and to galvanize popular support for halting nuclear testing and securing nuclear disarmament.

Although the movement in Australia was somewhat smaller, it too became an important feature of political life. Beginning in 1960, CND groups started to appear in Victoria, New South Wales, Queensland, and Western Australia, and in December 1963 activists established a nationwide CND. Appealing particularly to the youthful, educated middle class, CND held numerous meetings and distributed literature calling for an end to nuclear testing, the banning of nuclear weapons from Australia's soil, and the implementation of nuclear disarmament. Organizers developed the Australian movement's "radial walk," in which thousands of demonstrators marched from assorted suburbs to converge at a downtown rally, thus covering an H-bomb's area of destruction. Even though the movement had limited influence within the broader society, the Australian Council of Churches and the Labor Party did begin to take up its themes. Furthermore, polls found that overwhelming majorities of Australians favored an end to nuclear testing and a worldwide agreement to abolish nuclear weapons.

Inspired by events in Britain and, to a lesser extent, the United States, antinuclear activism accelerated in New Zealand. In 1959 and 1960, loosely affiliated nuclear disarmament groups in major cities held conventions that led to the formation of New Zealand CND, with Mary Woodward, a Quaker, serving as national secretary. By early 1963, it claimed some 1,700 members throughout the country, including ten branches in major population centers. Staging their own Aldermaston marches, youthful CNDers paraded along beaches and coastal roads before converging on the steps of parliament for mass rallies. Intellectuals, church members, and students were particularly active in New Zealand's antinuclear campaign, as were many women, who formed small women's peace groups. As U.S. nuclear tests in the Pacific lit up the skies over New Zealand and the French moved forward with their own testing program, the Federation of Labor grew increasingly critical of nuclear testing, the Council of Churches urged abandonment of the French program, and the Labour Party came out in favor of CND's proposal for a nuclear-free zone in the southern hemisphere.

In Scandinavia, too, antinuclear sentiment boiled over into nationwide movements. Enthusiastic about what he had observed in Britain, Carl Scharnberg, a Danish high school teacher, returned to his country and founded the Campaign Against Atomic Weapons in June 1960. It produced huge quantities of antinuclear literature, mobilized large numbers of people for antinuclear demonstrations (including 30,000 who turned out for its 1962 Easter march), and saw to it that none of Denmark's larger parties supported the deployment of nuclear weapons in their country. In neighboring Norway, a succession of nuclear disarmament organizations—Protest Against Nuclear Weapons, Action for Nuclear Disarmament, and the Campaign Against Atomic Weapons—held mass demonstrations, submitted an antinuclear petition to parliament, and helped swing popular sentiment in an antinuclear direction. Impressed, the governing Labor Party adopted a resolution in May 1963 proclaiming that it had "always been and is a peace movement." In Sweden, AMSA heightened its agitation against the military's proposal for Swedish nuclear weapons, dispatching antinuclear speakers to hundreds of meetings, widely distributing its journal, and organizing an anti-H-bomb exhibit in Stockholm that drew more than 20,000 people. Meanwhile, a new organization, the Campaign Against Atomic Weapons, founded in 1961, staged mass marches around the themes of halting nuclear tests and banning nuclear weapons. Public opinion turned increasingly hostile to nuclear weapons and, by the mid-1960s, antinuclear forces triumphed within the governing Social Democratic Party.

In West Germany, the vacuum left by the collapse of efforts to block the introduction of nuclear weapons into that nation was filled by a broader antinuclear campaign. In early 1960, two teachers, Hans-Konrad Tempel and Helga Stolle, convinced pacifist groups to hold a small Easter march that condemned the nuclear policies of East and West. In the following years, the Easter March of Nuclear Weapons Opponents blossomed into a mass movement. By 1964, these marches were occurring in almost every major West German city and town, with total participation of more than 100,000 people. Resembling their counterparts elsewhere, the Easter marches contained masses of youthful demonstrators sporting nuclear disarmament pins, carrying banners, and singing antinuclear songs. In addition, West German physicists—determined to press for their government's abandonment of plans for nuclear weapons—organized the Federation of German Scientists. Polls in the early 1960s found that the public opposed a West German nuclear force by a ratio of seven to one, that 71 percent supported a nuclear test ban, and that 84 percent favored the abolition of nuclear weapons.

In the Netherlands, antinuclear agitation heightened. Over 65,000 people signed a petition, circulated by the Albert Schweitzer Committee Against Nuclear Weapons, opposing deployment of nuclear weapons in their country. Impressed by the Aldermaston marches, a new Committee for Peace staged yearly Dutch antinuclear marches which, by 1964, had grown to 5,000 participants. In addition, Anti-Atom Bomb Action distributed an estimated 400,000 antinuclear leaflets, the Netherlands Society of Scientists warned of nuclear dangers, and a new Pacifist Socialist Party—entering the parliamentary elections of 1963—drew 180,000 votes, giving it six legislative seats. Swept up in the growing ferment, both the Protestant and the Catholic churches began taking antinuclear positions.

Meanwhile, in Belgium, a new National Federation of Initiatives for a Belgian Contribution to International Détente held mass marches denouncing nuclear testing and nuclear weapons and a small Committee for Non-Violent Action—protesting the resumption of nuclear testing—held silent vigils outside the Soviet and U.S. embassies. Starting in late 1961, Belgium's League of Large Families mobilized its own broadly based antinuclear campaign: the May 8 Movement. In response to its call, on May 8, 1962—the anniversary of the end of World War II in Europe—half of Belgium's population reportedly took part in a fifteen-minute work stoppage calling for an end to nuclear testing and for nuclear disarmament.

The movement also emerged as a substantial force in Europe's neutral nations. Petitioning for a nationwide referendum to constitutionally ban nuclear arms from Switzerland, the Swiss Movement Against Atomic Armaments gathered over 73,000 signatures, held 2,000 public meetings, produced five hundred articles for the press, and distributed three million antinuclear leaflets. Although the nuclear ban was defeated in the referendum, the government—disturbed by the hot controversy—abandoned further discussions of nuclear weapons. Meanwhile the movement pressed forward with youth marches and other demonstrations. In neighboring Austria, concerned scientists organized the Federation of Austrian Scientists, which sponsored antinuclear lectures and publicized the Pugwash conferences. Moreover, during early 1963 a group of intellectuals and young people organized the Austrian Easter March Committee, which distributed antinuclear literature and sponsored annual marches. In Ireland, the new CND group sponsored public meetings in Dublin, Limerick, and Belfast, canvassed door to door, distributed antinuclear publications, and protested the resumption of nuclear testing. Meeting in Dublin in 1962, representatives of Northern and Southern Irish students' groups merged their two organizations by forming Irish Students' CND.

Although France's antinuclear campaign developed more slowly, it eventually resembled its foreign counterparts. In early 1959, Claude Bourdet—now the influential editor of *France-Observateur*—managed to unite about twenty small organizations into a French Federation Against Atomic Armament, with André Trocmé (a leading pacifist) and Alfred Kastler (an eminent physicist) as co-presidents. Calling upon the French government to abandon its nuclear weapons plans and to support nuclear disarmament, the French Federation sponsored public meetings, issued statements signed by prominent individuals, and distributed antinuclear literature. Even so, thanks largely to France's preoccupation with its war in Algeria, the French Federation never developed into a mass campaign. Therefore, starting in early 1963, Bourdet—inspired by the rise of nonaligned activism elsewhere—renewed his efforts, this time forming the Movement Against Atomic Armament (MCAA). At the same time, Jules Moch (a Socialist Party leader), organized another organization to focus on opposing the French nuclear program: the League Against the Force de Frappe. Working together, the MCAA, the League, and other groups mobilized unprecedented displays of antinuclear sentiment. That November, the MCAA helped draw together some forty organizations—including the major union federations, the national students union, peace groups, and left-wing parties—for an estimated sixty antinuclear demonstrations throughout France. They also sponsored massive Easter marches, including one in 1964 that drew more than 100,000 demonstrators. Meanwhile, the French public gradually turned against France's nuclear weapons program and displayed overwhelming support for nuclear disarmament.

Italy's relative silence on the nuclear issue was broken in 1960, when Aldo Capitini decided that his Center for Nonviolence, located in Perugia, should organize a mass march, along the lines of Britain's. That September, thousands of marchers—bearing signs proclaiming "No More Nuclear Tests," "Disarmament of the East and West," and other antinuclear slogans—made the trek from Perugia to Assisi, finishing up with an assemblage of 25,000, including peasants, intellectuals, mayors, workers, and police (who joined the demonstration en route). Antinuclear ventures emerged in other parts of Italy, as well—for example, in Milan, where an Italian CND held a demonstration of 10,000 in October 1961. Gradually, much of this scattered activity came under the direction of Capitini, who helped form an umbrella organization, the Council for Peace. This new group staged further antinuclear marches and meetings, some of very substantial size. Although the movement found it difficult to influence Italian electoral politics, it had greater success with public opinion. Polls in the early 1960s showed that Italians supported a nuclear test ban by a ratio of seven to one, and that 96 percent of Italian respondents favored the abolition of nuclear weapons.

The antinuclear campaign made one of its most dramatic debuts in Greece. As news of antinuclear marches elsewhere filtered into that country, Michalis Peristerakis, a law student, decided to form a nonaligned peace group. During the Cuban missile crisis, he distributed a leaflet announcing this intention, leading to the formation of the Bertrand Russell Youth Committee for Nuclear Disarmament. Its first activity was an Aldermaston-style march, from Marathon to Athens, to be held in April 1963. Viewing the march as an incitement to revolution, Greece's conservative government banned it. On the day the march was to begin, Greek police arrested some 2,000 people, physically assaulting many of them and injuring about 300. The only person to complete the march was Grigoris Lambrakis, an independent parliamentary deputy, spared arrest by his parliamentary immunity. Excited by CND's work in Britain, Lambrakis had participated in the 1963 Aldermaston march, bearing the banner for

Greece. And with the completion of his one-man Marathon march, he emerged as the symbol of Greece's burgeoning nuclear disarmament campaign. A month later, leaving an antinuclear gathering in Salonika, Lambrakis was murdered by right-wing vigilantes, secretly mobilized for the task by leaders of the Greek armed forces.

The murder of Lambrakis generated a tidal wave of protest. On May 28, 1963, despite efforts by the Greek government to limit the turnout at his funeral, it erupted into the largest peace demonstration in world history. Athens came to a standstill. Construction workers went out on strike for the day, and the rest of the city deserted its desks or workshops. As the funeral procession of 500,000 people moved through Athens behind the coffin of Lambrakis, cascades of flowers rained down on it from the houses and shops along the route. Nuclear disarmament emblems appeared everywhere—on the silk banner borne by the Bertrand Russell Youth Committee, in the form of huge floral wreaths, and on the plain gray stone that marked his grave. Deeply embarrassed by the Lambrakis affair and other scandals, the government resigned. In the ensuing elections, the Center Union Party—which had denounced the government as "the moral perpetrator of Lambrakis' murder"—emerged triumphant, ushering in an era of freedom and reform in Greek politics. Meanwhile, the antinuclear movement flourished. In 1964, a new Marathon march—sponsored by all of Greece's peace groups—began with 70,000 people and concluded with an estimated 250,000. The 1965 antinuclear march proved even more successful, drawing half a million demonstrators.

In Japan, the antinuclear movement continued to exercise enormous influence in the nation's public life. Although political dissension within Gensuikyo undermined its strength, it still had very significant clout. In 1959, its director general estimated that some 10 million people participated in its Pilgrimage to Hiroshima, a nationwide demonstration in support of the Fifth World Conference Against Atomic and Hydrogen Bombs. With the resumption of nuclear testing by the Soviet Union and the United States in late 1961, Gensuikyo announced a three-month action campaign to petition for general disarmament, as well as to foster activities against nuclear weapons tests and military bases. Meanwhile, within the ranks of the Japan Science Council, the Pugwash conferences and their antinuclear conclusions stirred substantial support, leading to disarmament conferences among scientists in Japan. One of these meetings produced a forceful critique of nuclear testing and nuclear weapons that received front page coverage in all of Japan's major newspapers.

Other antinuclear elements rounded out Japan's extraordinarily powerful movement. Small pacifist and world federalist groups added their voices
to others criticizing nuclear testing, protesting Japan's use as a nuclear base,
and pressing for nuclear disarmament. The left-wing Zengakuren, claiming to
speak for more than half of Japan's university student population, organized
demonstrations by thousands of Japanese students against the resumption of
U.S. nuclear testing and even managed to stage a short-lived demonstration in
Moscow's Red Square, denouncing Soviet nuclear tests. In addition, Japanese
teachers had their students read tragic stories of nuclear destruction, unions
endorsed disarmament organizations and campaigns, university presidents
condemned nuclear testing, and most newspapers and magazines opposed
military programs on the part of their government and others. Naturally, visits
by U.S. nuclear-powered warships—which, despite U.S. government denials,
many feared were nuclear-armed—inspired storms of protest. In March 1963,
an estimated 30,000 demonstrators turned out at Japanese ports to condemn
the proposed entry of U.S. nuclear submarines. That June, about 70,000 union
members and students held similar demonstrations in Yokosuka and Sasebo.

The Japanese movement was quite in line with public opinion. According to
a poll taken in the spring of 1963, the Japanese public—by a ratio of nearly two
to one—favored a U.S.-Soviet agreement to ban nuclear testing. Furthermore,
71 percent of Japanese respondents supported nuclear disarmament and only
1 percent opposed it. Not surprisingly, then, all four opposition parties took
a strong antinuclear stand, and the largest of them, the Socialist Party, served
as a mainstay of the antinuclear movement. Although the misnamed Liberal
Democratic Party, the conservative party that governed Japan, was considerably
less sympathetic to the movement, it hesitated to challenge Japan's antinuclear
consensus. In October 1961, when the lower house of the Japanese parliament
approved a resolution calling for an immediate end to all nuclear testing, the
measure passed unanimously.

In the United States, SANE remained the largest, best-known antinuclear
organization. Although membership did not expand much above the 25,000
attained by late 1958, the number of chapters grew to some 150, reaching beyond the original urban core on both coasts to outlying areas like Grand Forks,
North Dakota, and Lincoln, Nebraska. Hollywood SANE, headed by Steve Allen
and Robert Ryan, mobilized top movie stars for the antinuclear cause. In May
1960, SANE put together an overflow rally at Madison Square Garden, drawing
nearly 20,000 people for speeches by Cousins, Norman Thomas, Eleanor Roos-

evelt, and United Auto Workers president Walter Reuther. Campaigning for a nuclear test ban treaty, SANE published numerous creative advertisements. The best-known of them, headed "Dr. Spock is Worried," showed the famed pediatrician looking down sadly at a little girl and warning: "As the tests multiply, so will the damage to children—here and around the world. Who gives us this right?" In addition, SANE opened a lobbying office in Washington, endorsed candidates for election, and, in 1961, played the major role in organizing the nation's first Easter marches. Drawing some 25,000 Americans, they were the largest peace demonstrations in the United States for a generation.

Other Americans turned to civil disobedience. After organizing small-scale civil disobedience actions at an ICBM base outside Omaha and at a Polaris nuclear missile-carrying submarine base at Groton, Connecticut, the Committee for Nonviolent Action (CNVA), led by the pacifist A. J. Muste, began its most dramatic venture in December 1960: a San Francisco to Moscow Walk for Peace. Calling on the governments of all nations to disarm, the marchers hiked and distributed leaflets across the United States, Western Europe, Eastern Europe, and the Soviet Union. Ten months later, after numerous arrests, beatings, and deportations, the intrepid walkers marched into Moscow's Red Square.

The largest U.S. civil disobedience actions against nuclear war, however, grew out of earlier ventures. Ever since 1955, small groups of pacifists had courted arrest by refusing to take shelter in New York City during yearly civil defense drills. With the approach of the 1960 drill, two young mothers, Mary Sharmat and Janice Smith, organized a Civil Defense Protest Committee to broaden resistance efforts. Consequently, on May 3, as the sirens sounded, approximately 2,000 New Yorkers staged antinuclear demonstrations at scattered sites. In City Hall Park, where a thousand protesters gathered—many of them women with baby carriages—half of them defied the authorities by standing their ground and refusing to take shelter. During the nationwide drill the following year, 2,500 protesters turned out in City Hall Park, while similar demonstrations took place at universities, colleges, high schools, and other public spaces around the country.

Another sign of rising U.S. resistance to nuclear war was the formation of Women Strike for Peace (WSP). On November 1, 1961, WSP startled observers by staging women's antinuclear protests, with an estimated 50,000 participants, in sixty American cities. Beginning the previous September, a handful of women in the Washington, DC area, outraged by the resumption of nuclear testing, had begun mobilizing for the event. And its success convinced them to persist. Although WSP never developed a coherent national organization or formal membership, it soon claimed approximately 145 local groups. Certainly it tapped enormous energy and talent among American women. WSP organized visits by WSP delegations to congressional representatives and administration officials, picketed the White House, and fired off messages to Khrushchev demanding that he renounce nuclear testing. It also urged women to have their children's baby teeth tested for strontium-90 and, then, mail the teeth along with the lab report to their senators. WSP leaders, including its beloved founder, Dagmar Wilson, liked to portray their movement as a rebellion of unsophisticated, middle-class "housewives." But the reality was that—though most WSP activists were married, middle-class mothers—they were considerably better educated than most American women and were veterans of political causes.

At roughly the same time, the Student Peace Union (SPU) sprang up on U.S. college campuses. Founded in 1959 by a small group of pacifists and Socialists, SPU argued that "neither human freedom nor the human race itself can endure in a world committed to militarism." Although SPU's official membership was never very large—reaching perhaps 5,000 at its zenith—in 1963 it claimed some two hundred chapters or affiliates on college campuses and 12,000 subscribers to its monthly *Bulletin*. Local groups held peace marches, sponsored talks by leading proponents of disarmament, and churned out enormous quantities of literature. Enthusiastic about activism in Britain, SPU popularized CND's nuclear disarmament symbol in the United States. In February 1962, SPU and smaller groups brought some 5,000 students to Washington, DC for the largest student demonstration yet held in that city. Demanding that the U.S. government halt plans to resume nuclear testing, they picketed the White House on a round-the-clock basis, demonstrated at the Soviet embassy, and met with members of Congress and administration officials. Their picket signs read: "Neither Red nor Dead, but alive and free."

Although hawkish forces in the United States denounced this surge of disarmament activism, claiming that it was all part of a Communist conspiracy, its antinuclear message had considerable appeal among Americans. In November 1959, a Gallup poll reported that 77 percent of U.S. respondents wanted the great power nuclear testing moratorium extended. Even in November 1961, after the Soviet Union had resumed atmospheric nuclear tests, opponents of resuming U.S. atmospheric tests outnumbered supporters. Asked, in September 1960 and August 1963, about a disarmament agreement with the Soviet Union, a plurality of U.S. respondents (46 percent on each occasion) expressed its approval.

The movement also gained traction in U.S. politics. As the 1960 presidential race heated up, two of the Democratic hopefuls—Hubert Humphrey and Adlai Stevenson—sent messages of greeting to SANE's Madison Square Garden rally. John F. Kennedy, chosen as the Democratic nominee, announced that he opposed resumption of underground nuclear testing and pledged that, if elected, he would not be the first to resume atmospheric testing. He also promised to pursue "vigorous" test ban negotiations at Geneva and "earnestly seek an overall disarmament agreement." Even the Republican presidential candidate, Richard Nixon, pledged his support for a nuclear test ban and maintained that U.S. nuclear tests should not be resumed as long as any chance existed of obtaining a treaty. The following year, determined to fund the races of peace candidates for the U.S. Senate, Leo Szilard established the Council for a Livable World. In 1962, it made substantial financial contributions to George McGovern and four other peace-minded politicians—all of whom were elected.

Nuclear disarmament activism was also taking root in Africa. In August 1959, a Ghana Council for Nuclear Disarmament had been launched. This fact, plus the anti-imperialist stance of Ghana's president, Kwame Nkrumah, convinced overseas activists to turn their attention to that nation as France made preparations for its first nuclear weapons tests, in Algeria. With the support of the Direct Action Committee and CNVA, leading Western pacifists—including Michael Randle, A. J. Muste, and Bayard Rustin—flew to Accra, where they engaged in intense planning sessions with the leaders of Ghana CND. After addressing numerous mass meetings, attended by tens of thousands of people, they pulled together a small team of protesters from Ghana, Nigeria, Basutoland, Britain, the United States, and France that plunged into French-governed Africa en route to the French test site. In late 1959 and early 1960, they made three successive attempts to disrupt the Bomb tests, as French troops blocked their passage, captured them, and deported them. Meanwhile mass demonstrations against the French weapons tests broke out in Tunis, Tripoli, and Rabat, as did smaller ones in Upper Volta, Ghana, Nigeria, and Western nations. Following up, Nkrumah organized a Conference on Positive Action for Peace and Security in Africa that met in April 1960. Bringing together overseas pacifists and leaders of the African liberation struggle, the conference unanimously backed the development of larger-scale action against French nuclear tests and—in this connection—called for the establishment of training centers for "positive nonviolent action." Although Nkrumah's follow-up disappointed peace activists, they did secure important footholds in Ghana, Zambia, and Tanzania.

In the Near and Middle East, too, antinuclear sentiment was on the rise. When the Soviet Union resumed nuclear testing in the fall of 1961, the Arab press denounced it, with one Cairo newspaper proclaiming "Entire World Opposes Nuclear Explosions." Similarly, surveying public reaction in the Middle East to Kennedy's 1962 announcement that the U.S. government would resume atmospheric nuclear tests, the USIA found "over-all opposition." In early 1963, a secret U.S. government survey of Teheran residents found that 77 percent favored the abolition of nuclear weapons. Although peace activism in the region remained weak, within Turkey criticism of nuclear weapons came from the student association, left-wing groups, and the Turkish Labor Party. In Israel, as well, nuclear weapons inspired revulsion, and in late 1961 Israeli activists formed the Committee for Nuclear Disarmament of the Arab-Israeli Region. Organized by prominent scholars and scientists, the Committee held protest meetings, issued pamphlets, produced books, and published antinuclear statements in the Hebrew and English language press.

In other parts of the Third World, antinuclear sentiment usually exceeded activism. Only in India did the movement develop a significant organizational base, and even here it proved a rickety one. Although Gandhians organized an impressive Anti-Nuclear Arms Convention in New Delhi during June 1962, with every Indian newspaper giving it front-page coverage, the antinuclear campaign declined later that year, when an armed border clash between India and China sent political shock waves through the nation. Yet, despite the absence of widespread activism, strong antinuclear sentiment existed in Asia and Latin America. According to pollsters, in early 1963 support for the worldwide abolition of nuclear weapons stood at 65 percent in Rio de Janeiro, 72 percent in New Delhi, 76 percent in Bangkok, 79 percent in Saigon, 84 percent in Buenos Aires and Singapore, 87 percent in Mexico City, and 90 percent in Caracas.

In the Soviet Union, antinuclear activism quickened. At the Pugwash conferences, Soviet scientists grew increasingly relaxed and friendly with their Western counterparts, challenging official verities and even, on occasion, telling anti-Communist jokes. At a time when the Soviet government was equating test ban verification measures with Western espionage, Alexander Topchiev, the head of the Soviet Pugwash delegation, argued that verification was quite feasible. In July 1961, learning to his horror that Khrushchev was about to order resumption of Soviet nuclear testing, Sakharov spoke up at a meeting of top Soviet government officials and atomic scientists, objecting to the tests. Khrushchev flew into a rage and, for half an hour or more, denounced Sakharov before the assemblage. Despite what should have been a terrifying rebuff, Sakharov and nuclear research director Yuli Khariton met again with Khrushchev, in August 1961, in an effort to dissuade him from resuming nuclear testing. Rebuked once more, Sakharov stubbornly persisted, phoning Khrushchev the day before the first test of the 1962 series and insisting that it would "kill people for no reason." Tired of dealing with Sakharov, Khrushchev fobbed him off on Frol Kozlov, an influential member of the Politburo, who proved just as implacable. Appalled, Sakharov decided to devote himself to ending nuclear testing.

Indeed, the Soviet intelligentsia, encouraged by its Western counterpart, became an important source of pressure for peace, disarmament, and political liberalization. In the early 1960s, particularly, antiwar books, plays, and films by Western authors and artists engendered a growing pacifist mood among Soviet writers and filmmakers, with nuclear testing, fallout, and the arms race putting in a significant appearance. A major controversy broke out over what the Soviet *Literary Gazette* called the "de-heroicing" of war, with *Pravda*'s Yuri Zhukov bemoaning the fact that it appeared as "something quite unsavory, as one continuous human slaughter." In February 1964, Soviet military and defense officials held a special meeting with writers and artists on the proper treatment of war in literature and the arts. An army general complained to the gathering that, in the cultural realm, there had been "excessive attention" to "descriptions of suffering and fear, horror and confusion," and too little discussion of "the international duty of the Soviet armed forces."

With government repression blocking Soviet citizens from forming independent disarmament organizations, overseas peace groups undertook their own operations in the Soviet Union. Quaker delegations from Britain and the United States traveled to that nation, where they met with small groups of ordinary citizens, established volunteer work camps, and participated in seminars to foster international understanding. Activists from abroad had an unusual opportunity to reach Soviet citizens in 1961, when Khrushchev authorized the San Francisco to Moscow marchers to hike unimpeded across 660 miles of the Soviet Union. Delighted, the marchers distributed materials condemning nuclear testing and war to everyone within sight (ultimately distributing some 100,000 leaflets), addressed frequent meetings (with up to a thousand Russians present at each event), held demonstrations outside Soviet military installations, and appeared on television. Perhaps because the marchers were met with disturbingly strong approval by average Russians, Soviet officials shut the door thereafter on outside peace agitation.

But even arrests and deportations did not stop its occurrence. Taking to the streets of Moscow in July 1962, British Committee of 100 members distributed thousands of copies of two leaflets ("Mankind Against War" and "Against All Bombs") and twenty-five nonaligned activists from six countries unfurled a banner only a hundred yards from Lenin's tomb, attacking nuclear tests in East and West. That October, when the *Everyman III* entered Leningrad's harbor and sought to land members of its leaflet-wielding pacifist crew, Soviet soldiers shoved them back on board. Undaunted, some activists opened the vessel's sea-cocks to sink it in the harbor, while others leaped into the near-freezing water and sought to swim ashore.

Although government restrictions on peace activism prevented it from playing a major role in influencing Soviet opinion, other factors reinforced its message. Traveling exhibits and other media portrayed the terrible destruction of Hiroshima. The goal was usually to encourage hostility toward the U.S. government for dropping the Bomb, but an unintended consequence was to give viewers a chilling picture of nuclear war. Soviet citizens also gained a negative impression of the Bomb from statements by their leaders and visiting dignitaries, whose comments on the destructiveness of nuclear weapons frequently appeared in the Soviet press. As in the United States, despite government efforts to foster a major civil defense program, many people had little confidence that it would work. A common joke in the Soviet Union during the early 1960s went:

Q: What should you do in case of a nuclear attack?
A: Get a shovel and a sheet, and walk slowly . . . to the nearest cemetery.
Q: Why slowly?
A: You mustn't start a panic.

In 1963, when a group of Western Sovietologists was called together by a U.S. government agency, they reported that "the general 'peace' mood" in the Soviet Union established "a predisposition in favor of disarmament and arms control arrangements."

In some other Communist nations, as well, independent peace activism proved irrepressible. Traversing Poland, the San Francisco to Moscow marchers distributed thousands of pacifist leaflets. For the most part, the people they

met seemed quite enthusiastic—surrounding them in great crowds, present-
ing them with flowers, and joining their procession. But the marchers' reception in East Germany was more subdued, perhaps because of official hostility,
which finally culminated in their deportation. Another nonviolent invasion of
the East bloc occurred in May 1963, when a team of British CND members
crossed into East Berlin and began handing out leaflets calling for the abolition of nuclear weapons, East and West. "Ordinary people accepted them with
interest," one leafleter recalled, "and sometimes people came back and shook
our hands to show their support." East Berlin police proved less enthusiastic,
however, and after an hour the activists were arrested and deported to the West.
Sometimes, domestic peace proponents took the lead. In East Germany, the
tiny, beleaguered FOR group held street meetings protesting nuclear warfare
and thousands of young men defied a new draft law by refusing induction into
the armed forces.

Increasingly, the movement took on international dimensions. Emphasizing
the nuclear menace, the three pacifist internationals expanded in size and influence. Meanwhile, the Pugwash conferences provided a key forum for discussions of disarmament by scientists and other experts from around the world.
Between 1958 and 1965, twelve additional Pugwash conferences were convened,
with the largest, held during September 1962, drawing participants from thirty-
six countries. As in the past, the World Council of Churches pressed for a nuclear test ban and disarmament. However, Pope John XXIII's 1963 encyclical,
Pacem in Terris, had a greater impact, for it "urgently" demanded the banning
of nuclear weapons and strengthened the international Catholic peace organization, Pax Christi. In addition, as the new ban-the-bomb organizations appeared in diverse countries, they began to swap ideas, literature, and speakers.
Sometimes, specific activist constituencies, such as women and students, drew
together across national boundaries. In 1962, when WSP sent a delegation to
meet with disarmament negotiators in Geneva, it was joined there by women
activists from Austria, Britain, Canada, France, Norway, Sweden, Switzerland,
West Germany, and other nations. But it was the Easter marches that provided
the most striking evidence of the movement's international strength. In 1964,
the marchers numbered 500,000, from twenty countries.

Could this new energy be harnessed into an international organization?
In 1959, most of the new West European antinuclear groups united to form a
European Federation Against Nuclear Arms. But the European Federation did

not draw together the full range of peace organizations and, also, remained geographically limited. Consequently, prodded by Homer Jack (SANE's executive director) and other activists who gathered at an Accra Assembly, in Ghana, during 1962, the European Federation invited nonaligned nuclear disarmament groups in numerous nations to participate in a conference to establish a worldwide peace organization. Meeting in Oxford in January 1963, delegates representing forty peace groups from eighteen countries voted unanimously to form an umbrella group, the International Confederation for Disarmament and Peace (ICDP). Member organizations would be welcome in the new international if, "by consistent deeds and stated policies," they actively opposed the testing, manufacture, and use of nuclear weapons by any country, all nuclear bases, and the proliferation of nuclear weapons. The ICDP grew steadily, and by 1967 was composed of fifty-six independent peace groups from eighteen nations.

Although the Communist-led WPC and many of its national affiliates remained substantial organizations, they continued to lose ground to their independent competitors. The mass participation attracted by the antinuclear campaign flowed largely into the new ban-the-bomb groups, which kept their distance from Communist-controlled organizations and projects. Furthermore, even when a small number of nonaligned delegates did participate in the 1962 WPC conference in Moscow, they made speeches and staged unauthorized demonstrations that scandalized their hosts and underscored their differences with this Soviet-controlled body. For the WPC, the formation of the ICDP represented a culminating disaster, and its "observers" came away fuming from the Oxford conference.

The division between aligned and nonaligned activism was just as clear on the national level. Within some of the new organizations, like SANE, internal measures were taken to limit Communist influence and participation. In most, though, Communist elements simply remained marginal. Only in Japan, where Communists began with a strong foothold in Gensuikyo, did they actually manage to take over a powerful ban-the-bomb organization. Moreover, in this case, non-Communists, after a bitter battle over control of Gensuikyo, withdrew from it and, in 1965, formed a rival group, Gensuikin, the Japan Congress Against Atomic and Hydrogen Bombs. Powered largely by the Socialist Party and its union allies, Gensuikin assailed Gensuikyo's Cold War partisanship and trumpeted its own opposition to nuclear weapons in all nations.

Policymakers and Protest, 1958–1965

As the nuclear disarmament movement burgeoned into a major force, government officials developed ever-closer relations with it. The leaders of nonaligned and neutral countries remained the most sympathetic. Julius Nyerere of Tanzania, Nehru of India, Mohammed Ayub Khan of Pakistan, Tito of Yugoslavia, and Nkrumah of Ghana were among the many leaders of nonaligned nations who sent messages of greeting to conferences of nuclear disarmament organizations. At the 1961 Belgrade conference of nonaligned nations, antinuclear groups were accorded a privileged status, and Homer Jack had remarkable access to the conference sessions and heads of state. Nehru conferred closely with disarmament campaign leaders like Russell, while Nkrumah provided the movement's 1962 Accra conference ("The World Without the Bomb") with its site, funding, and publicity.

The Soviet government had greater ambivalence about the movement. When it came to domestic peace pressures, the authorities had limited tolerance. They confiscated pamphlets advocating nonviolence, kept news of Soviet nuclear tests out of the mass media, and lectured writers and artists on the "harmful note of pacifism" that had crept into their works. The WPC and its Soviet affiliate, the Soviet Peace Committee, remained their agitators of choice. Even so, the Kremlin recognized the remarkable strength of the worldwide nuclear disarmament movement and sought to cultivate it. Khrushchev carried on an extensive correspondence with Russell and Cousins, officials in the Soviet embassy held cordial meetings with the leaders of SANE (promising them new Soviet peace initiatives), and Khrushchev sent repeated, fulsome messages of greeting to the Pugwash conferences. During a visit to the United States in 1960, the Soviet party secretary held an extraordinary, two-hour meeting with Leo Szilard, during which they discussed Szilard's ideas on peace, disarmament, and a settlement of the Cold War.

The leaders of some Western nations also found it expedient to cultivate good relations with the movement. In 1962, New Zealand's Conservative prime minister told a delegation of New Zealand CND members that he would give serious consideration to the idea of a nuclear weapon–free zone in the southern hemisphere. Actually, New Zealand External Affairs officials confided to a U.S. diplomat that they opposed a nuclear-free zone, but did not dare say so for "internal political reasons." Similarly, Canadian Prime Minister Diefenbaker, after a meeting with antinuclear leaders, told the press that there was "considerable merit in their viewpoint" and that he favored "the complete elimination of nuclear weapons." He also proclaimed his antinuclear views in two subsequent meetings with VOW activists. But, in fact, popular pressure played a key role in determining Diefenbaker's position. As a number of Cabinet members complained, the prime minister was obsessed with his mail, including petitions from VOW. A visitor recalled that Diefenbaker remarked "that his mail was running nine to one against nuclear arms for Canada," a fact that "weighed heavily in his deliberations."

Other Western bloc nations proved less accommodating. Crossing West Germany in 1961, the San Francisco to Moscow peace marchers found their leafleting and public meetings restricted by government pressure, culminating in their arrest for demonstrating outside the Ministry of Defense in Bonn. The following year, the West German government began blocking the entry of overseas contingents who sought to participate in the Easter marches. In the spring of 1963, 2,500 Danish Easter marchers were barred from entering the Federal Republic by hordes of West German soldiers, armed with tanks, machine guns, water cannon, and pistols and employing newly dug trenches and snarling dogs. The authorities were also quite unwelcoming in France. In 1960, as 500 African students from French Community nations gathered to present an anti-testing petition to Premier Michel Debré, the French government had them arrested. In 1961, after the San Francisco to Moscow marchers were barred from entering France, French activists conducted their own antinuclear march, during which French police confiscated their banner twice, arrested them repeatedly, and handled them brutally. In Greece, a group of military officers—determined to prevent the further erosion of their influence—seized power, established a right-wing dictatorship, and banned all of their nation's peace groups.

Even in Britain, which prided itself on its civil liberties, the government took a hard line toward the movement. In August 1961, the British Cabinet decided to deny the Committee of 100 the right to use Parliament Square for a legal rally, the first rejection of a public meeting there since 1916. That September, as plans moved forward for the Parliament Square sit-down, the government arrested the 89-year-old Russell, his wife, and twenty-eight other leaders of the Committee under the Defence of the Realm Act, sentencing them to two months' imprisonment. To head off the later nonviolent demonstrations at Britain's military bases, the government also arrested all six staff members of the Committee, charging them with violations of the Official Secrets Act. Five were sentenced to eighteen months in prison and a sixth to one year. Reporting to Prime Minister Macmillan, the home secretary remarked hopefully that the Committee demonstrations seemed "played out" and that the police were "keeping a special watch" on its future plans. Macmillan commented: "This seems sensible."

Although the British government took a less confrontational approach to CND, it had little respect for it. Most British officials were too sophisticated to believe that CND was part of a Communist conspiracy. But this did not make the organization acceptable. Canon Collins repeatedly requested that Macmillan receive a deputation from CND, but the prime minister just as steadfastly refused. In 1962, the government briefly relented when the head of Macmillan's Conservative Party insisted that it would "be useful" for Macmillan to speak with a CND women's delegation, for "peace . . . has really captured people's imagination" and "it would give a bad impression if the Prime Minister did not meet" with the women. The conclave did nothing to change Macmillan's attitude and, when he conferred later that year with Kennedy, he twice spoke disparagingly of antinuclear activists. Covert operations against CND remain largely unknown, but according to the CIA, the British government had CND and other nuclear disarmament groups "well infiltrated."

By contrast, the British government gradually warmed toward the Pugwash movement. Asked by Rotblat if he would like to join the advisory body of the British Pugwash committee, J. D. Cockcroft, a member of Britain's Atomic Energy Authority, referred the matter to the Foreign Office. In response, the Foreign Office urged him to join, as it would help prevent Pugwash from "being exploited for propaganda purposes." Soon the Foreign Office began to argue that it might be useful to take over the Pugwash movement for its own purposes. But when the British government suggested topics for Pugwash meetings and government officials who should be invited to them, Rotblat resisted, much to government dismay. Rotblat, one Foreign Office official complained, was too committed to "independence and scientific integrity." Even so, British officials— anxious to influence Soviet nuclear experts and to pick up useful ideas on arms control and disarmament—made the best of it. In 1962, when the Home Office, clinging to past policy, remarked that Pugwash was "a dirty word," the Foreign Office retorted that the movement now enjoyed "official blessing."

Even so, the British government remained deeply concerned about the growth of antinuclear sentiment. Citing the popular demand for a test ban and disarmament, the Cabinet's public relations officer warned in 1961 that public opinion had reached a "difficult phase." By 1965, when a rising young producer,

Peter Watkins, was commissioned by the BBC to make a film, *The War Game*, about the horrors of life in Britain during and after a nuclear war, the government panicked. Granted the opportunity to preview it, Home Office, Defence Ministry, and other officials concluded that it should not be broadcast, for it was bound to increase support for CND. As a result, the BBC not only refused to televise *The War Game*—which won top film prizes, including a Hollywood Oscar and the British Film Academy award—but prevented its television broadcast anywhere in the world.

In the United States, police and intelligence agencies—determined to stamp out what they considered subversion—kept nuclear disarmament activities under close scrutiny. Even before Women Strike for Peace staged its first demonstration, the FBI began the first of its many investigations of that organization. SANE also attracted extensive FBI surveillance, with J. Edgar Hoover firing off memos to the White House on the danger that this antinuclear group could acquire "much influence." In addition the FBI targeted the WILPF for lengthy investigations, including one under its COMINFIL (Communist Infiltration) program, ordered in 1962 by Hoover because "many of the programs of the WILPF, such as peace, disarmament, and banning nuclear testing, paralleled the Communist Party line." Meanwhile, the CIA warned (falsely) that Communists dominated the British antinuclear movement and, in violation of its charter, spied on U.S. antinuclear groups. Under its mail-opening program, the CIA read the private correspondence of the AFSC, the FAS, and WSP, among other organizations. In efforts to expose alleged links to Communism, Senator Thomas Dodd's Senate Internal Security Subcommittee publicly assailed SANE, while the House Un-American Activities Committee held sensational hearings on WSP. According to Dodd, even clearly non-Communist groups were subject to "infiltration by the Communist termites."

These attitudes pervaded the Eisenhower administration. In 1959, when the president of Princeton University requested that Eisenhower join him in inviting Albert Schweitzer to the United States to accept an honorary degree at that institution, the State Department objected, claiming that the missionary's "articles and speeches have been highly critical of United States nuclear test policy and closely adhere to the Communist line." As a result, Eisenhower refused to join the venture and Schweitzer did not come to the United States. The State Department was not much fonder of SANE. Asked by the Deputy Undersecretary of State to draw up the kind of argument that could be used to answer SANE's antinuclear advertisements, an official developed a statement arguing that the disarmament group was "really inviting us to a strategic surrender," which would lead to the United States "being colonized by the population hordes of China." From Britain, U.S. diplomats dispatched numerous, lengthy reports on CND's growth and development, invariably with a hostile slant.

For Eisenhower and his circle, the negative public attitude toward nuclear fallout and nuclear war remained a major problem. In December 1959, with showings of the film version of *On the Beach*—depicting life after a nuclear war—scheduled to begin in the United States and fifteen other countries, administration officials grew particularly distraught. Frightened by the film's "strong emotional appeal for banning nuclear weapons," the State Department and the USIA dispatched lengthy guidelines for handling it to their posts in foreign nations. At the administration's December 11 Cabinet meeting, officials condemned the film and agreed on further measures to combat its "extreme pacifist and 'Ban the bomb' propaganda." Although Strauss had returned to private life, he kept up his discussions on nuclear issues with government officials. Together they explored the possibility that, as he argued, "an intelligently directed mass hypnosis is being inflicted upon the American people using the threat of atomic warfare or fall-out as its instrument."

In some ways, the attitudes of the new Kennedy administration showed elements of continuity with those of the Eisenhower administration. From Sierra Leone, the embassy warned that a CND group formed in that country had "all the earmarks of a trouble-maker." Although the U.S. ambassador to Britain transmitted to the White House a protest by Russell against renewed U.S. nuclear testing, he recommended that it "be ignored"—which it was. At home, White House officials gave WSP a chilly reception, consistently refusing to allow WSP delegations to meet with the President. Robert Kennedy, the U.S. attorney general, almost turned against the civil rights movement when he learned that one of the Freedom Riders, savagely beaten during his bus ride through the segregated South, was Albert Bigelow, the Quaker captain of the *Golden Rule*. "Do you know that one of them is against the atom bomb?" Kennedy remarked with disgust. "I wonder if they have the best interest of their country at heart."

Nevertheless, the Kennedy administration proved more receptive than its predecessor had been to disarmament activists. Kennedy met with a delegation from the AFSC, hosted a dinner for Nobel laureates that included the once-dreaded Linus Pauling, and—when thousands of students picketed the White House against resumption of nuclear testing—dispatched the White House butler to the front door with a huge urn of coffee. Although the President refused to send a message of greeting to SANE's fourth annual conference, the director of the Arms Control and Disarmament Agency did so. In addition, Kennedy adopted SANE's rhetoric about a "Peace Race," having picked up the phrase from someone present at a SANE national board meeting. Like their British counterparts, U.S. officials warmed toward the Pugwash movement, for they began to consider it a useful forum for discussions about halting the nuclear arms race. In September 1961, Kennedy sent a Pugwash conference a message of greeting—the first from a U.S. president—and he repeated the gesture in 1962 and 1963.

Yet the Kennedy administration remained uneasy about most agitation against the Bomb. Regarding itself as occupying the center of the nuclear debate, between naïve pacifists and reckless warhawks, it viewed disarmament activism as representing one of the extremes. Decades later, asked about antinuclear organizations, White House advisor Arthur Schlesinger, Jr. noted that, although the administration sometimes found them politically useful, it did not identify with them. "The Kennedy administration welcomed pressure from domestic arms control groups as an offset against the pro-arms-race pressure from Congress and the military," he observed. "The administration valued these groups for political reasons rather than as a source of ideas."

Consequently, antinuclear opinion remained a major problem. In 1961, a U.S. National Intelligence Estimate warned that "world opinion tends to recoil from nuclear weapons, submerging logical consideration of the subject in an emotional reaction of dismay." In addition, "renewed U.S. testing would also stimulate fears concerning health dangers from fallout," and even U.S. allies "would find it hard to allay the anxieties of their public." Disturbed by these findings, Kennedy administration officials ordered further opinion studies, always with similar results. Secretary of State Dean Rusk bemoaned the world-wide "emotionalism" over nuclear testing. Although U.S. officials considered domestic opinion less of a problem, upsurges of protest caused them sharp uneasiness. Interviewed in January 1962, the day after WSP put a picket line of 3,000 women outside the White House, Kennedy was remarkably flustered and inarticulate. To offset protests from SANE and WSP over the radioactive contamination of children's milk, the President drank a glass of it at his press conference, claiming that it offered "no hazards" from nuclear fallout. When government scientists produced studies that showed adverse health effects of fallout, the AEC had them suppressed.

Governments Change Policies, 1958–1963

Disturbed by the popular clamor against nuclear weapons, numerous governments continued to retreat from their earlier pro-nuclear positions. In New Zealand, the prime minister pointedly criticized both sides in the Cold War for resuming nuclear tests. "Given the prevailing state of public opinion," he told the British government, "I am sure you will understand why we regard the resumption of testing . . . as a matter for deprecation." NATO, too, was starting to crack. In November 1961, when its U.N. delegates met to consider a Swedish proposal for disarmament, Denmark, Norway, and Iceland shocked U.S. officials by demanding a positive vote—a position taken, as the Danish representative explained, "because of public opinion at home." The following summer, a Norwegian diplomat notified the U.S. government that "because of the strength of Norwegian public opinion," his country would "have to vote" for a U.N. resolution against renewed nuclear testing. Canada also broke with U.S. policy, outraging U.S. officials by refusing to arm its missiles and bombers with U.S. nuclear weapons. Explaining this rebuff, Diefenbaker told Kennedy in 1961 that Canada had experienced "an upsurge of feeling against nuclear weapons" that made it "politically impossible" to accede to Washington's wishes. In June 1962, Rusk complained bitterly that the United States "has had to go on its knees to plead for the deployment of its weapons." And even then, "half of the countries have said no."

Britain, too, grew increasingly dovish. In the late 1950s, convinced that nuclear tests would no longer be tolerated by public opinion, British officials believed that it had become politically impossible to resume nuclear testing. Thus, in the summer of 1959—with elections scheduled for that fall—the government decided that, if no formal test ban agreement were reached, "it would be politically expedient" to seek U.S. agreement to permanent cessation of Anglo-American atmospheric testing and a moratorium on underground tests. Moreover, in the aftermath of the elections, Britain's chief arms control negotiator told the U.S. ambassador that the British government was "firmly convinced it is impossible from the standpoint of British and world public opinion for [the] U.S. and British to resume testing." Even after the Soviet resumption of nuclear testing in the fall of 1961, the British government fiercely resisted U.S. plans to resume atmospheric tests. Writing to Kennedy, Macmillan declared that he was "concerned about the possible reactions of opinion in this country," where "public pressures" were running high against testing, and "deeply concerned about our joint position in the face of world opinion."

Given British officials' sensitivity to criticism of nuclear testing, it was hardly surprising that they championed a test ban treaty with a much more relaxed system for inspection than did the Americans. The prime minister was particularly keen on what he called "an unpoliced agreement on tests that cause fallout." In 1961 he told Kennedy that "some such move will be necessary to show that we are fully conscious of world-wide anxiety about fallout and ready to do our best to avoid it." Even after Soviet resumption of nuclear testing, London pressed hard for a test ban on terms Washington considered dangerously lax. Meeting with Kennedy in March 1962, the British ambassador promoted a new British plan that dropped the idea of control posts on Soviet territory. He explained that his government felt "strongly" that it was "necessary to put forward a proposal which seems reasonable both to our own and to world public opinion."

Although Soviet officials were more insulated from public opinion, they could not disregard it entirely. From late 1958 to early 1960, Khrushchev's government—anxious to concentrate Soviet economic resources on the civilian sector, avert a disastrous war with the United States, and court world opinion through a "peace policy"—grew more serious about arms control and disarmament negotiations. But the U-2 incident in May of 1960 strengthened the position of hard-liners within the Soviet party apparatus. In these new circumstances, the government increased the military budget, built the Berlin wall, and resumed nuclear testing. As titular head of the Soviet party and state, Khrushchev presided over these measures, but without much enthusiasm. Sensitive to the outpouring of foreign criticism that Soviet testing had generated, Khrushchev appeared quite uncomfortable in conversations with Nehru and other diplomats. The extraordinary access to Soviet territory that he granted the San Francisco to Moscow peace marchers seems likely to have resulted from a desire to refurbish his image as a supporter of peace.

For U.S. officials, as well, a reputation as supporters of nuclear arms control and disarmament became increasingly important. Responding to pressure from peace groups and Senator Humphrey, the Kennedy administration established the U.S. Arms Control and Disarmament Agency (ACDA). Although U.S. government officials placed disarmament largely in the realm of "propaganda," they did take arms control seriously—particularly halting nuclear testing. Test ban negotiations, begun in October 1958, dragged on fruitlessly, but the Eisenhower administration did not dare to abandon them and resume testing, largely because the President and his top advisors feared a popular outcry. Sharing these fears, Kennedy and his advisors followed the same course, with

Rusk warning the President of a "serious political reaction ... were we to resume testing."

Even the Soviet resumption of testing in the fall of 1961 did not lead immediately to similar action on the part of the U.S. government. For a time, Kennedy simply used the situation to turn public opinion against the Soviet Union. Meanwhile, he delayed a decision on resuming U.S. atmospheric tests. According to the deputy director of ACDA, Kennedy thought "that it probably made sense" for the United States to resume its test program. "But he also recognized that there were a lot of people that were going to be deeply offended by the United States resuming atmospheric testing. We had people picketing the White House, and there was a lot of excitement about it. ... And that's the reason we didn't resume atmospheric testing." Kennedy held out on resuming such tests until April 1962. And even then, as the President's speechwriter and biographer Theodore Sorensen has observed, "they received as little publicity as the President could 'manage.' He wanted no pictures of mushroom clouds, no eyewitness reports of each blast, and as little stimulus as possible to picketing and ban-the-bomb parades around the world."

Meanwhile, waging nuclear war became increasingly unacceptable. A late 1960 Defense Department report to President-elect Kennedy, recalled one of its drafters, contended that developing a U.S. "'win' capability" for a future nuclear war "probably was not feasible, given Soviet capabilities and the political mood of the country." This fear of the public response tempered administration action during the Cuban missile crisis, when Kennedy—as Rusk recalled—worried about "an adverse public reaction," including "demonstrations, peace groups marching in the streets, perhaps a divisive public debate." Rusk noted that, during one meeting at the height of the crisis, "I argued against a surprise attack, pointing out that world opinion would turn against us because we didn't first try diplomatic avenues." Furthermore, even in conflicts with non-nuclear powers, U.S. policymakers felt it necessary to rule out nuclear war thanks to the popular stigma it had acquired. Years later, Rusk explained that a nuclear power "would wear the mark of Cain for generations to come if it ever attacked a non-nuclear country with nuclear weapons."

The Atmospheric Test Ban Treaty and Beyond, 1962–1970

As the Cold War antagonists grew more serious about a nuclear arms control agreement, SANE's founder and co-chair, Norman Cousins, stepped forward to facilitate it. At a lengthy meeting he arranged with Kennedy at the White House in November 1962, Cousins asked the U.S. President if he could be of service by speaking to Khrushchev on his behalf. In response, Kennedy urged Cousins to convince the Soviet leader that his administration sought peaceful relations with the Soviet Union and that a test ban treaty would provide an important route toward this goal. That December, Cousins met with Khrushchev for an intense exchange, which lasted over three hours. The Soviet leader expressed his desire to meet the President "more than halfway" in the quest for peace, and added that they should move "right away . . . to conclude a treaty outlawing testing of nuclear weapons." Five days later, he dispatched a lengthy letter to Kennedy devoted entirely to the test ban issue, with proposals that left Kennedy exhilarated.

Despite this promising start, in early 1963 U.S.-Soviet test ban negotiations became bogged down in a sharp dispute over the number of on-site inspections. As a result, the White House once more turned to Cousins. In a meeting with Rusk, another lengthy meeting with Kennedy, and in a subsequent phone call from the President, the SANE leader was urged to speak with Khrushchev again and convince him of the administration's integrity and goodwill. That April, conferring with the Soviet premier at his country retreat, Cousins found Khrushchev angry and suspicious of the U.S. government. Nevertheless, Cousins marshaled all his persuasive powers to restore the momentum for a test ban. Finally, at the end of their six-hour conversation, Khrushchev relented and stated that he accepted the President's explanation that the dispute over inspections was "an honest misunderstanding." But he said that "the next move" was up to Kennedy.

Returning to the United States, Cousins again met with Kennedy and convinced him of the need for "a breathtaking new approach" to Soviet-American relations. In follow-up messages, he proposed "the most important single speech of your Presidency," a speech that would "create a whole new context for the pursuit of peace." Enthusiastic about the idea, Kennedy had Cousins discuss the speech with Sorensen, who—drawing on a draft by Cousins—prepared it for delivery. On June 10, 1963, speaking at American University, Kennedy focused on what he called "the most important topic on earth: world peace." In the nuclear age, he said, "total war makes no sense" and peace had become imperative. "A fresh start," he argued, should be made on "a treaty to outlaw nuclear tests," and he had ordered a halt to U.S. atmospheric testing and had arranged for the beginning of high-level treaty negotiations in Moscow. "Confident and unafraid," Kennedy concluded, "we labor on—not toward a strategy of annihilation but toward a strategy of peace."

The turning point had been reached. Although the conferees at Moscow failed to agree on the terms for a comprehensive nuclear test ban, on July 25 they signed an agreement for a ban on atmospheric testing: the Partial Test Ban Treaty. It was the first nuclear arms control treaty in world history.

Not surprisingly, the Partial Test Ban Treaty sparked worldwide enthusiasm. Although the Chinese and French governments denounced it as a hypocritical attempt by the great powers to maintain a nuclear monopoly, nearly all countries in the Western, Communist, and nonaligned blocs applauded it. By 1980, 125 nations had agreed to its provisions. In Britain, where Macmillan reported on the newly signed agreement to the House of Commons, he drew a standing ovation from members of both major parties. In the Soviet Union, the treaty enjoyed substantial popularity among average people and activists, as well as within Khrushchev's reformist circle in the party hierarchy. In the United States, Kennedy praised the treaty for ending "the atmospheric tests which have so alarmed mankind" and formed a Citizens Committee for a Nuclear Test Ban, led by Cousins, to promote its ratification by the U.S. Senate. Thanks to its efforts and to the breadth and depth of antinuclear feeling in the United States, the Senate ratified the treaty by an overwhelming vote.

Although Kennedy, Macmillan, and Khrushchev have received the credit for the treaty, some government officials have emphasized the importance of external pressure. According to McGeorge Bundy, Kennedy's national security advisor, the treaty "was achieved primarily by world opinion." Others were more specific. Recalling his years as White House science advisor, Jerome Wiesner gave the major credit for moving Kennedy toward the 1963 treaty to SANE, WSP, and Linus Pauling. Sir Solly Zuckerman, the top science advisor to the British Defense Ministry, argued that "the pressure brought to bear by Pugwash" on British officials "played a real part in pushing us along" to the test ban. Recognizing the extraordinary role Cousins had played, Kennedy presented him with one of the original signed copies of the treaty.

Nor was the atmospheric test ban the movement's only achievement. With the ice broken, numerous nuclear arms control measures followed. In 1966, the United States and the Soviet Union signed the Outer Space Treaty, banning the deployment of weapons of mass destruction in orbit or on celestial bodies. In 1968, most of the world's nations signed a nuclear Non-Proliferation Treaty, in which the non-nuclear powers pledged to forgo nuclear weapons development and the nuclear powers pledged to divest themselves of their nuclear weapons. Some nations went even farther. Giving way to enormous public pressure, the Japanese prime minister announced in December 1967 that his government would not possess, manufacture, or introduce nuclear weapons into Japan. In 1968, the nations of Latin America put the Treaty of Tlatelolco into place, establishing a nuclear-free zone for their continent. Reversing past policy, the Canadian government began phasing nuclear weapons out of Canada's defense program.

In this context, nuclear war grew increasingly unthinkable. When it came to the Vietnam conflict, recalled Rusk, the Kennedy, Johnson, and Nixon administrations deliberately "lost the war rather than 'win' it with nuclear weapons." Bundy, who served as the national security advisor to two of these Presidents, maintained that the U.S. government's decision not to use nuclear weapons in the Vietnam War did not result from fear of nuclear retaliation by the Russians and Chinese, but from the terrible public reaction that a U.S. nuclear attack would provoke in other nations. Even more significant, Bundy maintained, was the prospect of public upheaval in the United States, for "no President could hope for understanding and support from his own countrymen if he used the bomb." Nixon complained that, had he dared to use nuclear weapons in Vietnam, "the resulting domestic and international uproar would have damaged our foreign policy on all fronts."

Decline of the Movement, 1964–1970

As the nuclear crisis waned, so did the movement. In Britain, CND abandoned its yearly Aldermaston marches and its membership dwindled. By 1971, it had a staff of four people, debts that exceeded its annual income, and only 2,047 members. In Canada, the Voice of Women also experienced a serious decline, while Canadian CND disappeared entirely. Voting in December 1966 to terminate its operations, Denmark's Campaign Against Atomic Weapons closed its office and stopped publication of its journal. Much the same thing happened in Norway, Sweden, and Belgium, where antinuclear campaigns dropped out of sight in the mid-1960s. In the Netherlands and France, Easter marches and other antinuclear agitation persisted into the latter part of the decade, only to come to an abrupt end in its final years. In Australia, CND groups expired during 1965. By that time, branches of New Zealand CND were also becoming inactive, and several years later the national organization collapsed. In the Soviet Union, disarmament gradually ceased to be a central concern of dissident intellectuals. In the United States, the Student Peace Union disbanded and CNVA was absorbed by the War Resisters League. Although SANE and WSP survived, both groups lost momentum and support.

What had happened to the once-powerful nuclear disarmament movement? From the start, it had been contained to some extent by fear of other countries and fear that the antinuclear campaign was a Communist-directed enterprise. Nevertheless, it overcame these obstacles sufficiently to build a mass movement, mobilize public opinion, and alter public policy. Beginning with the signing of the Partial Test Ban Treaty, however, the movement became a victim of its own success. As governments drew back from nuclear weapons and nuclear war, many people became convinced that victory had been won or, at the least, that things were moving in the right direction. Not surprisingly, then, they dropped their antinuclear efforts. Their withdrawal from the disarmament campaign was reinforced by the exhaustion activists felt after years of antinuclear struggle. Moreover, there were other critical situations that peace organizations now confronted—most notably the Vietnam War—and other issues which became priorities for some of the movement's core constituencies: anti-imperialism, women's liberation, and human rights. As a result, the nuclear disarmament movement faded.

6   A Third Wave, 1971–1980

Despite the decline of the antinuclear campaign in the late 1960s, in the following decade it slowly began to revive and to become a force once more in the shaping of public policy. During the early 1970s, the movement remained weak, distracted, and largely unable to offer an effective challenge to the ongoing nuclear arms race. But the end of the Vietnam War, a growing controversy over "peaceful" nuclear power, and the 1978 U.N. Special Session on Disarmament helped to refocus the attention of peace groups and the public on nuclear issues. Furthermore, despite the professed détente between the Soviet Union and the United States, the nuclear arms race and the Cold War continued. In these circumstances, movement activism quickened.

Largely Forgotten: The Arms Race and the Movement, 1971–1975

During the early 1970s, key aspects of the nuclear arms race persisted. Although the United States and the Soviet Union abided by their nuclear arms control treaties and signed new ones—including the Strategic Arms Limitation Treaty (SALT I), which placed some limits on nuclear arms—they continued their reliance on nuclear weapons. Indeed, they moved their nuclear test explosions underground, which assisted them with the development of new and more sophisticated nuclear devices that they added to their devastating and expanding arsenals. By 1974, the nuclear stockpiles of the United States and the Soviet Union had reached the equivalent of a million times the destructive power of the atomic bomb that had destroyed Hiroshima.

Furthermore, the nuclear arms race was not limited to the two superpowers. The British, French, and Chinese governments devoted themselves to testing, upgrading, and increasing their nuclear arsenals. Having developed the Bomb in the late 1960s, the Israeli government, though careful to maintain ambiguity about its nuclear status, also cultivated its weaponry. In 1974, the Indian government conducted what it called a "peaceful nuclear explosion," but few were fooled by the rhetorical sugarcoating. Denouncing this "fateful development," Pakistan's prime minister spurred on his own country's effort to develop nuclear weapons. In addition, an estimated ten nations stood in line for entry into the once-exclusive nuclear club.

Although the buildup of nuclear arsenals did not necessarily reflect an eagerness to use them, the nuclear powers remained ready and willing to wage nuclear war. NATO policy was to reply to a conventional military attack upon Western Europe with the initiation of nuclear war against the Soviet Union and its allies. In turn, the Soviet government stated repeatedly that it stood ready to respond to Western "aggression" by fighting and winning a nuclear conflict. A White House official recalled that "personal activities were designed according to the time it would take a nuclear missile to fly from Russia to the United States. . . . Even the White House press corps designed its daily life around the possibility that the President might push the nuclear button at any moment." Sometimes that moment seemed perilously close. In October 1973, amid a war between Israel and Egypt that appeared to be spiraling out of control, the Soviet government sent a message to Washington suggesting joint—or if necessary Soviet—military action to end the conflict. With President Nixon reeling from the Watergate scandal and drunk in the White House, his top national security advisors responded by ordering a worldwide alert of U.S. nuclear forces. Aghast, Soviet Politburo members asked: "Are they crazy?" Ultimately, the situation was resolved peacefully. But it was the most dangerous nuclear confrontation between the great powers since the Cuban missile crisis. Furthermore, this time it occurred during a period of Soviet-American détente.

The nuclear buildup of the early 1970s reflected not only the ongoing conflict among nations, but the enfeebled state of the nuclear disarmament movement. In Britain, the once-vibrant CND had been reduced to a tiny remnant. In the Netherlands, the Interchurch Peace Council, formed by the powerful Protestant and Catholic churches, did little more than organize an annual Peace Week. In Scandinavia, too, the once-thriving antinuclear movement had largely dissipated. Meanwhile, the Japanese nuclear disarmament campaign, sharply divided and overshadowed by opposition to the Vietnam War, subsided into ritual protests. In Canada, the Voice of Women almost totally dropped the subject of the nuclear arms race from its agenda, focusing instead on ending the war in Vietnam. As its national components faded, the ICDP went into a long-term decline from which it never recovered.

Within the two superpowers, the movement was in the doldrums. In the Soviet Union, disarmament ideas and themes did appear on occasion among individuals in the artistic and scientific intelligentsia. Thanks to government harassment, however, organized antinuclear activism never got very far. In the United States, too, the movement faced great difficulties sustaining itself, and organizational membership dropped substantially. SANE, the movement's flagship, retained only a few thousand members. Although the FAS and the new Center for Defense Information helped sustain a focus on nuclear issues, the Vietnam War continued to preoccupy most peace groups.

Only in the Pacific did the antinuclear movement maintain a lively presence. Spurning the Partial Test Ban Treaty, the French government continued atmospheric nuclear testing on Moruroa in the South Pacific, sending deadly radioactive clouds drifting across Pacific island nations. In response, New Zealand activists began defying the French government during 1972 by sailing small vessels into the test zone. Joining the fray, the New Zealand Federation of Labour pledged a strict ban on French goods and the Labour Party took a principled stand against continued nuclear testing, leading to its election victory that November. In Australia, thousands of irate citizens joined protest marches in Adelaide, Melbourne, Brisbane, and Sydney; scientists issued statements demanding an end to the tests; unions refused to load French ships, service French planes, or carry French mail; and consumers boycotted French products. In Fiji, activists formed an Against Testing on Moruroa organization, which, in 1974, began planning a regional antinuclear conference.

Nuclear testing in the Pacific also triggered the establishment of Greenpeace. In 1971, Jim Bohlen and Irving Stowe, two antiwar Americans who had relocated to Vancouver, British Columbia, during the Vietnam War, decided to sail a ship north to Amchitka Island, off Alaska, to protest U.S. government plans to explode nuclear weapons there. En route, the crew read of a Cree grandmother's 200-year-old prophecy that there would come a time when all the races of the world would unite as Rainbow Warriors, going forth to end the destruction of the earth. Deeply moved, the crew enlisted in that cause. Although U.S. authorities arrested the crew members as they approached the nuclear test site, thousands of cheering supporters lined the docks in Vancouver upon their return. Furthermore, Bohlen and Stowe embarked on another voyage to Amchitka and, although they failed to reach it before the U.S. government exploded its nuclear bomb, a new movement had been born. In New Zealand, a former Canadian, David McTaggart, convinced Canada's Greenpeace group that he should sail his yacht into France's nuclear testing zone around Moruroa. When he arrived with a crew in June 1972, a French minesweeper, at the order of the French government, rammed and crippled the ship. But McTaggart returned with a new ship and crew the following year.

As before, government officials from nuclear nations viewed these ventures with alarm. Thoroughly contemptuous of those he derided as "peaceniks," Nixon stepped up FBI and CIA spying upon peace organizations and the disruption of their activities. By the early 1970s, the CIA's Operation Chaos had targeted over a thousand U.S. organizations and 200,000 individuals. Meanwhile, White House staffers placed both SANE and its executive director, Sandy Gottlieb, on the President's "Enemies List." Angered by the opposition of scientists to nuclear tests on Amchitka and to other administration programs, Nixon abolished the President's Science Advisory Committee. French officials, too, were quite hostile. When McTaggart and his crew returned to the international waters that the French government had staked out for its nuclear test zone, French sailors boarded their ship, beat them savagely with truncheons, and threw their cameras and other equipment overboard.

On the other side of the "iron curtain," the reception was much the same. Soviet militiamen broke up a planned pacifist march in June of 1971, while Soviet party conservatives waged a fierce counterattack on antimilitary and libertarian trends. Indeed, Soviet police regularly dispersed gatherings of Soviet pacifists or arrested their participants. When Sakharov was awarded the Nobel Peace Prize in 1975, Kremlin officials barred his travel to Oslo and denounced him as a "laboratory rat of the West." Nor did foreign activists receive an enthusiastic reception. In 1973, Moscow denied entry visas to two top Western peace movement leaders: Gottlieb of SANE and Michael Randle of the War Resisters' International.

But the agitation of the early 1970s did produce some results. New Zealand's new Labour government dispatched a stiff letter of protest to the French authorities, condemning their plans for nuclear testing. Moreover, joined by its Australian counterpart, it went to the International Court of Justice to seek an injunction against the French tests. When the French refused to accept the court's jurisdiction, the New Zealand government, following the trail blazed by antinuclear activists, dispatched two protest vessels to the French testing zone, one with a cabinet minister on board. Although the French government refused to halt its nuclear tests during 1973 and 1974, it grew increasingly rattled. Near the end of the latter year, it announced that it had finally abandoned atmospheric nuclear testing.

And there were other concessions to activism, as well. In October 1975, the governments of New Zealand, Fiji, and Papua New Guinea sponsored a proposal at the United Nations for a South Pacific Nuclear Weapon Free Zone, a venture endorsed by the world body that December. Countervailing pressure from the U.S. government, however, plus conservative election victories in New Zealand and Australia, undermined this project. Nevertheless, the tide was beginning to turn. Even the hostile Nixon administration, acting for what a U.S. government spokesperson called "political and other reasons," responded to the Greenpeace campaign by canceling the remaining U.S. nuclear tests on Amchitka. Eventually, it turned the island into a bird sanctuary.

Movement Revival, 1975–1980

In the latter part of the decade, the movement began a renaissance. In part, this revival reflected the end of the Vietnam War in April 1975—an event that released peace groups and activists from their preoccupation with that conflict. In addition, growing public concern about the environmental hazards and nuclear weapons potential of nuclear power plants resurrected nuclear fears, while the 1978 U.N. Special Session on Disarmament focused activist and public attention on the menace of nuclear annihilation. And great power military activity provided plenty of potential along these lines. In 1977, a fierce controversy arose over the U.S. government's plan to produce and deploy an enhanced radiation warhead—better known as the neutron bomb. The Soviet Union began deploying a new and far more devastating generation of intermediate-range (INF) nuclear missiles, the SS-20s, on its territory. In 1979, NATO decided to install its own INF Euromissiles, cruise and Pershing II missiles, in Britain, West Germany, the Netherlands, Belgium, and Italy. Moreover, the U.S. government pressed forward with the development of the MX missile, a new strategic nuclear weapon. By 1980, there existed over 60,000 nuclear warheads around the world.

The response was particularly dramatic in the Netherlands. Concluding that the great powers were not serious about nuclear disarmament, the Interchurch Peace Council (IKV) embarked on an antinuclear campaign in 1977, epitomized by its new slogan: "Help rid the world of nuclear weapons; let it begin in the Netherlands." IKV grew rapidly and, by January 1980, it had more than 350 local branches in operation. In addition, a "Halt the Neutron Bomb" movement swept across the nation, generating a March 1978 protest demonstration with 50,000 participants and a petition to the Dutch parliament signed by 1.2 million people. Antinuclear agitation heightened after the announcement of the NATO plan to deploy cruise and Pershing II missiles, with IKV sparking countless parish meetings, marches, vigils, and picket lines against missile deployment. The National Council of Churches raised its voice against the missile plan, as did the synods of the two largest Protestant churches and the Catholic bishops. In November 1979, some 25,000 people turned out for an anti-missile demonstration organized by IKV, the Stop the Neutron Bomb group, the powerful Dutch Labor Party, and other opposition parties. With even the ruling Christian Democrats split on the Euromissiles, there was a clear parliamentary majority against the NATO deployment decision. Moreover, on the broader—and more radical—issue of withdrawing the nuclear weapons already in place, Dutch opinion was overwhelmingly antinuclear. An October 1980 survey found that 65 percent of the Dutch public favored removing all nuclear weapons from the Netherlands.

The movement also experienced a rebirth in Britain. Led after 1977 by Monsignor Bruce Kent, a Catholic prelate with strong social convictions, CND was once again at the forefront of Britain's antinuclear crusade—sponsoring showings of *The War Game*, condemning the planned deployment of the neutron bomb, Euromissiles, and Trident nuclear submarines, and decrying the revival of the Cold War. When the British government published *Protect and Survive*, a manual on how to survive a nuclear war, the historian E. P. Thompson responded with a scathing, highly publicized riposte, *Protest and Survive*. Appearing in April 1980, it became a CND best-seller. Meanwhile, the British Council of Churches voted overwhelmingly to oppose building the Trident submarine—a position echoed by the national pastoral congress of the Roman Catholic Church. Long dwindling, CND's influence within the Labour Party began to revive. In June 1980, Labour organized an "Against Nuclear Weapons" rally and march in downtown London, and later that year its national convention passed strong antinuclear resolutions. Polls found substantial support among Britons for new limits on nuclear weapons and a speed-up of strategic arms talks.

With CND's membership rising and a new excitement in the air, its leaders decided to call for a mass march in honor of U.N. Disarmament Week—a risky venture in light of the pathetic turnout at CND marches in the recent past. On the morning of October 26, 1980, the day of the demonstration, Kent recalled, "we already knew that we were on to a winner. Coaches were coming from all over the country, trains had been booked, and there was an astonishing feeling of expectation." Soon, Trafalgar Square "was full and kept on filling. . . . Great banners kept on flowing down from Piccadilly like the sails of ships. By half past four it was already getting near dusk, and still they came." Addressing the antinuclear throng, estimated at as many as 80,000 Britons, Thompson sent a surge of energy through it as he cried out: "Feel your strength!" Even the conservative London *Times* acknowledged "the second coming of CND."

Although the nuclear disarmament movement in West Germany was less unified and visible, it, too, started to revive. Veterans of the Federal Republic's youthful, extra-parliamentary opposition began to gravitate to local citizens' initiatives, where they continued their anti-Establishment activities on a grassroots level. Many of these citizens' initiatives focused on environmental protection, and none proved more dramatic than the struggle against nuclear power. Storming the nuclear reactor site at Wyhl in 1975, some 20,000 activists tore down the surrounding fence and proceeded to occupy it for the next month. Within church circles, as well, there was a growing concern about nuclear weapons. Action Reconciliation/Peace Service and Live Without Armaments (among Protestants) and Pax Christi (among Catholics) began to tackle disarmament issues. As plans for Euromissile deployment went forward, protest demonstrations erupted in West Germany's cities and towns, some drawing as many as 15,000 participants. Building upon this resistance, antinuclear leaders launched the Krefeld Appeal—a critique of the NATO missile deployment—in late 1980. In addition, during 1979 young activists organized a new political party, the Greens. Committed to ecological balance, feminism, and peace, the Greens emerged as leading advocates of nuclear disarmament in electoral politics and in the streets.

Disarmament activism also began to flourish in the Nordic countries. Plans for the neutron bomb touched off a wave of concern in Denmark and, especially, in Norway, where a Campaign Against the Neutron Bomb was launched in January 1978. In Sweden, activists moved from a groundswell of protest against nuclear power plants to a mobilization against nuclear weapons, usually under the leadership of the Swedish Peace and Arbitration Society. In Finland, the defunct Committee of 100 revived and became the key component of the Finnish Peace Union, which in 1978 began serving as an umbrella organization for Finland's small, independent peace organizations. To protest U.S. and Soviet Euromissile plans, veteran Norwegian activists issued a petition signed by prominent personalities, held public meetings, and by November, had organized fifteen to twenty local groups in Norway's major cities and towns. Within a short time, union federations, most branches of the ruling Labor Party, and other small parties of the Center-Left endorsed the anti-missile campaign. In January 1980, activists reorganized their venture as a broader, non-hierarchical disarmament movement, No to Nuclear Weapons, committed to dismantling nuclear weapons in East and West. Much the same thing happened in Denmark, where veteran peace activists began an anti-missile campaign that included petitions, newspaper advertisements, and protest marches in several cities. Here, too, a grassroots No to Nuclear Weapons organization was launched in January 1980. Moreover, dynamic Women for Peace organizations appeared in all four Nordic nations. Founded in early 1980, they launched a mass antinuclear petition drive of their own, declaring that "women of the Nordic countries have had it. Enough is enough!"

Indeed, non-Communist Europe once again buzzed with antinuclear activity. In Belgium, peace groups mobilized public sentiment against the neutron bomb and, led by the National Action Committee for Peace and Development, turned out 10,000 demonstrators in Brussels during May 1978 under the slogan "Disarm to Survive." In Italy, eight religious groups published an open letter on the arms race, denouncing "the new threat imposed by the political policy of the 'balance of terror.'" In France, the Movement for Disarmament, Peace, and Liberty sponsored small-scale antinuclear ventures opposing French nuclear testing and calling for a Europe free of nuclear weapons. The most surprising upsurge occurred in Turkey, where a broadly based peace organization had never existed. In 1977, during a time of substantial democratization in Turkish life, the Istanbul Bar Association helped launch the Turkish Peace Association (TPA), which soon claimed representatives from almost fifty groups, including professional bodies and Turkey's largest labor, women's, and youth organizations. Campaigning for nuclear disarmament, the TPA sharply criticized deployment of the neutron bomb and the NATO missile decision.

Across the Atlantic, in the United States, the movement underwent a dramatic revival. WSP demanded a comprehensive test ban treaty, assailed the neutron bomb, and distributed a brochure entitled "Human Beings are an Endangered Species." Members of the War Resisters League staged simultaneous demonstrations in Red Square and on the White House lawn, unfurling banners that called upon the two Cold War antagonists to disarm. The AFSC organized campaigns against local nuclear weapons facilities, drawing an ever-larger response. In 1975, when the AFSC's Rocky Flats Action Group held its first demonstration, only 25 people took part; four years later, the number of participants rose to 15,000. These organizations and others sometimes worked together—as in the campaign to stop the B-1 bomber, a proposed $50 billion Pentagon weapons system with both nuclear and conventional capabilities. In January 1977, activists staged demonstrations against the B-1 in 145 U.S. cities.

Fed up with the nuclear arms race, small groups of religious pacifists began to take nonviolent direct action. The best-known incident occurred in September 1980, near Philadelphia. Entering the General Electric plant in the town of King of Prussia, eight Catholic pacifists—including the priest Daniel Berrigan and his brother, Philip—followed the biblical injunction to beat swords into plowshares by hammering nuclear missile cones out of shape and, then, pouring blood upon blueprints, work orders, and equipment. Their task finished, they knelt, joined hands, and sang hymns. Eventually, the "Plowshares Eight" were tried and convicted, receiving three- to ten-year prison terms. But they were not repentant. "Who expects politicians, generals, and bomb makers to disarm?" asked Philip Berrigan. "People must disarm the bombs."

In the United States, as elsewhere, opposition to nuclear power plants spurred disarmament activism. Organized by the Clamshell Alliance, thousands of antinuclear demonstrators staged a nonviolent occupation of the Seabrook, New Hampshire, nuclear reactor site in April of 1977, leading to 1,400 arrests. Most of the arrested refused bail, and had to be held in jail for days or weeks. This dramatic incident led to the appearance of similar antinuclear power groups elsewhere, and the struggle at Seabrook was reenacted nationwide. Although, superficially, this was an environmental movement, the underlying reality was that many of the activists viewed nuclear reactors and nuclear weapons as inseparable. Bumper stickers, books, and buttons depicted nuclear power as the "silent bomb," while activists referred to both nuclear reactors and nuclear weapons simply as "nukes." Many other Americans also connected the two, particularly in the dazed aftermath of the 1979 Three Mile Island reactor disaster. In July of that year, the mayor of Harrisburg, Pennsylvania—the city nearest the devastated nuclear power plant—proposed a sister city affiliation with Hiroshima.

The kinship of the two campaigns was recognized by a new organization that united them: Mobilization for Survival. Organized in 1977 by peace and antinuclear power groups, Mobilization for Survival had four official goals: "Zero Nuclear Weapons"; "Ban Nuclear Power"; "Stop the Arms Race"; and "Fund Human Needs." In fact, though, the first two generated most of its activities. That August, in commemoration of the Hiroshima and Nagasaki bombings, the Mobilization sponsored more than a hundred public gatherings. By the time of its first nationwide conference in December, it claimed 330 affiliates. In May 1978, it played the central role in organizing a march and rally, focused on the U.N. Special Session on Disarmament, that drew an estimated 15,000 to 20,000 people—probably the largest single disarmament demonstration up to that point in U.S. history.

Concerns about nuclear power initially provided the focus for yet another entrant in the disarmament campaign. In the summer of 1978, Helen Caldicott, an Australian pediatrician working at Harvard Medical School, was convinced that radiation from nuclear power plants constituted a serious hazard to human health. When she held a meeting of physicians to consider the issue, they agreed and decided to adopt the name of a now-defunct group, Physicians for Social Responsibility (PSR). During 1979, PSR gathered momentum, becoming a nationwide organization. But, with the deterioration of Soviet-American relations, PSR shifted its emphasis to nuclear weapons. In February 1980, when it held a symposium at Harvard Medical School on the medical consequences of nuclear war, more than a thousand people showed up and the national media covered the event. After two days of discussing horrifying scenarios, sixty physicians sent a telegram to Carter and Soviet party secretary Leonid Brezhnev, warning them that "recovery from a nuclear war would be impossible." In the following months, PSR grew rapidly, not only because of the substantial publicity it received, but because of the enormous energy and persuasiveness of Caldicott. Resigning her position at Harvard, she barnstormed across the country, mobilizing doctors, addressing the general public, and leaving vigorous PSR chapters in her wake. By late 1980, PSR had 10,000 members.

SANE, too, experienced a burst of energy, as well as a rising membership and influence. Under the new, dynamic leadership of David Cortright (a prominent GI resister during the Vietnam War), Seymour Melman (a professor of industrial engineering), and William Winpisinger (president of the International Association of Machinists), SANE sought to build a labor-peace alliance—focused on converting the U.S. economy from a wartime to a peacetime basis. But the revival of the nuclear arms race made economic conversion appear utopian. By contrast, defeating the U.S. government's MX missile project seemed feasible.

Considering the MX a dangerous, first-strike weapon, SANE organized a powerful resistance coalition, the National Campaign to Stop the MX. It brought together not only peace groups, but local ranchers, Native Americans, environmental organizations, and unions. As peace activists publicized the fact that MX missile sites would cover a substantial portion of Utah and Nevada, the normally super-patriotic residents of these states grew alarmed. Local organizers placed MX referenda on the ballot in eight rural counties in Nevada and, in the 1980 elections, voters rejected the MX by a ratio of two to one.

Determined to halt the nuclear arms race, most U.S. peace organizations united behind the idea of a Nuclear Freeze. Randall Forsberg, a defense and disarmament researcher who had been addressing peace groups for years, was convinced that they needed greater organizational and programmatic unity. At a December 1979 meeting of the Mobilization, she pointed out that the AFSC, the FOR, and Mobilization for Survival, among other groups, had been promoting a nuclear moratorium by the United States. But, she argued, if U.S. peace groups turned this unilateral moratorium proposal into one calling for a Soviet-American agreement to halt the testing, production, and deployment of nuclear weapons, it would become politically irresistible. Later that month, encouraged by peace movement leaders, Forsberg drew up a "Call to Halt the Nuclear Arms Race." The "Call" emphasized that the Freeze would retain "the existing nuclear parity between the United States and the Soviet Union" and open the way for the sharp reduction or elimination of nuclear weapons in the future. In the spring of 1980, when Forsberg and leading peace groups formally issued the "Call," most U.S. peace organizations started signing on to it. The campaign's potential was shown in western Massachusetts, where, prematurely, a Freeze referendum was placed on the November 1980 ballot and emerged victorious in 59 of the 62 towns voting on it.

As the Massachusetts victory suggested, Americans felt a strong aversion to nuclear weapons. In 1977 and 1978, opinion surveys revealed that three-quarters of the U.S. population favored a comprehensive test ban treaty. Although the deterioration of Soviet-American relations and relentless Republican attacks did erode popular backing for a SALT II treaty, polls in 1978 and 1979 found that support for it among Americans consistently surpassed opposition. Asked, more abstractly, if they favored a new Soviet-American agreement to limit nuclear weapons, Americans responded affirmatively by ratios that varied from two to one to six to one.

Canadians, too, were quite dovish. Although the Voice of Women and other peace groups joined the struggle against nuclear power, with the approach of the U.N. Special Session they changed their focus to the nuclear arms race. They were joined by a new disarmament organization, Project Ploughshares. Launched at the beginning of 1977, Project Ploughshares was adopted in the middle of that year by the Canadian Council of Churches and, henceforth, its funding came from twelve church and civic groups. By the fall of 1980, the Canadian movement was thriving. That year's Disarmament Week, coordinated by Project Ploughshares, drew more than 10,000 Canadians to 160 events in all ten provinces. Churches and religious organizations emphasized disarmament education, while disarmament events took place on the campuses of 22 Canadian universities. Mayors or city councils issued disarmament proclamations in numerous cities and towns. Films like *War Without Winners* and *Dr. Strangelove* were widely shown. Asked in August 1978 how they would vote on nuclear weapons if a worldwide referendum were held, Canadians—by a ratio of three to one—responded that they would vote in favor of complete nuclear disarmament.

In Australia, the disarmament campaign developed obliquely, thanks to the growth of widespread public opposition to uranium mining. In this uranium-rich country, critics of such mining pointed out that it caused radioactive contamination of the environment, encouraged the growth of dangerous nuclear reactors, and provided the raw material for the building of nuclear weapons. In 1979, activists formed the Movement Against Uranium Mining (MAUM), which drew the backing of both the Australian Congress of Trade Unions and the Labor Party. Campaigning against uranium mining, MAUM came around to championing nuclear disarmament. Indeed, it joined disarmament groups in protesting French nuclear testing, calling for a nuclear-free Pacific, and sponsoring Hiroshima Day activities. In turn, disarmament groups endorsed MAUM's anti-uranium campaign. The two themes for the 1980 Hiroshima Day march and rally in Sydney were: "Keep uranium in the ground" and "No to nuclear war." Later that year, the Sydney city council officially proclaimed Sydney nuclear-free, an action similar to that taken by numerous other municipal councils throughout Australia.

In New Zealand, public protest developed over the visits of U.S. nuclear-armed and nuclear-powered warships. In late 1975, calling for nonviolent action to make New Zealand "an island of sanity in an ocean of peace," the Rev. George Armstrong, an Auckland peace activist and theologian, proposed the development of Peace Squadrons to block their entry. As a result, when a U.S.

nuclear warship, the *Truxton*, arrived at Wellington, it was met by a small Peace Squadron, as well as by a union ban on the waterfront, which prevented it from berthing. Similarly, in October 1976, when the U.S. nuclear cruiser *Long Beach* arrived at Auckland, a Peace Squadron of some 150 small yachts, dinghies, canoes, and kayaks obstructed its passage, as did individual surfboarders, flying the nuclear disarmament symbol. As the confrontations grew more intense, Friends of the Earth, Greenpeace, CND, and other groups joined the Peace Squadrons in seeking a court injunction to block future visits by nuclear warships. Joining the controversy, the leader of the Labour opposition fervently committed his party to the struggle for a nuclear-free Pacific. Meanwhile, the confrontations heightened. In 1979, when the *Haddo*, a U.S. nuclear submarine, rammed its way into Auckland's harbor, sinking a number of small protest craft, one activist—to the delight of the demonstrators—managed to board the nuclear behemoth. According to a news account: "Like Zorba the Greek he began a dance, half of defiance, half of joy on the very nose of the incoming sub." By 1980, nuclear disarmament groups were emerging throughout New Zealand.

In Japan, too, the movement was on the upswing. The Soka Gakkai, a peace-oriented Buddhist group, held antinuclear exhibitions in Japan's cities and gathered 10 million signatures on petitions calling for nuclear abolition. The most important factor behind Japan's antinuclear revival, however, was the shift toward greater unity in the divided nuclear disarmament movement, spurred on by the entreaties of non-political citizens' groups and by the approach of the U.N. Special Session. In May 1977, Gensuikyo and Gensuikin agreed to hold a united world conference against atomic and hydrogen bombs, and to establish a united delegation for the U.N. gathering. Although organizational unity proved elusive, joint world conferences occurred in subsequent years and the joint delegation to the 1978 U.N. conclave brought with it a nuclear abolition petition containing 19 million Japanese signatures.

Elsewhere in the Pacific, a variety of nuclear hazards contributed to the growth of disarmament activism. In the Philippines, a lively, popular antinuclear campaign was organized in the late 1970s to protest the construction of a giant nuclear power plant on the slope of a live volcano in Morong, Bataan. Although constrained by martial law imposed by the dictatorship of Ferdinand Marcos, the movement mobilized thousands of local Filipinos against the project and, gradually, began taking on nuclear weapons issues, as well. Furthermore, during 1978, in the Marshall Islands, some 500 people staged a nonviolent occupation of eight islands from which they had been forcibly evicted years before by the U.S. military to accommodate U.S. nuclear missile tests. The next year, in Palau—another small island trust territory, located in the Caroline Islands—92 percent of the voters in a U.N. referendum gave their support to a constitution, drafted in preparation for independence, that would make the island nuclear-free. As U.S. officials had nuclear plans for the island, they declared the U.N. referendum unofficial, and sponsored a second ballot, this time on a constitution without the nuclear ban. Despite a massive U.S. public relations campaign, Palau's voters rejected this U.S.-imposed constitution and, then, proceeded to adopt yet another nuclear-free charter for the island.

These events added momentum to the emerging nuclear-free movement throughout the Pacific. In April 1975, representatives of dozens of antinuclear organizations, meeting in Suva, Fiji, launched the Nuclear Free Pacific Movement. Its People's Charter called for prohibiting: the tests of nuclear weapons and delivery vehicles; the presence of such weapons, support systems, or bases; nuclear reactors and waste storage; and uranium mining. Three years later, the Nuclear Free Pacific Movement held a second conference at Ponape, in the Caroline Islands, and in 1980 it convened again, in Honolulu. Sponsored by over 50 organizations from 20 Pacific and Pacific Rim nations, the Honolulu conference voted to enlist the help of doctors to examine the people of the Marshall Islands and French Polynesia for radiation-caused illness, to mobilize international support for Palau, to oppose nuclear exercises and nuclear tests in the Pacific, and to work for a nuclear-free Pacific treaty. Activists were particularly outraged at the dumping of nuclear waste in the Pacific by the great powers, which they perceived as yet another facet of colonialist exploitation. A popular Nuclear Free Pacific poster read: "If it's so safe, Dump it in Tokyo, Test it in Paris, Store it in Washington."

Although dictatorial governments in Communist nations narrowed the opportunities for citizen activism, it displayed a new liveliness there, as well. In the Soviet Union, intellectuals once again spoke out for nuclear disarmament. Sakharov assailed the nuclear arms race, while Roy Medvedev, a dissident Soviet historian, publicly applauded the campaign to remove all nuclear weapons, Soviet and American, from Europe. Meanwhile, Communist party reformers defended détente and disarmament against what they called "Stalinist conservatism." In articles published in 1978, the reformer Georgi Arbatov argued that there would be no winners in a nuclear war and that "no one will return" from one—statements that rankled in official circles.

Elsewhere in Eastern Europe, antinuclear activism took on a sharply dissident quality. In Hungary, Catholic "base communities"—following the teachings of György Bulanyi, a Catholic priest—developed rapidly in the late 1970s, preaching not only a new way of life, but resistance to militarism. Although the Catholic Church hierarchy condemned these ventures, many young priests and Catholic laypersons became involved in them. Furthermore, prominent independent Hungarians risked imprisonment by lending their support to the European nuclear disarmament campaign. In East Germany, the Evangelical Church, the major Protestant denomination, undertook a growing number of peace activities. In November 1980, it organized a "Peace Week" under the slogan "Make Peace Without Weapons." As part of this "Peace Week," the Church produced a sew-on badge bearing this slogan, together with the words "Swords into Plowshares" and an accompanying emblem. Particularly among young people, there now developed an informal "Swords into Plowshares" movement, in which wearing the badge came to be regarded, by participants and the authorities alike, as a subversive activity.

These stirrings of East European dissent were encouraged by the rise of the nuclear disarmament movement in the West. Watching reports of Western antinuclear demonstrations broadcast on West German television, which could be viewed equally well in East Germany, many citizens of the German Democratic Republic, and especially the young, were favorably impressed. Furthermore, since 1977, East Germany's Evangelical Church had been widening its contacts with the Dutch IKV. In the Soviet Union, Sakharov did his best to keep in touch with the FAS, with which he closely identified.

Soviet physicians, too, were roped into the international movement thanks to the efforts of a Western activist, Bernard Lown, a prominent American cardiologist. Having founded the original PSR and returned to it upon its revival, Lown, in early 1979, sent a highly emotional letter urging joint action against the arms race to a distinguished Soviet cardiologist, Evgenii Chazov. When Lown followed up by speaking with him in Moscow in April 1980, Chazov was reluctant to proceed, arguing that Lown's plan would destroy his career and sacrifice the modern hospital he was building—all for a clearly quixotic venture. But after his daughter intervened and told him that he should take on the project for the sake of his six-month-old grandson, Chazov spent the whole night agonizing over his career, his life's work, and the meaning of medicine. The next day, he told Lown that he would do it. As a result, a small group of U.S. and Soviet physicians, meeting later that year, laid the groundwork for a new organization: International Physicians for the Prevention of Nuclear War (IPPNW).

By the end of the decade, IPPNW was but one of numerous international organizations participating in the growing nuclear disarmament campaign. In addition to the three pacifist internationals and Greenpeace, these included the Pugwash movement, the World Disarmament Campaign, the Socialist International (the world body of social democratic parties), the Catholic Pax Christi, and the Buddhist Soka Gakkai. Women, too, were organizing for disarmament on an international level. During the spring of 1980, antinuclear Women for Peace groups sprang up not only in the Nordic countries, but in West Germany, the Netherlands, and Switzerland.

The best known of the new international movements was European Nuclear Disarmament (END). In early 1980, a group of veteran British antinuclear activists, convinced that the time had come for a mass mobilization against the arms race, began to work on an Appeal for European Nuclear Disarmament. Drafted by E. P. Thompson and subsequently edited by other movement stalwarts, the Appeal was released in April 1980 at a press conference in the House of Commons. "We are entering the most dangerous decade in history," it declared, capped by "a demented arms race." Appraising this situation, "we do not wish to apportion guilt between the political and military leaders of East and West. Guilt lies squarely upon both parties." The genuinely novel part of the END Appeal was its dramatic call for a people's movement to reverse the deadly momentum of the arms race. As little could be expected of missile-wielding governments, "the remedy lies in our own hands. We must act together to free the entire territory of Europe . . . from nuclear weapons." Indeed, "we must learn to be loyal, not to 'East' or 'West,' but to each other." Thereafter, the Appeal garnered the signatures of thousands of prominent individuals in the West and of a small, courageous group of people in the East. Even more important, Europe's nonaligned antinuclear organizations rallied to the END campaign.

By contrast, the Communist-led World Peace Council (WPC) was on the wane. Although the WPC retained some strength thanks to munificent Soviet funding and its revival during the Vietnam War, by the late 1970s its popular appeal was ebbing. Many of its national branches existed only on paper, and its massive world conferences were heavily based on people seeking all-expenses-paid junkets to Eastern Europe. In large part, this weakness reflected the WPC's continued fierce, pro-Soviet partisanship. Condemning the United

States, NATO, Japan, and China in the harshest of terms, the WPC heaped praise upon the Soviet Union and its foreign adventures, including the Soviet invasion of Afghanistan. Nor did the rise of popular protest against the Bomb benefit the WPC. Quite the contrary; the vibrancy and mass mobilization of its nonaligned competitors merely exposed the WPC's marginality.

The Impact on Public Policy

This upsurge of nuclear disarmament activism coincided with more serious efforts by governments to grapple with the nuclear arms race. Part of this tilt in public policy can be attributed to the advent of a more antinuclear leadership at the governmental level in a number of key countries during the late 1970s. In the United States, particularly, the new administration of Jimmy Carter opened opportunities for progress in arms control and disarmament. Although some members of his administration, such as Zbigniew Brzezinski, his National Security Advisor, were more hawkish than the new President, Carter entered office promising to work toward "the elimination of all nuclear weapons from this earth." In addition, most other NATO nations also leaned toward nuclear disarmament, largely because they were governed by relatively antinuclear Center-Left parties. Addressing the 1978 U.N. Special Session, the Canadian Prime Minister, Pierre Elliot Trudeau, a Liberal, reported that his country was divesting itself of nuclear weapons and, furthermore, outlined a "Strategy of Suffocation" for the nuclear arms race. In India, the new prime minister, Morarji Desai, a Gandhian, declared that his government opposed nuclear weapons and would not manufacture them. Nevertheless, numerous nations—including the Soviet Union—had governments with a more traditional approach. And even the new officials hesitated to move as decisively as the antinuclear campaign urged.

In the United States, peace groups enjoyed unusual access to power with the advent of the Carter administration. Officials at ACDA, the State Department, and the White House met with leaders of the disarmament movement—providing them with briefings on key issues and, on occasion, soliciting their opinion. Administration officials not only considered them an important Democratic constituency, but, sometimes, a useful force for promoting the Carter administration's agenda. "I thought they were a plus," recalled Paul Warnke, Carter's top arms control negotiator. When it came to mobilizing support for the SALT II treaty, "we were counting very heavily on them." Carter commended WSP for its disarmament efforts, issued a public testimonial for SANE, and appointed peace group leaders as members of the official U.S. delegation to the U.N. Special Session.

On the other hand, Carter kept aloof from most antinuclear campaigners. Numerous peace groups found that they had no access to the President. Even Harold Willens, a peace-oriented businessman who had grown very close to Carter during his 1976 presidential campaign, was shunted aside thereafter by White House aides. In part this standoffishness seems to have reflected the irritation of more hawkish officials, who were affronted by peace groups' opposition to deployment of the neutron bomb. Furthermore, some degree of political calculation seems to have been involved. Beginning in the fall of 1977, reports from Brzezinski and from the President's pollster emphasized growing public dismay at America's foreign policy "weakness." In these circumstances, While House political operatives discouraged presidential meetings with leaders of peace groups.

Overall, governments reacted to the revival of antinuclear agitation in direct proportion to their commitment to nuclear disarmament. Developing nations, recognizing that peace groups shared their position on the arms race, had their leaders address meetings at the U.N. Special Session and drew eagerly upon their expertise. The social democratic Nordic countries were also fairly open to exchanges with disarmament NGOs, as was the social democratic government of Turkey, which sent representatives to many of the seminars and international symposia organized by the TPA. By contrast, the conservative-led government of the Netherlands was less forthcoming, with the Dutch foreign minister telling American officials that he was "worried about the emergence of new 'ban the bomb' movements." In Britain, the May 1979 election victory of the Conservatives opened the door for intense government spying on antinuclear activists. In 1980, a military takeover of the Turkish government led quickly to the dissolution of the TPA, the seizure of its files, and to a government investigation of its leaders.

The Soviet government continued to follow a more complex policy. Lavishly funding the WPC and its operations, the Kremlin leaned heavily upon this Soviet-dominated organization and upon Communist parties to further its "peace" agenda, including vigorous opposition to the neutron bomb and Western missile deployment. But Soviet authorities took a considerably less charitable view of independent peace activism. Thus, they worked to keep independent peace groups out of the U.N. Special Session and, when Sakharov publicly condemned the Soviet invasion of Afghanistan, had him seized by Soviet security police, stripped of his rights, awards, and privileges, and flown to Gorky, where he remained isolated from foreigners and under constant police surveillance. To be sure, the nonaligned antinuclear campaign began to draw the respectful attention of Soviet officials like Aleksandr Yakovlev, the ambassador to Canada. Moreover, Soviet authorities tolerated the early meetings of Chazov with Lown and the establishment of IPPNW. But Yakovlev was a party reformer whom the leadership had farmed out for his suspiciously independent ideas, while Chazov managed to avoid difficulties because he was the personal physician to Brezhnev and other top party leaders. For the most part, Soviet policy remained hostile to nonaligned peace activism.

Naturally, then, antinuclear campaigners made greater progress on the other side of the Cold War divide. In his first months in office, Carter met twice with Terry Provance, director of the Stop the B-1 Bomber Campaign, and also conferred with leaders of the anti-B-1 liberal bloc in Congress, who pointed to polls showing majority opposition to the weapon. Even so, after years of lobbying by the Rockwell corporation and the Air Force, the weapon had a powerful array of supporters in Congress and in many parts of the country eager to secure defense contracts. Thus, the expectation grew that the B-1 would go forward, though perhaps in reduced form. But on June 30, 1977, just as Pentagon generals reportedly were ordering champagne to celebrate their victory, Carter canceled the B-1 project.

Public pressure also had some impact on Carter administration policy for the use of nuclear weapons. Although the President did not want to undermine the credibility of a U.S. nuclear response to a conventional Soviet attack upon Western Europe, he did favor some softening of U.S. policy. Thus, on July 22, 1977, in response to a query from Carter, Brzezinski proposed that the President issue "a statement to the effect that we would not be the first to use nuclear weapons, except as a response to the invasion of territory of the U.S. or of U.S. Allies." This "would highlight the notion that nuclear weapons are designed only for defensive purposes." Considering this "a good public position to take," Carter asked government officials to work out the details. In September, he ran the idea past West German Chancellor Helmut Schmidt, pointing out that a statement on "non-use of nuclear weapons" would "deprive the Soviet Union of its propaganda monopoly over this issue." Finally, in June 1978—after strong pressure for a U.S. disarmament initiative from the U.S. delegation to the U.N. Special Session—the administration used the U.N. conference to unveil its modification of first use doctrine.

The Carter administration's greatest concession to public pressure, however, came when it decided to scrap the neutron bomb project. In June 1977, an article in the *Washington Post* revealed administration procurement plans for this enhanced radiation warhead. A carryover from the Ford administration, the neutron bomb was designed for use by the U.S. Army's short-range Lance missile in Western Europe for the purpose of offsetting the Warsaw Pact's advantage in tank forces. The *Post* article, which emphasized that this was the first weapon with the explicit purpose of killing people through radiation, touched off what Brzezinski called "a political explosion that reverberated throughout the United States and Europe."

Although the administration won a difficult funding battle in Congress, the neutron bomb became exceptionally problematic in Western Europe. According to U.S. Secretary of State Cyrus Vance, news of the weapon "set off an explosive political and public reaction," led by "antinuclear groups." In this context, West European government leaders shied away from requesting deployment. On July 22, Brzezinski complained to Carter that, although NATO officials wanted the new weapon, "they are terrified by the political consequences of seeming to approve nuclear warfare on their territory and of endorsing a weapon which . . . seems to have acquired a particularly odious image." With West European leaders refusing to share responsibility for the neutron bomb, Carter found himself in a very awkward position. At an August 17 meeting with top U.S. government officials, Brzezinski noted in his diary, Carter said "he did not wish the world to think of him as an ogre, and we agreed that we will press the Europeans to show greater . . . willingness to absorb some of the political flak."

But European leaders shunned accepting any blame for this very unpopular weapon. In February 1978, Brzezinski informed Carter that the British had "a lot of trouble with publicly supporting a decision to produce and deploy." The "Labour Party was split" and the Cabinet ministers "would prefer to avoid a decision." On February 22, the Danish prime minister told Carter that he would not support deployment. The following day, the West German government announced that a "decision on the production of neutron weapons falls into the exclusive responsibility of the United States." In March, the Dutch parliament passed a resolution declaring that production of the neutron bomb was undesirable, and the prime minister reported to Washington that, in these circumstances, he could not agree to deployment. Later that month, British Prime Minister James Callaghan told Carter that, if the neutron bomb were scrapped, he would find it "the greatest relief in the world," for otherwise it would provide "a very difficult political issue" for him. To Carter, the situation had become intolerable. He fumed: "Why should I go forward and take all the onus for having produced this infamous weapon, if they're not prepared to take their fair share of the opprobrium?" Consequently, on April 7, 1978, he canceled plans for its production and deployment.

As indicated by the Carter administration's initial support for the neutron bomb, it did not oppose the development of all new nuclear weapons or plans for their use. Carter's MX missile program, for example, was a massive one. It entailed building and deploying 200 MX missiles, each carrying ten nuclear warheads, in a mobile, racetrack form, with thousands of missile silos dug in the Southwest to house the weapons on their constant travels. Carrying an estimated price tag of $60 billion, it constituted the largest construction project in human history, dwarfing the building of the Egyptian pyramids. Members of the Carter administration rallied behind this scheme because of their belief that, having canceled the B-1 bomber, the administration had to back an alternative nuclear weapons system. In July 1980, Carter also issued Presidential Directive 59, which outlined a new strategy for U.S. nuclear war-fighting. To hawks and doves alike, PD-59's leakage to the press indicated that, in the midst of an election campaign, Carter was firming up his anti-Soviet credentials.

If, however, the Carter administration sought to appease American hawks, it also tailored its policies to conciliate the doves. On December 12, 1979, NATO adopted what became known as its "two-track" policy for intermediate range nuclear missiles. Track one provided that, in the fall of 1983, the U.S. government would begin installing 464 cruise and 108 Pershing II missiles in five West European nations. But track two provided that NATO would begin negotiations with the Soviet Union for the reduction or elimination of all nuclear missiles in Europe. As Vance recalled, "the arms control aspect of this so-called two-track approach was politically essential to contain expected internal opposition to the proposed deployments within most of the member countries." Or, as McGeorge Bundy, an administration advisor, put it, the second track "was necessary for domestic political reasons."

Nor was it clear that, even with this concession, all NATO nations would support the two-track package. Although Margaret Thatcher, who replaced Callaghan that spring, was thoroughly committed to it, her subsequent talks with West European leaders left her appalled at their equivocation. Schmidt remained "very concerned at the effect on German public opinion of stationing more nuclear missiles on German soil" and the Dutch prime minister "explained to me in some detail the difficulties he was facing. Apparently, half the sermons in Dutch churches were now dealing with nuclear disarmament and the issue of deployment was endangering his government's survival." In addition, the Dutch parliament rejected the proposed NATO decision in a non-binding vote, while the Belgian and Danish governments called for a postponement of the decision for six months. Although U.S. officials finally managed to secure unanimous support within NATO for the two-track policy, it remained very difficult to implement, for NATO governments placed onerous conditions on their participation.

Furthermore, West European antinuclear pressures became so intense that they began to transform the arms control track into the most radical, far-reaching of its possibilities: what became known, in later years, as the "zero option." Most NATO officials wanted some deployment of their new missiles in Western Europe, regardless of what the Russians did about the SS-20s. But the zero option—the removal of all intermediate range nuclear missiles from Europe—began to make headway, particularly after the summer of 1979, when it was proposed by the West German and Dutch social democratic parties. Naturally, it took on an increasing political significance as protest grew against the missiles. "The zero option," Schmidt recalled, was "first thought up in Bonn; I had first proposed it publicly in December 1979 and repeated it several times." With his own Labor Party badly split by the two-track decision, the Norwegian foreign minister adopted a similar approach.

Soviet nuclear weapons policy also had cautious aspects. Underneath Soviet propaganda calls for banning the Bomb, there did lurk a genuine, if more modest, Kremlin interest in détente and nuclear arms control. This attempt to set limits to the nuclear arms race and reduce the danger of nuclear war was reflected in negotiations with the U.S. government over a SALT II treaty. In addition, the Soviet leadership, while considering its deployment of SS-20 missiles merely a modernization of its intermediate range nuclear forces, ultimately agreed to open negotiations on Euromissile reduction. The Soviet government was also quite serious about a comprehensive test ban treaty, apparently based on its fear of nuclear proliferation and its desire to curb nuclear advances by China. Perhaps most important, Brezhnev, speaking at Tula in January 1977, broke new ground for a Soviet leader by declaring the impossibility of victory in a nuclear war. According to Soviet ambassador Anatoly Dobrynin, this speech "was made as a signal of goodwill," in the hope that it would breathe new life into détente and the SALT process.

At the same time, however, in areas not covered by arms control treaties or Kremlin promises, the Soviet Union continued its military buildup. In addition to its SS-20s, it deployed a new generation of ICBMs with improved accuracy and MIRVed warheads, as well as improved longer-range, sea-launched ballistic missiles. Although the Kremlin was on relatively good behavior toward Western Europe and Japan, it engaged in a variety of military adventures in the Third World. Channeling arms and other aid to "national liberation" movements and friendly governments in underdeveloped nations, especially in Africa, it contributed thereby to an atmosphere of international insecurity. In the final days of 1979, the Soviet government sent its armed forces into Afghanistan, where they battled Afghan rebels in an attempt to prop up the Communist government of that nation. When Dobrynin pointed out that Soviet policy in the Third World was undermining its relationship with Washington, Soviet officials "invariably responded: 'Why does the United States raise such complaints about us when they are themselves so active around the globe?'"

The contradictions in Soviet policy were exemplified by Brezhnev, the aging, increasingly incompetent Soviet party secretary, caught in a bind between his revulsion at nuclear war and his fear of U.S. aggression. According to Dobrynin, although "détente in Soviet-American relations was Brezhnev's true objective . . . he failed to comprehend fully what it entailed." He "saw no need of any major corrections" in Soviet policy, despite the fact that "reality demanded changes." At a 1979 summit meeting, Dobrynin was struck by the contrast between Carter's capability and Brezhnev's physical and mental decrepitude. Similarly, young Mikhail Gorbachev, a party reformer, was also disturbed by the fact that Brezhnev seemed "more dead than alive." But most Politburo members were quite content with current arrangements, which enabled them to continue ruling their fiefdoms without interference. Dominated by tradition-bound, authoritarian, and sickly leaders and shielded, to a great degree, from popular pressures, the Soviet government was simply incapable of changing course.

Even so, there was some joint effort toward halting the nuclear arms race, principally because Carter was determined to secure a SALT II agreement. In his opinion, a new SALT treaty was imperative to deal with the threat to human survival posed by the thousands of Soviet and American ICBMs. Furthermore, Carter was influenced by public opposition to the nuclear arms race. "It was important not to appear as a warmonger," Carter recalled. "Such a posture would . . . isolate the United States within the community of nations," while an "unequivocal commitment to nuclear arms control . . . would signal that

America was a peaceful and reliable country." At home, too, nuclear arms controls made good political sense. Hamilton Jordan, his White House political advisor, assured him that "if we ratify a SALT II agreement . . . and the economy is in reasonably good shape, I believe that it will insure your re-election." Although sharp Republican attacks on a SALT treaty led to doubts about securing the two-thirds vote necessary for Senate ratification, the President took heart at its widespread public backing. In May 1979, Carter's pollster assured him: "One fact stands out in the recent survey on SALT—the American people stand firmly behind the idea of arms limitation and . . . behind the SALT treaty"; indeed, there was "overwhelming support for the idea of limiting nuclear arms among the whole population." Impressed by the report, portions of which he underlined and commented upon, Carter ordered that it be made the basis for all his speeches and those of his Cabinet.

Nevertheless, the results fell far short of Carter's hopes. Determined to secure deep cuts in strategic nuclear arsenals, Carter proposed that earlier, more modest understandings between Henry Kissinger and Brezhnev be scrapped. Soviet leaders were horrified, assuming, incorrectly, that this turnabout indicated that Carter had adopted an aggressive posture toward the Soviet Union. With the SALT negotiations suddenly near collapse, the anxious Carter administration brought less ambitious arms control proposals to the bargaining table. But the Russians, now wary, proved tough negotiators, while elements of the Carter administration, led by Brzezinski, argued that, without good behavior by the Soviet Union, the U.S. government should take a hard line on the SALT II treaty. As a result, the final treaty-signing did not take place until June 1979, when Carter met with Brezhnev at a summit conference in Vienna. Aware that the treaty set rather high limits on strategic arms, Carter also used the meeting to produce a list of proposals for SALT III, which included "deep cuts in weapons," a halt to the production of nuclear warheads and launchers, and a comprehensive test ban treaty. Although this advanced position again dismayed the Soviets, they need not have worried. Not only did SALT III never materialize but, after Soviet military intervention in Afghanistan, SALT II stood no chance of Senate ratification.

The Rise of the Hawks

Although Soviet aggression in Afghanistan played a key role in torpedoing the SALT II treaty, that agreement also fell afoul of rising U.S. militarism.

During the late 1970s, alarm spread among hawkish elements that the Soviet government stood on the verge of dominating the world. Frightened of the Soviet Union, many Americans had never accepted the idea of Soviet-American détente or of limits upon their nation's nuclear weapons program. In November 1976, Paul Nitze, Eugene Rostow, and other veterans of the nation's policy-making elite who shared these views established the Committee on the Present Danger (CPD), which demanded major increases in spending for U.S. land, sea, and air forces, including nuclear weapons. Responding to the new organization's venomous attacks on his administration, Carter and his top national security officials tried to conciliate the CPD. But to no avail. During Senate hearings in the fall of 1979, CPD leaders testified against the SALT II treaty on seventeen different occasions, arguing that it would leave the United States ripe for conquest by the Soviet Union. This contention—though quite dubious—proved very effective, for it came from a group of influential national security officials. According to Richard Allen, a CPD executive committee member, the CPD "managed to destroy SALT II, which was our objective."

In the wake of the SALT II fiasco, the CPD had no regrets about the collapse of the nuclear arms control process. Determined to secure a rapid U.S. nuclear buildup, the CPD and its leaders had no use for arms control or disarmament. Rostow wrote in November 1980: "The nuclear weapons issue has probably gotten beyond the possibility of control through arms limitations agreements like SALT. So? What arms limitation agreements have ever done much good?" To the CPD, there were more important concerns. The following month, in a memo to another CPD member, William Casey, Rostow wrote: "One question now haunts the world: Who is going to win the war we still call Cold?"

In fact, thanks to the ascendancy of the Republican Right, now rallying behind California Governor Ronald Reagan, the hawks had an excellent chance to sweep arms control from the board and pursue Cold War victory. A fervent anti-Communist and proponent of a U.S. military buildup, Reagan became a member of the CPD in 1976. On his weekly radio programs, he lauded the CPD and assailed peace movement leaders (such as Dr. Spock) and organizations (such as the AFSC) as agents of a Communist conspiracy. Rarely did Reagan see a weapon that he did not like. Enthusiastic about the neutron bomb, he called it "the dreamed-of death ray weapon of science fiction" and "a moral improvement" over other means of modern war—perhaps even "the ideal deterrent weapon." In September 1979, he asked his radio audience: "Do arms limitation agreements—even good ones—really bring or preserve peace?" He replied: "History would seem to say 'no.'" Repeatedly denouncing the SALT II negotiations, Reagan called the treaty "an act of appeasement." Indeed, by late 1980, Reagan had opposed *every* nuclear arms control agreement negotiated by Democratic and Republican administrations.

As the 1980 Republican presidential nominee, Reagan drew upon these themes in his election campaign. He championed building the B-1 bomber, the neutron bomb, the Trident nuclear submarine, and the MX nuclear missile, as well as many additional navy warships and air force planes. The Russians, he explained, were "monsters," who kept the Cold War alive with their relentless drive to spread "Godless communism." Indeed, he declared, "the Soviet Union underlies all the unrest that is going on. If they weren't engaged in this game of dominoes, there wouldn't be any hot spots in the world." In these circumstances, Reagan could see little reason for nuclear constraints. The SALT II treaty, he declared, was "fatally flawed." Questioned about the prospect of his using nuclear weapons, Reagan declared that he would never reveal what the United States "won't do." His vice presidential running mate, George H. W. Bush, insisted that nuclear war was winnable.

For a time, it seemed that this extremist stance might jeopardize Reagan's election. Seizing upon the Republican candidate's hawkish statements, Carter's re-election strategists developed the theme of Reagan as "a mad bomber." This included a TV ad in which Carter spoke earnestly about the dangers of nuclear war and a lengthy radio talk in which he charged that Reagan was bringing the United States closer to a "nuclear precipice." Worried that Reagan's hawkishness might prove his undoing, Republican strategists pressed him to soften his belligerent comments on national defense issues (including arms control) and to focus on economic issues, both of which he did. Even this shift, however, did not entirely halt the clamor, and in late October Reagan was forced to deliver a lengthy television speech complaining that his views on war and peace had "been distorted in . . . an effort to scare people." Fortunately for Reagan, though, his folksy, appealing style soothed fears of his nuclear recklessness. As Richard Wirthlin, who directed his campaign strategy, later remarked, despite Reagan's beliefs, "the persona of the man was such that he didn't really scare people down to their boots." As a result, Reagan secured a decisive victory at the polls that November.

Although the hawks made their greatest political advances in the United States, they also were on the march elsewhere and, particularly, within NATO nations. NATO's military command had disliked the alliance's two-track decision, for the disarmament track left an opportunity open for canceling the deployment of U.S. intermediate range nuclear missiles in Western Europe. Furthermore, as in the United States, hawkish pressures for a nuclear buildup received powerful support from conservative parties and governments.

Nowhere was this more evident than in Britain, where the victory of Margaret Thatcher's Conservatives in the spring of 1979 caused a defense policy turnabout as dramatic as the one in the United States. By the beginning of the new decade, the British government had come out against a comprehensive test ban treaty, warned about compromises on the Euromissiles, and laid plans for a nuclear buildup, including the deployment of Trident submarines and cruise missiles. Fiercely committed to a nuclear-armed Britain, Thatcher was a sharp critic of arms control and disarmament policies. When she first met Reagan, Thatcher recalled, "I knew that I was talking to someone who instinctively felt and thought as I did."

Opponents of arms control were also on the move elsewhere. During the SALT II debate in the United States, West German hard-liners sought to kill the treaty by leaking information that the German military opposed it. Furthermore, the conservative Christian Democrats, out of power at the time of NATO's two-track decision, championed deployment of Western nuclear missiles and scorned the idea of a "zero option" as nonsense. Although they were defeated at the polls in 1980, they felt a new surge of hope with Reagan's election. Meanwhile, their counterparts in Japan, the hawkish Liberal Democrats, won an overwhelming victory in parliamentary elections that same year.

Within the Soviet Union, hawkish tendencies grew. Arbatov recalled that, in the late 1970s, "our military policy and arms industry completely escaped political control. The leadership made the decisions, but the military and the military-industrial agencies prompted these decisions." The "military-industrial complex" increased its "strength and influence and . . . skillfully put Brezhnev's patronage and weaknesses to its own good use." Brezhnev viewed the military "as a very important power base" and, also, had a "sentimental" attachment to it, "which grew in proportion to his age and illness."

The rise of the hawks, however, did not rest upon a solid base of popular support for nuclear weapons. In the United States, as Wirthlin noted, the 1980 campaign was "fought primarily on the grounds of economic issues." Furthermore, although it is true that, at the end of the decade, an increasing number of Americans favored spending more on defense, this appears to have reflected the growing frustration they felt in dealing with a world beyond their control. The

Iranian hostage crisis, more than any other foreign policy issue, contributed to this trend and to Carter's political demise. But the crisis in Iran had nothing to do with nuclear issues.

Similarly, the hawkish rise elsewhere did not reflect a rise of pro-nuclear sentiment among the public. During Thatcher's first years in office, she was a very unpopular prime minister. In West Germany, the hawkish Franz Josef Strauss was defeated resoundingly by the more moderate Schmidt in the 1980 election for chancellor. In Japan, the ruling conservatives carefully avoided challenging the "three non-nuclear principles." Opinion polls in NATO nations found that the public much preferred nuclear arms controls to a nuclear buildup.

Thus, as the 1980s began, all was not lost. Although hawkish forces held office in a number of powerful countries, their ability to fully implement their program for a nuclear buildup and, if necessary, nuclear war, remained problematic. Furthermore, the movement's successes during the 1970s—especially the cancellation of the neutron bomb, the negotiation of SALT II, and the second track of NATO's two-track decision—provided a basis for later advances. Indeed, these concessions to the force of antinuclear sentiment would prove to be like the seed in the snow—ready to germinate in later years, when more favorable developments warmed the earth with new hope.

7   Peace Begins to Break Out, 1981–1985

During the 1980s, the reaction to the rise of the hawks was widespread and stormy. Both the peace movement and ever-widening circles of the public believed that, with nuclear weapons enthusiasts controlling major governments and talking glibly of nuclear war, a nuclear conflagration was becoming more likely. In response, millions of people around the world mobilized against the policies of their rulers. Peace and disarmament groups burgeoned into mass movements of unprecedented size and intensity. Major cities were swept by vast nuclear disarmament marches and rallies—in many cases, the largest political demonstrations in their history. Furthermore, powerful social institutions threw their weight behind the antinuclear campaigns. Ultimately, these forces proved irresistible, and many of the same government officials who entered office roaring like lions began bleating like lambs.

Preparing for Armageddon, 1981–1983

Some of the would-be lions governed the United States, where the Reagan administration took office in January 1981. Appointed Secretary of Defense, Caspar Weinberger told his first news conference that "a strong confident America" was now ready to "fight for its freedom." As Weinberger had no foreign or military policy experience, he leaned heavily for advice and expertise upon his new Assistant Secretary, Richard Perle. Smart and relentless, Perle was a staunch opponent of nuclear arms control and advocate of a nuclear buildup. For Secretary of State, Reagan chose General Alexander Haig, a zealous proponent of U.S. military power. Nancy Reagan recalled that "once, talking about Cuba in a meeting of the National Security Council, he turned to Ronnie and said, 'You just give me the word and I'll turn that f____ island into a parking lot.'" She concluded: "If Ronnie had given him the green light, Haig would have bombed everybody and everything."

Numerous other top national security officials shared this militarist approach. Richard Allen, Reagan's National Security Advisor, used his first public statement to warn against the "advocacy of arms control negotiations as a substitute for military strength." Eugene Rostow, appointed director of the Arms Control and Disarmament Agency (ACDA), insisted that "arms control thinking drives out sound thinking." Questioned at a Senate hearing about whether he thought the United States and the Soviet Union could survive a full-scale nuclear war, he responded cheerfully: "The human race is very resilient." Others, like William Casey (appointed director of the CIA), Jeane Kirkpatrick (appointed U.S. ambassador to the United Nations), and Paul Nitze (appointed chief negotiator for theater nuclear forces in Europe) were full-blown Cold War ideologues. By November 1984, 60 of the 182 CPD members occupied key posts in the Reagan administration, among them Kenneth Adelman, Allen, Casey, Kirkpatrick, Nitze, Perle, Rostow, Donald Rumsfeld, George Shultz, Edward Teller, and, of course, the new President of the United States, Ronald Reagan.

In Reagan's view, any agreement with the Soviet Union was impossible. Speaking at a press conference only nine days after taking office, the new President declared that the Russians were ready "to commit any crime, to lie, to cheat" in a relentless campaign to promote "world revolution and a one-world socialist or communist state." Reagan's strident pronouncements culminated in a public address on March 8, 1983, in which he denounced the Soviet Union as "the focus of evil in the modern world," an "evil empire." Conflict between the United States and the Soviet Union, he said, represented an apocalyptic "struggle between right and wrong and good and evil." In these circumstances, the United States should be girding for battle. Addressing West Point cadets, Reagan contended that any argument in his administration over national security policy "will be over which weapons, not whether we should forsake weaponry for treaties and agreements." A believer in biblical prophecy, Reagan insisted that "the day of Armageddon isn't far off. . . . Ezekiel says that fire and brimstone will be rained down upon the enemies of God's people. That must mean that they'll be destroyed by nuclear weapons."

Once in office, the Reaganites began implementing their priorities. The Pentagon's new military program called for simultaneous across-the-board modernization of all U.S. strategic forces, including cruise missiles, the MX missile, and the Trident submarine. Furthermore, the administration laid out plans to produce the once-canceled B-1 bomber and the discredited neutron bomb.

This program for a nuclear weapons buildup was accompanied by statements displaying a rather relaxed attitude toward using them. Reagan chatted with a group of newspaper editors about the feasibility of "limited" nuclear war, while Haig declared that a NATO contingency plan for a conventional war in Europe called for the explosion of a nuclear weapon for "demonstrative purposes." In May 1982, when the administration's first Defense Guidance was leaked to the press, it revealed that the U.S. military was being readied for a "protracted" nuclear war with the Soviet Union, in which U.S. nuclear forces "must prevail and be able to force the Soviet Union to seek earliest termination of hostilities on terms favorable to the United States."

Soviet leaders were horrified by these developments. In May 1981, amid the new President's anti-Soviet tirades, Brezhnev delivered a secret address to a major KGB conclave in Moscow, denouncing Reagan's policies and warning that the Soviet Union and the United States stood on the brink of nuclear war. He was followed by Yuri Andropov, the KGB director, who told the gathering that the new U.S. administration was not only preparing for such a war, but for the possible launching of a nuclear first strike. In response, the Kremlin fostered a rapid buildup and mobilization of Soviet military might. The Reaganite military surge, recalled Arbatov, "forced us to spend more on defense and to pay even greater heed to the opinions of the military." To counter deployment of Pershing II missiles, Soviet officials decided to preserve the ABM system around Moscow (which they were planning to dismantle), to build a new, ground-launched, high-speed missile to attack them, and to place SS-20 missiles in a position where they could devastate the northwestern United States. According to a member of the Soviet General Staff, the Soviet military used Reagan's "evil empire" speech "as a reason to begin a very intense preparation . . . for a state of war." In addition, "we started to run huge strategic [nuclear] exercises." Thus, "for the military, the period when we were called the evil empire was actually very good and useful, because we achieved a very high military readiness. . . . We also rehearsed the situation when a non-nuclear war might turn into a nuclear war."

In this context of heightening military tension, U.S.-Soviet diplomatic relations went into a deep freeze. By mid-1982, recalled George Shultz, Haig's successor as Secretary of State, "relations between the two superpowers were not simply bad; they were virtually nonexistent."

The Revolt of the Doves: Non-Communist Europe

In Britain, the general public, appalled by the spiraling militarism of the early 1980s, flooded into the Campaign for Nuclear Disarmament. By early 1985, CND's national membership topped 100,000, and local membership, dispersed in more than a thousand groups, numbered in the hundreds of thousands. CND sponsored numerous mass rallies, including one in October 1983 that drew an estimated 400,000 participants for what was probably the largest demonstration in British history. CND leaflets drew on testimonials from prominent figures in the nation's cultural life, such as actress Susannah York and writer Salman Rushdie. Although CND's membership far surpassed that of the past, its primary constituency remained much the same—the middle class, particularly the well-educated middle class.

When it came to program, CND called for both unilateral and multilateral nuclear disarmament as steps toward the creation of a nuclear-free world. It devoted most of its energy to opposing the deployment of cruise, Pershing II, and SS-20 nuclear missiles in Europe and Britain's purchase of Trident submarines. In addition, it threw itself into opposing civil defense exercises. Work on the latter was facilitated by sympathetic local city councils, which began declaring their cities nuclear-free zones. During 1982, CND and the nuclear-free zone movement—which had grown to more than 120 local jurisdictions—joined forces to block government plans for a nationwide civil defense drill. CND also protested government persecution of independent disarmament activists in Eastern Europe (e.g. in the Soviet Union and East Germany) and in Western Europe (e.g. in Turkey).

Although CND was by far the largest of Britain's nuclear disarmament campaigns, others also flourished. The best-known of these began in August 1981 with a march by a small group of women from Cardiff, Wales to the proposed cruise missile deployment site: the U.S. air force base at Greenham Common, England. When government officials refused to meet with them, the women established a women-only peace camp at the site, declaring that it was time to "take the toys away from the boys." Protests and demonstrations multiplied, leading to a growing number of arrests. On December 12, 1982, responding to a call for action, 30,000 women from across Britain appeared at the nine-mile military fence surrounding the base, adorning it with children's pictures and other decorations—symbols of the life the nuclear missiles would destroy. That night, television news carried aerial shots of the miles of women holding glowing candles and encircling the base. In the ensuing months and years, thousands of women activists settled in at Greenham Common to continue resistance efforts—blocking the gates with their bodies, cutting or pulling down the perimeter fence, painting peace symbols on U.S. warplanes, and even dancing and singing defiantly atop the cruise missile silos. Buffeted by icy storms in winter, evicted from their tent colonies repeatedly (and sometimes brutally), assailed as bizarre and disreputable by the mass media, the women of Greenham Common hung on tenaciously.

As Britain's nuclear disarmament campaign swept forward, it won important victories within civil society. At the 1981 conference of the Trades Union Congress, delegates adopted a resolution calling for Britain's unilateral nuclear disarmament, and followed that up in 1982 and 1983 with resolutions demanding the removal of all nuclear bases from Britain. In turn, the movement's strength within the unions had a substantial impact on the Labour Party, which adopted a unilateralist resolution by a two-thirds majority and elected Michael Foot, a longtime CND activist, as party leader. Although the ruling Conservatives took a fiercely pro-nuclear position and venomously attacked CND, two other small parties—the Liberals and the Social Democrats—condemned the Thatcher government for escalating the arms race and called for multilateral nuclear disarmament. Among the churches, some of the smaller Protestant denominations adopted unilateralist stands, while others opposed the deployment of the new nuclear missiles. Even the traditionally pro-nuclear Church of England insisted that there existed "a moral obligation on all countries publicly to forswear the first use of nuclear weapons."

The movement clearly had the ear of the British public. Although the Labour Party was defeated in the June 1983 parliamentary elections, support for the pro-nuclear Tories also fell, a fact that would have cost them the election if the three antinuclear parties had been united. Moreover, in nearly every instance polls found pluralities or majorities of the public—ranging from 48 to 61 percent—opposed to the deployment of cruise missiles. A large majority of Britons also opposed the purchase of Trident submarines.

In the Netherlands, the movement was even stronger. IKV, headed by a young mathematician, Mient Jan Faber, expanded to some 400 groups functioning on a local or parish level. Championing a step-by-step approach away "from the brink of nuclear disaster," IKV played the dominant role in the massive Dutch antinuclear effort. But other major peace organizations in the campaign included the Stop the Neutron Bomb movement, Pax Christi, and Women for

Peace. Working together, some nine peace groups, seven political parties, and the nation's trade union federation formed the No Cruise Missiles Committee. It staged anti-missile rallies of 400,000 people in Amsterdam in November 1981 and 550,000 people at The Hague in October 1983—the largest demonstrations ever held in the Netherlands. In 1985, 3.75 million people signed an anti-missile petition—an all-time petitioning record for that tiny nation.

The Dutch movement's primary effort went into pressuring the nation's parliament to reject NATO's plan for cruise missile deployment. But the campaign also had wider dimensions. In early May 1984, as part of an action week to illustrate the broad popular resistance to the Euromissiles, about 560 local groups put together 2,000 antinuclear ventures in cities and villages throughout the country, including special church services and vigils, a strike staged by union members and students, and demonstrations at military bases and in provincial capitals. This local focus had a significant impact on the grassroots level, and some 200 Dutch townships declared themselves nuclear-free zones. Meanwhile, IKV fostered an international program—protesting repression of peace groups in East and West and, in addition, defending the rights of dissident movements like Solidarity in Poland and Charter 77 in Czechoslovakia. Indeed, IKV became the leading force within the world peace movement for bypassing national governments and generating "détente from below."

The campaign also made extraordinary progress within major social institutions. In addition to the Dutch labor federation, women's organizations emerged as important components of the antinuclear struggle. The greatest source of the movement's strength, however, lay in the support it mobilized within the Dutch churches. Prodded by IKV, the synods of the two main Protestant bodies issued public proclamations opposing cruise missile deployment. Meanwhile, pressed by Pax Christi, the Roman Catholic bishops issued a pastoral letter in June 1983 that opposed the deployment of new missiles, approved unilateral steps as a means to halt the arms race, and declared that the use of nuclear weapons was impermissible.

Ironically, despite the movement's strength within the Christian churches, it had far less impact upon the Christian Democrats than on the secular parties to their left, most notably the Labor Party, which staunchly opposed missile deployment. Occupying the political Center, the Christian Democrats formed a coalition with a party on the Right, the pro-nuclear Liberals. But, although the Christian Democratic majority favored missile deployment, a party minority opposed it. Consequently, with a small bloc of Christian Democratic deputies threatening to vote with the Labor Party against missile deployment, the governing coalition lacked the votes necessary to push the measure through parliament.

The antinuclear state of public opinion bolstered the parliamentary deadlock. Between 1981 and 1985, polls reported that the Dutch public opposed cruise missile deployment by about two to one. Surveys found that up to 85 percent of respondents favored the removal of all nuclear weapons from the Netherlands through multilateral action, and that as much as 56 percent backed it through unilateral action. Antinuclear sentiments were most widespread among the well-educated, women, youth, the secular, and people with a left-wing orientation.

In neighboring Belgium, the movement was nearly as strong. The Flemish VAKA and the Walloon CNAPD—both coalitions of peace groups, unions, churches, and political organizations—worked closely together to oppose the deployment of nuclear missiles in Western Europe, to support the dismantling of SS-20 missiles in Eastern Europe, to call for the creation of a European nuclear-free zone, and to demand an independent peace policy by their country. In October 1981, they mobilized 200,000 people in Brussels for an antinuclear protest, the largest demonstration in Belgium's history. Two years later, again in Brussels, they doubled that turnout. As in the Netherlands, local committees did much of the antinuclear work—organizing meetings, promoting peace education, and distributing circulars, posters, and petitions. By the fall of 1982, more than 150 Belgian townships had declared themselves nuclear-free zones.

The antinuclear campaign also made substantial progress within Belgian society. Labor unions placed their influence behind it and, in July 1983, the Catholic bishops weighed in with an official statement, "Disarmament for Peace," that buttressed the campaign's legitimacy. Belgium's political parties took positions on nuclear issues roughly along the lines of their counterparts in the Netherlands. Public opinion was less divided. In general, surveys during the early 1980s reported that opposition to NATO's missile deployment ranged between 60 and 78 percent, while a majority of Belgians opposed *any* nuclear armament for their country.

In West Germany, an unusually diverse, decentralized, and powerful movement shook yet another nation slated for missile deployment. Although no organization predominated, political parties, religious groups, unions, women's groups, pacifists, youth groups, and environmentalists worked together to produce unprecedented outpourings of antinuclear sentiment. In October 1981, 300,000 people protested in Bonn against the Euromissiles—the largest political demonstration in West Germany's history. In 1983, when a loose Coordinating Committee brought together thirty of the major organizations, it led to a week of action against missile deployment that drew an estimated three million participants nationwide. It culminated on October 23 in rallies staged in four cities and attracting over a million people.

The movement's constituency in West Germany was rather typical, including a disproportionate number of the well-educated, professionals, youth, and women. Although the Catholic bishops remained rather cautious on nuclear issues, the Catholic Church as a whole moved closer to the position of the antinuclear movement—especially Catholic youth groups, which turned out large numbers of young people for demonstrations. Considerably greater support for the antinuclear campaign came from the Protestant (Evangelical) Church. In 1982, over 5,000 Protestant parishes (more than 50 percent of the total) hosted Peace Weeks, which emphasized the dangers of missile deployment and the need for nuclear-free zones. This antinuclear ferment, particularly among the young, led to the transformation of the Kirchentags, the nation's biannual Protestant lay conferences, into vast antinuclear festivals. Although the labor movement initially kept its distance from the antinuclear campaign, it eventually came around to supporting it. In 1983, warning of the missile danger, the union federation staged a five-minute strike, symbolizing "five minutes to midnight," in factories around the country.

The movement also made important gains within West Germany's political party system. Thoroughly identifying themselves with the antinuclear movement, the Greens campaigned for unilateral rejection of Euromissile deployment and for the withdrawal of all nuclear weapons from the Federal Republic. Led by the charismatic Petra Kelly, they played a key role in West Germany's anti-missile demonstrations and, also, publicly demonstrated in East Berlin and in Moscow against Soviet SS-20 missiles and government repression of independent peace activists. In the 1983 elections, the Green vote rose above the 5 percent hurdle, producing the new party's first parliamentary delegation, a group of 27 antinuclear activists. Although the Greens sniped at their much larger rivals on the Left, the Social Democrats, for compromising with militarism, the latter, in fact, were running to catch up with the antinuclear movement. After the fall of 1982, when the Social Democrats were forced out of office thanks to abandonment by their centrist coalition partner, they took a hard line against the NATO missiles. In November 1983, at a nationwide party congress, the Social Democrats voted to reject the stationing of the missiles in West

Germany and to call upon the Soviet Union to begin the reduction of its SS-20 missiles. By contrast, the Christian Democrats, headed by the new Chancellor, Helmut Kohl, applauded missile deployment, staged pro-missile rallies, and denounced antinuclear demonstrators. Everyone who joined the antinuclear marches, charged the Christian Democratic Party secretary, served as "the tool of Soviet foreign policy."

Although the Christian Democrats and their centrist allies emerged victorious in the March 1983 elections, this did not reflect popular support for their position on nuclear weapons. Opinion polls consistently reported that a majority of West Germans opposed Euromissile deployment in their country. According to a Harris poll, public acceptance of the missiles dropped to a mere 15 percent by late 1983. Furthermore, between July 1981 and May 1984, the percentage of the population opposed to NATO's use of nuclear weapons "under any circumstances" rose from 29 to 44 percent.

Within the small Nordic countries, too, the movement made dramatic advances. In Norway, No to Nuclear Weapons burgeoned into an organization with 100,000 members, operating in about 300 local groups. Conducting one of the largest petition campaigns ever seen in Norway, No to Nuclear Weapons gathered 540,000 signatures on its call for a Nordic nuclear-free zone. In Denmark, No to Nuclear Weapons also grew into an exceptionally powerful organization, with some 45 local branches. Together with Women for Peace and pacifist groups, it stirred up tremendous antinuclear fervor. This included antimissile demonstrations of about 100,000 people in Copenhagen in 1981 and 1983, antinuclear Easter marches with escalating numbers of participants, and a nuclear-free zone petition that garnered 260,000 signatures. In Sweden, more than thirty peace groups now existed, with the largest of them, the Swedish Peace and Arbitration Society, growing by 150 percent between 1980 and 1984. The Swedish antinuclear campaign held demonstrations against the Euromissiles and for a Nordic nuclear-free zone that ranged from 50,000 to 100,000 people and secured the signatures of more than a million Swedes on a petition calling for peace, nuclear disarmament, and a nuclear-free zone. In Finland, too, the movement swept like a storm across the country, with the Peace Union and the Committee of 100 playing key roles. In November 1983, an estimated 215,000 people (about 5 percent of the population) turned out across Finland to demonstrate simultaneously against nuclear weapons—the largest demonstration in the Nordic countries since the Second World War. Furthermore, 1.2 million Finns signed petitions calling for a Nordic nuclear-free zone.

As in other parts of Northern Europe, the movement in the Nordic countries appealed disproportionately to the educated middle class—particularly to youth, and especially to that portion of it with avant-garde political, social, and cultural views. Affiliates appeared among teachers, journalists, doctors, engineers, psychologists, architects, artists, and lawyers. In Sweden, Physicians Against Nuclear Weapons enrolled more than half the nation's medical doctors. Furthermore, powerful social democratic parties, labor federations, and women's organizations backed the antinuclear campaign, as did many religious bodies. In Sweden, the sweeping election victory of the Social Democrats in September 1983 was particularly welcome to peace and disarmament activists. Olof Palme, the new prime minister, had very close relations with Western Europe's antinuclear campaign, and announced his government's commitment to a Nordic nuclear-free zone in the first 60 seconds of his inaugural address.

Nordic public opinion, too, was strikingly antinuclear. Throughout the region strong pluralities or majorities opposed missile deployment and supported building a nuclear-free zone. In 1981, the Norwegian public favored such a zone by 69 to 14 percent. In 1985, 78 percent of Finns backed rapid movement toward general and complete disarmament.

In France, the movement, though weaker, was still quite substantial. Formed in November 1981 by twenty-five peace, political, and women's groups, the Committee for Nuclear Disarmament in Europe (CODENE) opposed nuclear missiles in East and West and called upon the French government to dismantle the French nuclear arsenal. CODENE sponsored conferences, campaigned to have cities and towns declare themselves nuclear free, and organized demonstrations. In June 1982, it turned out 30,000 people in Paris to protest the visit of Ronald Reagan. It also established close contacts with independent peace groups in Eastern Europe. Although France's antinuclear movement made little headway within the Catholic Church, it did far better among Protestant bodies and unions, including the French Democratic Federation of Labor. Unlike its counterparts in Northern Europe, the movement could not count on support from the Socialists, for France's new Socialist president, François Mitterrand, strongly backed the *force de frappe* and the deployment of NATO missiles. But two smaller parties on the Left opposed this stand, and many Socialist officials felt uncomfortable with it. The public, too, was antinuclear. Opinion surveys usually found backing for Euromissile deployment running at no more than 35 percent. Although polls revealed stronger support for French nuclear weapons, modernization of these weapons met with substantial opposition. The French preferred arms controls and, between 1982 and 1984, consistently favored them by two to one or more over maintaining a military balance with the Soviet Union.

Like its counterparts to the north, the Italian nuclear disarmament campaign mushroomed into a mass movement. In October 1981, responding to the Christian Democratic-led government's announcement of plans to deploy cruise missiles, a loose coalition of left-wing political parties, religious groups, unions, ecologists, feminists, pacifist groups, and youth organizations mobilized some 500,000 people for a protest demonstration in Rome. They demanded the rejection of the cruise missiles and the dismantling of the SS-20s as the first steps toward the demilitarization of Europe. Although activists had difficulty agreeing upon a unified policymaking body for the campaign, it continued to generate mass participation—including a crowd estimated at from 500,000 to a million people who, in October 1983, participated in an anti-missile demonstration in Rome. In Sicily, a fierce battle broke out over the proposed cruise missile site, in Comiso, where massive demonstrations erupted and two-thirds of Comiso's population signed a petition demanding the cancellation of the missile base plan. Women from Italy and abroad poured into Comiso and established peace camps, which were brutally assaulted by police and by the Mafia. Although the Catholic Church hierarchy and the Vatican discouraged antinuclear activism, a small number of Catholic prelates supported the antinuclear campaign, as did the tiny Protestant denominations, unions, and peace, feminist, and student groups. Political parties evaded nuclear issues, but public opinion was clear. Pluralities or majorities of Italians told pollsters that they unconditionally opposed cruise missile deployment, with opposition peaking at two-thirds of respondents in the spring of 1984. According to surveys conducted from 1981 to 1983, from 38 to 55 percent of Italians opposed the use of nuclear weapons under any circumstances.

Elsewhere in Southern Europe, the movement grew increasingly vibrant. In Greece, the Movement for National Independence, International Peace, and Disarmament—linked closely to PASOK, the Greek socialist party—emerged as the dominant force within the peace movement. It opposed Euromissile deployment, agitated for the closure of U.S. military bases in Greece, and championed the creation of a nuclear-free zone in the Balkans. The movement also could count on the support of public opinion, as illustrated not only by the socialists' smashing election victory in 1981, but by polls showing overwhelming opposition to deployment of cruise and Pershing II missiles and majority opposition to any use of nuclear weapons.

In Spain, recently freed from the grip of Franco's dictatorship, massive anti-military and antinuclear rallies swept the nation. The rising Socialist Workers Party played an important role in this agitation, and was rewarded with a dramatic election victory in 1982, bringing it to office for the first time since the 1930s. Meanwhile, the demonstrations continued, backed by peace collectives, Socialists, ecologists, and Pax Christi, and culminated in a rally of half a million people in Madrid in June 1984. By the mid-1980s, more than 350 Spanish villages, towns, and cities had proclaimed themselves nuclear-free zones. An October 1983 survey found that 55 percent of Spaniards favored unilateral nuclear disarmament by the West and that 61 percent opposed use of nuclear weapons under any circumstances.

Elsewhere, too, antinuclear agitation reached new heights. The Swiss disarmament movement underwent a dramatic surge, staging mass marches and demonstrations in Bern, Geneva, Basel, and Alsace. In Austria, the antinuclear campaign rapidly escalated, with mass protests and marches, culminating in October 1983, when, according to the *New York Times*, "some 100,000 demonstrators brought Vienna to a standstill." Here, as in neighboring Switzerland, the movement drew heavily upon Socialists, pacifists, women's and religious groups, and environmentalists. Meanwhile, Irish CND revived and grew rapidly, with some 40 local branches by early 1983. That year, this sprightly antinuclear organization organized a demonstration of 4,000 people in Dublin protesting Euromissile deployment. By the beginning of 1983, more than half of Ireland's population lived in cities and towns that had proclaimed themselves nuclear-free zones.

Opinion surveys during the early 1980s found that very substantial portions of the public in non-Communist Europe sympathized with antinuclear demonstrators, including 50 percent in France, 52 percent in Britain, 59 percent in Germany, 60 percent in Norway, 63 percent in Belgium, 79 percent in Italy and the Netherlands, and 82 percent in Finland.

The Revolt of the Doves: North America

Similarly, among Americans, Reagan's bellicose rhetoric rang like an alarm bell, setting off a vast antinuclear campaign. Determined to heighten popular understanding of nuclear dangers, Roger Molander, a former NSC staffer, put together Ground Zero Week in April 1982. In some 650 cities and towns, it drew more than a million people to "nuclear war awareness and education" events, ranging from street theater to lectures, from town meetings to tours of the area of devastation that would result from a nuclear attack. Other disarmament proponents adopted a more confrontational approach. Following the example of the Plowshares activists, religious pacifists conducted another seventeen nonviolent civil disobedience actions by 1985. Despite sentences that ranged up to eighteen years in prison, priests, nuns, teachers, students, anti-poverty workers, and lawyers entered nuclear weapons facilities, hammered and poured blood on MX missiles, Trident submarines, and other components of the U.S. nuclear weapons system, and often left behind "indictments" charging the U.S. government and corporations with crimes against international law and against God.

Women's groups, too, plunged into the nuclear disarmament campaign. The antinuclear efforts of WSP and the WILPF were reinforced by those of Women's Action for Nuclear Disarmament—a new organization, founded by Helen Caldicott, which by mid-1984 had affiliated groups in 30 states. Furthermore, following the example of activists at Greenham Common, American women established antinuclear peace camps. The best-known of these appeared at Seneca Falls, New York, a town that, in 1848, had hosted the nation's first women's rights conference but, in the early 1980s, served as the site of a U.S. army depot that shipped Pershing II missiles to West Germany. In July 1983, vowing to "create a women's community of resistance," thousands of activists set up a Women's Encampment for a Future of Peace and Justice not far from the depot. Thereafter, defying arrests, they organized numerous anti-missile rallies and waves of nonviolent civil disobedience at its gates.

Meanwhile, SANE grew into a very significant political entity—larger and more powerful than ever before. It denounced the Reagan administration's military buildup, condemned Euromissile deployment, and backed the Freeze campaign. Its most important venture, however, remained the struggle against the MX missile, now a formidable campaign in which it continued to play a central role. SANE's executive director, David Cortright, recalled that "the letters we would send to the Hill sometimes had as many as a hundred organizations signed on." Leaders of the House of Representatives worked closely with the anti-MX coalition, and on a number of occasions SANE dragged legislators from their sickbeds for key votes. These and other activities contributed to SANE's meteoric revival. Between 1981 and 1984, its membership grew by 800 percent.

Although dozens of disarmament groups developed among professionals, the one with the highest profile remained Physicians for Social Responsibility.

PSR held symposia on the medical consequences of nuclear war in virtually every major city in the United States, often drawing crowds in the thousands. Termed by PSR insiders "the bombing run," a symposium described in chilling detail what would happen to the host city in the event of a nuclear attack. In October 1982, moving beyond informational work, the PSR board of directors agreed to challenge national policies presupposing that nuclear war could be won or survived. Henceforth, PSR opposed civil defense planning, supported a Nuclear Freeze, advocated a comprehensive nuclear test ban, and rejected U.S. and Soviet development of first-strike weapons. Despite a nasty internal conflict that emerged when senior figures in the PSR hierarchy maneuvered Caldicott—the organization's best-known, most popular leader—out of the presidency, PSR continued to flourish. By 1985, it had ten times its membership of 1981, as well as 150 active chapters. Given the considerable prestige physicians enjoyed in American life, PSR had good access to community leaders, to the mass media, and to members of Congress.

None of these organizations, however, compared in size, popular mobilization, and impact to the Nuclear Weapons Freeze Campaign. Determined to capture the mainstream of American life, activists brought Freeze resolutions before religious bodies, professional associations, unions, town meetings, city councils, and state legislatures. These and other activities generated a massive outpouring of support. Voting on March 12, 1982, 159 of 180 Vermont town meetings backed a U.S.-U.S.S.R. nuclear weapons Freeze. On June 12, 1982, when a broad coalition of peace groups sponsored an antinuclear demonstration in New York City around the theme of "Freeze the Arms Race—Fund Human Needs," it turned into the largest political rally in American history, with nearly a million participants. But the most stunning display of antinuclear sentiment occurred that fall, when Freeze referenda appeared on the ballot in ten states, the District of Columbia, and 37 cities and counties around the nation. Over the intense opposition of the Reagan administration, the Freeze emerged victorious in nine out of ten states and in all but three localities. In this largest referendum on a single issue in U.S. history, covering about a third of the electorate, over 60 percent of the voters supported the Freeze. By November 1983, the Freeze had been endorsed by more than 370 city councils, 71 county councils, and by one or both houses of 23 state legislatures.

As the antinuclear campaign gathered momentum, major religious bodies placed their weight behind it. The National Council of Churches endorsed the Nuclear Freeze, with Bishop James Armstrong, its president, declaring that

"Jesus Christ stands in direct opposition to everything nuclear weapons represent." Although fundamentalist Protestant denominations generally stayed clear of the antinuclear movement or opposed it, the more liberal ones endorsed the Freeze and condemned nuclear war. Speaking for all branches of Judaism, the Synagogue Council of America called upon U.S. and Soviet leaders to "implement a bilateral mutual cessation of the production and deployment of nuclear weapons." The most important breakthrough, however, involved American Catholics, who constituted the largest religious denomination in the United States. In May 1983, the Conference of Catholic Bishops, by an overwhelming vote, adopted a pastoral letter, *The Challenge of Peace*, supporting a Nuclear Freeze, a rejection of nuclear war, and the ultimate abolition of all nuclear weapons.

Other mainstream organizations also lent their strength and credibility to the movement. Leading professional bodies—ranging from the American Psychiatric Association to the Association of American Geographers—endorsed the Freeze campaign, and many participated actively in the overall movement. Prodded by PSR, the American Medical Association called upon its state and local affiliates to educate physicians and the public about the medical consequences of nuclear war. Law school deans lobbied Congress on behalf of the Nuclear Freeze. Major unions, angered by the Reagan administration's antilabor policies and caught up in the antinuclear mood of the time, became Freeze supporters. The flood of union endorsements of the Freeze became so great that, in October 1983, the AFL-CIO executive council voted unanimously to add its own and to call for "radical reductions" in nuclear arsenals. Ultimately, 25 national unions joined the Freeze campaign.

Within a short time, the enormous momentum of the antinuclear campaign attracted the support of mainstream politicians. In early 1982, U.S. Representative Edward Markey and U.S. Senator Edward Kennedy introduced Freeze resolutions in both houses of Congress. Democratic congressional leaders jumped on board, although their Republican counterparts continued to insist that a U.S. nuclear buildup was imperative. After midterm congressional elections substantially strengthened the Democratic majority in the House of Representatives, a Freeze resolution—vigorously opposed by the Reagan administration—sailed through that body by a vote of 278 to 149. Despite the defeat of the resolution in the Republican-controlled Senate, Democrats made plans to reintroduce the measure, while leading candidates for the Democratic presidential nomination met with peace movement leaders and promised to back an array of nuclear disarmament measures. In 1984, the Freeze was adopted as an official part of the Democratic national platform, and the party's presidential nominee, Senator Walter Mondale, promised that, if elected, he would make it his top priority.

Despite the movement's newfound strength, it also faced serious difficulties. Within the mass communications media, it drew a chilly response. The *New York Times* pontificated: "Few knowledgeable Americans actually favor a freeze or think it can work." In November 1982, when American voters overwhelmingly endorsed Freeze referenda, CBS Evening News—the nation's highest-rated TV newscast—devoted only 20 seconds to this extraordinary event. Sometimes, the media were particularly unscrupulous, as when the *Wall Street Journal* portrayed the movement as pro-Soviet and *Reader's Digest* depicted it as part of a KGB plot. Although ABC planned to provide one of the first realistic television portrayals of nuclear war by screening a film, *The Day After*, the corporate and governmental backlash was so great that the film was censored and followed immediately on the air by top current and former US. government officials, who assured Americans that they had nothing to worry about.

Moreover, the Freeze stirred up furious resistance on the political Right. Denouncing "the freezeniks," Phyllis Schlafly contended that "moaning and groaning about the horrors of nuclear weapons . . . is evidence of juvenile immaturity." The Bomb, she insisted, was "a marvelous gift that was given to our country by a wise God." In May 1982, the Heritage Foundation distributed a "Backgrounder" on "Moscow and the Peace Offensive," urging a massive campaign to block the growth of the antinuclear movement. The Christian Right also rallied behind the pro-nuclear campaign. The Rev. Jerry Falwell, the nation's most popular evangelical preacher and a confidant of the President, used his weekly Sunday morning sermons, broadcast over 400 television stations, to lash out again and again at the antinuclear movement. In March 1983, he told listeners: "In the Kremlin, Andropov or somebody decides that we need 300,000 to march in Stockholm or Berlin or New York, and the robots stand up and start marching for a nuclear freeze," a measure that ensured "slavery for our children."

Whatever the movement's difficulties, however, it had become a powerful force. Membership and financial support for American disarmament groups soared, and by early 1985, SANE had over 100,000 members, PSR more than 30,000, and WAND some 25,000. In 1982 alone, private foundations contributed over $6 million to nuclear disarmament groups. Although the largest of the peace organizations, the Freeze, did not maintain a formal membership, by early 1985 it claimed about 1,400 local chapters with hundreds of thousands of activists. In an October 1983 study, Patrick Caddell, one of the nation's leading pollsters, called the Freeze campaign "the most significant citizens' movement of the last century. . . . In sheer numbers the freeze movement is awesome; there exists no comparable national cause or combination of causes . . . that can match . . . the legions that have been activated."

Furthermore, the movement could take heart at U.S. public opinion. A March 1982 poll indicated that Americans—by 50 to 31 percent—believed that the United States did not need more nuclear weapons. Indeed, polls throughout the early 1980s revealed that the Freeze drew the support of between 70 and 85 percent of the public. Asked their opinion of an international agreement to destroy all nuclear weapons, Americans backed it by 61 to 37 percent in March 1982 and 80 to 17 percent in March 1983. Above all, Americans did not want a nuclear war. Polled in May 1984, 74 percent of U.S. respondents agreed that "even relatively small nuclear weapons should never be used in a battlefield situation," and 79 percent said that there was "nothing on earth that could ever justify the all-out use of nuclear weapons."

To the north, in Canada, the nuclear disarmament campaign also made dramatic gains. A new organization, Operation Dismantle, placed a proposal on the ballot in cities and towns across Canada that supported a global referendum on nuclear disarmament, and in November 1982 the proposal received the support of 77 percent of the voters. Meanwhile, Project Ploughshares backed an idea that cut closer to home: the establishment of Canada as a nuclear-free zone. Begun in early 1981, the campaign drew widespread public support—including endorsements ranging from the National Farmers Union, to the United Church of Canada, to the New Democratic Party—and more than 75 cities and towns proclaimed themselves nuclear-free zones. The movement's popularity was evident in April 1983, when a nuclear disarmament march in Vancouver drew 65,000 participants, the largest single peace demonstration in Canadian history. Surveys found that, between 1962 and 1982, the percentage of Canadians believing that "the West should take all steps to defeat Communism, even if it means risking nuclear war," plummeted from 42 to 6 percent. In July 1982, a survey reported that 68 percent of the population favored worldwide nuclear abolition.

Canada's nuclear disarmament campaign drew upon constituencies similar to those in most other Western nations. Not only small pacifist churches, but the major religious denominations gave it their support. In an antinuclear appeal sent to the prime minister in December 1983, the leaders of the Canadian Council of Churches, the Canadian Conference of Catholic Bishops, the Anglican Church, the Presbyterian Church, the Lutheran Church, and the United Church declared that they opposed the deployment of cruise, Pershing II, and MX missiles, sought reductions in SS-20 missiles, supported a no first-use pledge and a nuclear freeze, and rejected Canadian testing of cruise missiles. In addition, important antinuclear groups formed among professionals, while labor unions rallied behind the campaign. Denouncing the nuclear arms race—"this global game of chicken"—the Canadian Labour Congress proclaimed its support for Operation Dismantle, the establishment of Canada as a nuclear-free zone, and the end of cruise missile testing. Women and young people, particularly, flocked to the campaign.

The Revolt of the Doves: Asia and the Pacific

Across the Pacific, in Japan, the movement was also at high tide. Faced with the approach of the 1982 U.N. Special Session on Disarmament, Gensuikyo and Gensuikin, the major *hibakusha* organizations, labor federations, women's and youth associations, religious groups, and eminent individuals established the Japanese National Liaison Committee for Nuclear and General Disarmament. This set the stage for the greatest burst of antinuclear activism in Japanese history. Record numbers of people turned out for antinuclear rallies: 200,000 people in Hiroshima in March 1982 and 400,000 in Tokyo that May. Nuclear disarmament petitions were presented to the United Nations by the Liaison Committee (with 29 million signatures), by religious groups (with 36.7 million), and by political parties (with 16 million). Although the movement made little headway with the governing Liberal Democratic Party, other parties were far more responsive, and about two hundred local governments proclaimed themselves nuclear free. Furthermore, 76 percent of the public supported Japan's "three non-nuclear principles," 86 percent wanted their government to promote abolition of nuclear weapons, and 58 percent opposed the use of nuclear weapons under any circumstances.

Australia, like its counterparts elsewhere, experienced a phenomenal growth of nuclear disarmament activism. Antinuclear professional organizations sprang up, and hundreds of small, local antinuclear organizations appeared. Religious groups backed the campaign, as did women's groups, which established peace camps outside U.S. military bases and, in one case, staged a non-violent invasion of a U.S. base and tore down its gates. Although the newly formed People for Nuclear Disarmament sought to coordinate activities at the state level and the Australian Coalition for Disarmament and Peace at the national one, the movement usually lacked central direction. Even so, the few united events illustrated its unprecedented popularity. On Palm Sunday 1982, an estimated 100,000 Australians took to the streets for antinuclear rallies in the nation's biggest cities. Growing year by year, the rallies drew 350,000 participants in 1985. For the most part, the movement focused on abolishing nuclear weapons, halting Australia's uranium mining and exports, removing foreign military bases from Australia's soil, and creating a nuclear-free Pacific. Surveys found that about half of Australians opposed uranium mining and exporting, as well as the visits of U.S. nuclear warships, that 72 percent thought the use of nuclear weapons could never be justified, and that 80 percent favored building a nuclear-free world.

In neighboring New Zealand, the movement attained even greater popularity. Older organizations like CND were reinvigorated, while hundreds of newer ones were formed, including a crop of professional groups. Union, church, and Maori organizations joined the antinuclear campaign. In May 1983, 25,000 women participated in an antinuclear rally in Auckland—the largest public gathering of women in New Zealand's history. Continuing their program of resistance, Peace Squadrons sought to prevent visiting U.S. nuclear warships from entering their nation's harbors. In June 1982, when a U.S. cruiser tried to enter Wellington, maritime workers and seamen closed the port for three days through work stoppages, and 15,000 other workers halted labor for two hours to hold protest meetings. In August 1983, 50,000 people turned out for an anti-warship protest in Auckland. Meanwhile, a Nuclear Free Zone Committee pressed to have local governments proclaim their jurisdictions nuclear free. As a result, by 1984, 65 percent of New Zealanders lived in nuclear-free zones.

The New Zealand struggle reached a critical point during 1984–85. With the governing National Party (the conservatives) barely able to sustain an effective parliamentary majority against antinuclear resolutions, the prime minister scheduled an election for July 1984. Assuming that a warships ban (and the necessary revision of the Australia-New Zealand-United States alliance) would be unpopular, the Nationalists made the Labour party's antinuclear policy the centerpiece of their campaign. In turn, Labour and two minor parties spoke out vigorously for a nuclear-free New Zealand. On election day, 63 percent of the voters cast their ballots for the three antinuclear parties, catapulting Labour into power. Taking office as prime minister, David Lange announced a four-part program. It included barring nuclear weapons from New Zealand, halting French nuclear testing in the Pacific, blocking nuclear waste dumping in that ocean, and establishing the South Pacific as a nuclear-free zone. When the U.S. government requested entry for a nuclear-capable destroyer, Lange announced in January 1985 that the warship was banned from his country. Although U.S. officials and the opposition Nationalists bitterly condemned this action, it proved enormously popular. Between 1978 and early 1984, polls found that opposition to allowing nuclear armed ships into New Zealand's ports rose from 32 to 57 percent. And once Lange defied the United States, opposition soared to 76 percent. New Zealand had become a nuclear-free nation—and was proud of it.

Protest was rising elsewhere in Asia, as well. In the Philippines, the building of a giant nuclear power plant inspired growing opposition, as did the U.S. military bases at Subic Bay and Clark Field, which housed nuclear-armed planes and warships. With the government's nominal lifting of martial law in 1981, representatives of church, labor, women's, student, and other groups organized the Nuclear Free Philippines Coalition, dedicated to halting construction of the power plant and closing down U.S. military bases. By early 1983, it claimed the support of 82 organizations. In South Korea, the presence of large numbers of U.S. nuclear weapons and the frightening promises of U.S. officials to employ them in a future war led to a growing public fear of nuclear disaster and protests by church groups. Furthermore, in India, a newly formed Committee for a Sane Nuclear Policy issued numerous public statements by prominent citizens warning against the activities of their nation's "nuclear bomb lobby" and pressed the government to reject nuclear weapons.

The antinuclear struggle reached a crescendo in the scattered island nations of the Pacific. Decades of western use of the region for thermonuclear explosions, nuclear missile tests, and nuclear warship ports, topped off by the latest great power nuclear confrontation, led to a surge of resistance among native peoples. In Fiji, church, union, and student organizations established the Fiji Anti-Nuclear Group to work for the creation of a nuclear-free Pacific. In Tahiti, thousands of people marched through the streets protesting French nuclear tests and demanding independence from France. On Kwajalein atoll, some 1,000 Marshall Islanders—reacting to a U.S. government plan to extend its military rights by fifty years—escaped their crowded squalor on Ebeye Island by staging "Operation Homecoming," an illegal occupation of eleven islands they had left years before to accommodate U.S. nuclear missile tests. In Palau, the U.S. government, stymied by that nation's antinuclear constitution, sponsored new referenda to overturn its antinuclear provision. When the third and fourth referenda proved unsuccessful, U.S. officials waged a $500,000 campaign to sway the nation's 7,000 voters in a fifth referendum. But the people of Palau stubbornly voted yet again to keep their islands nuclear free. Deeply resenting their mistreatment by the nuclear powers, delegates to the 1983 Nuclear Free Pacific conference renamed their organization the Nuclear Free and Independent Pacific movement. By 1985, it had 185 constituent organizations.

The Revolt of the Doves: Elsewhere

Only limited activism surfaced in areas of the Third World farther removed from the nuclear arms race and subject to political repression. In Africa, a small antinuclear group developed in Zimbabwe and public denunciations of nuclear weapons appeared on occasion in the press, but no mass movement emerged. In Turkey, the movement collapsed when the new military government arrested leaders of the TPA. The situation proved somewhat better for activists in Latin America, especially in countries that had freed themselves from the grip of military dictatorships. In August 1982, continued fears that the Brazilian government's nuclear power program was designed to produce nuclear weapons led to the first substantial antinuclear demonstration in Brazil, with a thousand participants. Similarly, in January 1984, a group of prominent Argentine intellectuals organized that country's Movement for Life and Peace, which assailed the threat of militarism to democracy and of nuclear weapons to survival. But these efforts remained relatively small-scale.

The movement made more impressive strides in Eastern Europe. Certainly, the antinuclear campaign faced major obstacles in this region. The Communist authorities, horrified by grassroots activism, did their best to stamp it out. Furthermore, much of the population had more immediate concerns than the nuclear arms race and, also, felt a deep cynicism about the propaganda-laden "peace" activities of Communist governments. Even so, East European nations were on the front lines of the Soviet-American confrontation and, as such, were prime targets for a nuclear war. Moreover, they housed a restless intellectual-professional class, the cutting edge of antinuclear activism in so many countries. Finally, East Europeans were well aware of the antinuclear campaign in Western Europe, and some, at least, found it inspirational and a source of outside assistance. Taken together, these factors had an explosive potential.

East Germany proved one of the more inflammatory locales. Although the official leadership of the Evangelical Church remained cautious about challenging the regime, some activists proved quite daring. East Berlin Pastor Rainer Eppelmann dispatched a letter to Communist Party boss Erich Honecker, complaining of his country's militarism and warning of "the imminent annihilation of Europe." Together with Robert Havemann, a prominent East German scientist and Marxist, Eppelmann launched the Berlin Appeal, a public plea for a Europe free of nuclear weapons, beginning with the demilitarization and denuclearization of all of Germany. Although the regime resisted ferociously, activists circulated the Berlin Appeal in factories, schools, and churches, drawing 2,000 signatures. In February 1982, when the Evangelical Church sponsored a Peace Forum in Dresden, it attracted some 5,000 people, mostly young and flaunting "Swords into Plowshares" emblems. Inspired by the forum, thousands of participants poured into the streets to stage an illegal peace demonstration. Meanwhile, East German writers spoke out against the nuclear arms race and young people leafleted and adorned walls with antinuclear slogans.

In Czechoslovakia, the antinuclear rebellion drew the support of Charter 77, a group of intellectuals and workers attempting to monitor their government's compliance with the human rights provisions of the 1975 Helsinki Accords. In late 1983, when the press announced that Soviet nuclear missiles were slated for deployment in Czechoslovakia, Charter 77 activists joined workers, students, church groups and others in leafleting, circulating anti-missile petitions, and organizing protests. Although Charter 77 participants initially viewed Western disarmament activists with suspicion, eventually they recognized that both constituencies shared a common objective. Dispatching an open letter to END's 1984 convention, the Chartists proclaimed that "your hopes are our hopes," and called for efforts to "unite all those opposed to the nuclear madness in a mighty democratic coalition."

In neighboring Hungary, a group of Budapest University students organized their own independent organization, the Peace Group for Dialogue, in September 1982. Subsequently, they met with Thompson and other END leaders, produced their own publication, made contacts with East German activists, and organized affiliates in other parts of the nation. Determined not to be marginalized, hundreds of Dialogue members plunged into an official peace march, bearing their own banners aloft with suspiciously independent slogans, including: "All nuclear weapons out of Europe!" In addition, followers of Father Bulanyi formed a Committee for Human Dignity, which announced its approval of the Western peace movement and its opposition to nuclear weapons in both Cold War blocs.

In spite of a December 1981 declaration of martial law in Poland, the movement emerged there, as well. The Workers Defense Committee (KOR)—an organization composed mostly of students and intellectuals—championed nuclear disarmament and cooperation with the Western antinuclear campaign. Two of its leaders, Adam Michnik and Jacek Kuron, were particularly prominent in this regard. Moreover, one of the nation's leading underground organizations, the Committee for Social Resistance (KOS), which maintained a network of cells in factories and schools that overlapped with those of the powerful Solidarity movement, felt particularly close to Western nuclear disarmament activism. Addressing the West European movement in a May 1983 open letter, KOS maintained that "like you, we say NO to the arms race" and, consequently, anticipate "future joint activities in defense of peace."

The antinuclear campaign also gathered significant strength within the Soviet Union. Forming a group called Independent Initiative, countercultural youth staged anti-military demonstrations in Moscow. Prominent writers, drawing upon their prestige, assailed nuclear weapons on both sides of the "iron curtain." In open letters, Latvians, Estonians, and Lithuanians urged the inclusion of the Baltic republics in a nuclear-free zone. The best-known of the new, independent peace organizations, however, was launched in June 1982, when a group of young people held a press conference in Moscow. Announcing the formation of the Moscow Group to Establish Trust Between the USSR and the USA, they then proceeded to hold peace meetings and seminars, petition for peace, organize a photo exhibit on the nuclear disarmament campaign, and welcome hundreds of visitors from the Western antinuclear campaign, with whom they exchanged ideas. Despite the constant harassment of the Moscow Trust Group by the authorities, people in other parts of the Soviet Union felt inspired, and formed their own local Trust Groups.

The movement gathered such momentum that it began to permeate official Soviet ranks. In early 1983, Evgenii Velikhov, a top physicist, established the Committee of Soviet Scientists for Peace and Against the Nuclear

Threat (CSS). Although the Kremlin planned to use the new organization for propaganda purposes, the CSS developed along quite different lines, for it brought together a group of intellectuals acquainted with Western antinuclear scientists and opposed to the nuclear arms race. Thus, the CSS churned out studies reporting that nuclear war would be suicidal and, therefore, that Soviet policy should facilitate a drastic reduction of nuclear arsenals. At the same time, liberal intellectuals—often working in academic, think tank, or advisory posts—began to promote antinuclear ideas. Criticizing Cold War confrontation, Georgi Arbatov sought to advance a program of "common security." As liberal ideas gained ground, Arbatov and Velikhov became foreign and defense policy advisors to a young Soviet party reformer, Mikhail Gorbachev. Speaking to the British parliament in December 1984, Gorbachev argued that "the nuclear age inevitably dictates new political thinking," and "preventing a nuclear war is the most burning issue for all people on earth."

International Dimensions

With protest against nuclear weapons sweeping around the world, the antinuclear campaign became the largest, most dynamic movement of modern times. IPPNW grew rapidly and, by 1985, had affiliates in 41 nations, representing 135,000 physicians. Similarly, lawyers, teachers, engineers, journalists, psychologists, and scientists created international disarmament organizations. Women were particularly inclined to join the antinuclear movement, as evident from the emergence of Women for Peace groups and from the appearance of women's peace camps—usually modeled on the one at Greenham Common—in the United States, West Germany, Canada, Italy, the Netherlands, and elsewhere. The Catholic Pax Christi International took a sharply antinuclear stand, while the General Assembly of the World Council of Churches resolved, in 1983, that "the churches must unequivocally declare that the production and deployment as well as the use of nuclear weapons are a crime against humanity." In addition, the pacifist internationals, the Socialist International (with particular enthusiasm in northern Europe), and environmental groups mobilized their global networks behind nuclear disarmament. Greenpeace challenged nuclear weapons testing, uranium mining, and nuclear waste dumping in the Pacific, publicized efforts to create nuclear-free zones, and—to highlight Soviet nuclear practices—staged dramatic, nonviolent invasions of Soviet territory.

The international dimensions of the movement were exemplified by the European Nuclear Disarmament campaign. Thousands of antinuclear activists—mostly from Western Europe, but also from Eastern Europe, the United States, and Australia—flocked to its annual conventions. At these exciting, turbulent events, demonstrations broke out not only in the streets—for example, in May 1983, when Green Party participants, led by Petra Kelly, demonstrated in East Berlin in support of the Swords into Plowshares movement—but inside the convention halls as well. Arguing that hawkish behavior in one Cold War camp fed hawkish behavior in the other, END contended that dovish practices could reverse the process. Therefore, it was vital for movement activists to support unilateral initiatives in each Cold War bloc. Along the way, END's Western activists fostered "détente from below," building close relationships with the Hungarian Dialogue group, Charter 77, the Moscow Trust Group, and other intrepid antinuclear forces in the East. Although hostile East European governments blocked most East European activists from attending END conventions, the Easterners regularly sent messages to these gatherings, affirming their solidarity. In turn, END dispatched delegations to meet with embattled Eastern activists in their homelands, publicly defended them against their governments, and insisted upon the indivisibility of peace and freedom.

The situation was quite the reverse within the Communist-led WPC. Continuing its partisan approach, the WPC contrasted "the principled stands" for peace "taken by the Soviet Union" with "the U.S. drive towards a global apocalypse." Naturally, when Ronald Reagan publicly charged that the European antinuclear campaign was controlled by the WPC, Romesh Chandra, the WPC's general secretary, was thrilled. But as Rob Prince, the organization's U.S. secretary, recalled, other WPC officials were "looking at each other and saying: 'If only it were true!' But it wasn't." The WPC was "totally isolated from the major peace movements—from any of the groups. . . . We were not part of it." Enraged by the WPC's marginal status, Yuri Zhukov of the Soviet Peace Committee sent a letter in December 1982 to 1,500 disarmament groups and individuals in Western Europe and the United States, charging that END was trying to "split the anti-war movement." END's talk of "equal responsibility" for the arms race was merely an attempt "to conceal and justify an aggressive militarist policy of the USA and NATO." But these and other WPC-directed attacks upon the nonaligned peace movement could not reverse the WPC's growing isolation and decrepitude.

By contrast, the nonaligned campaign had emerged as a global movement of unprecedented size and power. Backed by mainstream groups and public opinion, it represented a remarkable success in grassroots political mobilization. In the fall of 1983, it turned out more than five million antinuclear demonstrators on the streets of Europe and North America. Addressing hundreds of thousands of protesters in Hyde Park, E. P. Thompson called it "one of the greatest concerted international manifestations of the political will of ordinary people ever known in world history." Could such an outpouring of popular protest be resisted indefinitely? "At some point," he predicted, "the old structures of militarism must buckle . . . and . . . peace must and will break through."

Confronting the Movement

The vast upsurge of citizen activism posed significant problems for the officials of nuclear nations. Queried years later about the Freeze campaign, Robert McFarlane, President Reagan's National Security Advisor, recalled: "We took it as a serious movement that could undermine congressional support for the [nuclear] modernization program, and potentially . . . a serious partisan political threat that could affect the election in '84." According to White House communications director David Gergen, "there was a widespread view in the administration that the Freeze was a dagger pointed at the heart of the administration's defense program." Another of Reagan's National Security Advisors, Richard Allen, recalled that "we did a careful study" of European antinuclear protest and the conclusions were deeply disturbing. "We were swimming upstream," Allen remarked. "The President was swimming upstream, against the current."

Confronted with these difficulties, the Reagan administration began what McFarlane called "a huge effort" to discredit the Freeze campaign. Tapped to head the venture in March 1982, McFarlane dispatched government officials around the country, including Haig, Weinberger, and a host of others. Reagan began publicly denouncing the Freeze as opening the United States to "nuclear blackmail." That fall, as the Freeze seemed increasingly likely to emerge victorious at the polls and in Congress, the President began charging that the Freeze was not inspired by "sincere, honest people who want peace, but by some who want the weakening of America and so are manipulating honest people." On November 11, he told a press conference that "foreign agents" had helped "instigate" the Freeze campaign. Somewhat later, he charged that "the originating organization" for the Freeze was the WPC, and that it had been proposed initially by Leonid Brezhnev—contentions so patently absurd that the mass media quickly dropped them from consideration and the administration scuttled them in embarrassment.

Nevertheless, the Reagan administration continued its rollback campaign. During the drafting of the Catholic bishops' peace pastoral, Weinberger and other top officials lobbied fiercely to alter it, going so far as to intervene with the Pope. Reagan himself made numerous telephone calls to Republican members of the House of Representatives, pleading with them to oppose the Freeze resolution. Forging a close alliance on nuclear issues with evangelical Protestant groups, the President met with and mobilized the Rev. Jerry Falwell and, in March 1983, delivered his "evil empire" address to the annual convention of the National Association of Evangelicals. On this occasion, Reagan denounced the Freeze as "a very dangerous fraud," leading to "the betrayal of our past, the squandering of our freedom."

Undermining the nuclear disarmament campaign abroad was at least as important. According to Robert Gates, then the CIA's deputy director, that U.S. intelligence agency "devoted tremendous effort" to investigating Soviet participation in the West European campaign against the Euromissiles, only to conclude that "the Soviets did not 'control' the peace movement . . . and that much of the protest was genuine." Even so, the Reagan administration devoted enormous resources to countering it. This included secret financial subsidies to pro-nuclear groups in Western Europe, as well as a major campaign of "public diplomacy." Through a special program of worldwide broadcasts, massive distribution of propaganda literature, and speeches by government leaders, the U.S. Information Agency—in the words of its director—sought "to mitigate the impact of anti-nuclear movements on publics and governments abroad." Reagan, too, at the request of West European officials, traveled to Europe to deliver speeches justifying the U.S. nuclear buildup. He revealed years later that his trips to Britain and West Germany in mid-1982 were designed "to demonstrate that I wasn't flirting with doomsday." Conflating (as he often did) the European with the American movement, Reagan explained: "Several of our European allies . . . had their hands full with the nuclear freeze movement, which was being fired up by demagogues depicting me as a shoot-from-the-hip cowboy aching to pull out my nuclear six-shooter."

Certainly the administration dramatically altered its rhetoric. In April 1982, upon the advice of aides who urged him to counter the antinuclear campaign, Reagan began declaring publicly that "a nuclear war cannot be won and must never be fought." He added, on that occasion: "To those who protest against nuclear war, I can only say: 'I'm with you.'" In line with this approach, Vice President Bush proclaimed the following January, in West Berlin, that NATO was "the real peace movement." Addressing the Japanese Diet in November 1983, Reagan sounded remarkably like a leader of the antinuclear campaign, reiterating his declaration that nuclear war should never be fought and concluding: "Our dream is to see the day when nuclear weapons will be banished from the face of the earth."

The Soviet government felt just as dismayed by independent nuclear disarmament activism. Although Soviet officials hoped that the movement would blunt the nuclear ambitions of the Reagan administration, they were appalled by its criticism of their own policies. As a result, even before NATO's deployment of the Euromissiles, they authorized the vitriolic propaganda campaign against END by the Soviet Peace Committee and the WPC, declared END leaders *persona non grata* in Eastern Europe, and supported the crackdown upon independent peace groups in the Eastern bloc. In the Soviet Union, as two Moscow Trust Group representatives reported, Trust Group activists underwent "detentions, arrests, threats, interrogations, 'talks' with the police, 'talks' with their bosses, searches, job dismissals, 24-hour shadowing . . . beatings, incarceration in psychiatric hospitals, provocations, automobile accidents, imprisonment, official warnings and charges, vilification in the press, house arrest," and "psychological terrorizing." Even IPPNW, an officially approved movement, faced serious difficulties thanks to opposition from senior party, military, and Foreign Ministry officials. Lown recalled that only Chazov's position as the personal doctor for top Kremlin potentates spared him from being "thrown to the wolves." Of all the peace groups, only the WPC drew the Soviet government's staunch support. Thompson concluded: "If the Geneva negotiations had been, not about cruise, Pershing and SS-20s, but about how to rub out the non-aligned peace movements . . . then the negotiators would have come out smiling and arm-in-arm."

Thompson's analysis certainly applied to the junior partners of the Western bloc. The French military rammed and impounded antinuclear vessels, West German officials threatened to punish teachers and students participating in anti-missile demonstrations, and the Turkish government sentenced eighteen leaders of the Turkish Peace Association to eight years of hard labor (plus 32 years of probation) and another five of them to five years in prison. In Britain, Prime Minister Thatcher, worried that CND had become "dangerously strong," assigned Defense Minister Michael Heseltine to coordinate a campaign to destroy it. CND's "purpose," proclaimed Heseltine, was "the advancement of the Socialist and Communist cause," including "the cause of the Soviet Union at the expense of the free societies of the West." Heseltine also announced to a stunned parliament that the Greenham Common women who ventured near the missile bunkers would be shot. Subsequently, the British government deployed thousands of soldiers and police to destroy the Greenham Common peace camp and to force nonviolent activists from the peace camp at Molesworth. In addition, the British government placed intelligence agents within CND headquarters, installed taps on CND's telephones, and opened files on thousands of CND activists. It also began pumping money into front groups that supported nuclear weapons programs and harassed CND. Defending Conservative weapons policies, Thatcher announced: "We are the true peace movement."

East European Communist regimes followed much the same pattern. In June 1983, when independent Czech peace activists demonstrated in Prague, they were assaulted by club-wielding policemen. That July, the Czech government sentenced Charter 77 spokesman Ladislav Lis—the foremost figure responsible for initiating a dialogue between his organization and Western antinuclear groups—to fourteen months' imprisonment and three years under house arrest. In Hungary, members of the independent Dialogue group were issued with warnings by their universities and employers. During July 1983, when Western peace activists arrived to participate in a peace camp organized by Dialogue, the authorities arrested twenty Dialogue members and deported most of the Western visitors. In East Germany, Pastor Eppelmann was arrested and, though released, routinely told to visit the security police for interrogation. Other activists, not as well known, received harsher treatment. Beginning in late 1982, the East German authorities cracked down on the thriving antinuclear community in Jena, arresting some activists and expelling others. In October 1983, the secret police detained hundreds of independent activists to block a planned "die-in" in East Berlin. Nor were East German officials any fonder of West European activists. In May 1983, when leaders of West Germany's Green Party entered East Berlin for an antinuclear demonstration, the police attacked them, tore up their banners, and deported them to the West. Condemning the independent nuclear disarmament movement, East Germany's defense minister declared: "Our soldiers bear their arms for peace, and the better command they have over their weapons, the better peace is assured."

Public Policy Shifts

A more significant indication of the movement's growing strength was its impact on public policy. Besieged by protest, NATO nations retreated from their plan to install cruise and Pershing II missiles. Reagan recalled that "some European leaders, feeling the heat, began expressing doubts about NATO's 1979 decision to deploy the new weapons." Weinberger, too, lamented the erosion of the alliance position. "As more and more demonstrations were held," he complained, "more and more defense ministers . . . urged . . . that more be done on the 'second [disarmament] track.'" This meant, first, pressing the Reagan administration to resume INF negotiations. And, later, when this was accomplished, urging the U.S. government to soften its negotiating position. To head off a political crisis, the Dutch and Belgian governments followed yet another tack—delaying missile deployment. "We simply cannot get a yes from the Dutch parliament," the Dutch foreign minister told Shultz. "Therefore, the strategy is to avoid a no and also to avoid losing both the cabinet and the missiles." Although Reagan reversed Carter's neutron bomb decision by producing the weapon for deployment in Western Europe, no government dared to accept it; thus, ultimately, production was halted. Even the hard-line Thatcher government pressed Washington to soften its missile negotiating position and scrapped civil defense exercises.

Public policy changed even more dramatically in the Pacific. In New Zealand, the new Labour government of Prime Minister Lange not only defied Washington by barring nuclear-armed warships, but became a leading proponent of a comprehensive test ban treaty and of a South Pacific nuclear weapons-free zone. In Australia, after the victory of the Labor Party in the 1983 elections, the new prime minister, Bob Hawke, appointed Australia's first minister for disarmament, instructed Australia's representative at the United Nations to support a Nuclear Freeze resolution, withdrew his earlier offer to have Australia test the MX missile, and made his country into a key force in world efforts to secure a comprehensive test ban treaty. Moreover, New Zealand and Australia joined the other eleven nations of the South Pacific in negotiating the Treaty of Rarotonga, designed to prohibit the testing, production, acquisition, or stationing of nuclear weapons in the region. Although nations lacking antinuclear movements, such as China and Pakistan, made progress on their nuclear weapons programs during these years, the Japanese government—beset by waves of protest—proved more cautious, and Japan's "three non-nuclear principles" remained officially enshrined.

Some policy changes occurred even within the Soviet Union. In June 1982, at the U.N. Special Session on Disarmament, the Soviet government pledged never to be the first nation to use nuclear weapons. Meanwhile, Soviet officials issued new arms control proposals, some of them clearly modeled on the Freeze. Also, the Soviet government took action against the militarization of space. In March 1983, Velikhov and another CSS leader, Roald Sagdeev, returned from meetings in Washington with American scientists anxious to ban the testing of anti-satellite (ASAT) weapons. Lobbying Soviet officials, they convinced them of the virtues of this measure. Consequently, that August, the Kremlin announced a unilateral Soviet moratorium on ASAT weapons tests. In addition, the CSS successfully fended off pressures to copy Reagan's SDI plan by insisting that the real alternatives to the U.S. initiative were arms controls and, if necessary, inexpensive countermeasures.

Nevertheless, the fundamentals of Soviet policy did not change. Through all its discussions of Euromissile deployment, the Kremlin insisted that it should retain hundreds of its SS-20s while, at the same time, NATO should forgo installation of all cruise and Pershing II missiles. Taking office as Soviet party secretary in November 1982, Andropov declared that peace could "be upheld only by relying on the invincible might of the Soviet armed forces." After withdrawing from nuclear arms control talks in December 1983, the Soviet government resumed SS-20 missile deployment, placed SS-23 nuclear missiles in East Germany and Czechoslovakia, and moved Soviet nuclear submarines closer to the coasts of the United States. In late 1984, as Kremlin officials prepared their next five-year plan, they incorporated into it a 45 percent rise in military spending.

For the time being, the Soviet government remained unable to depart from its military approach to national security. Returning from a briefing on U.S. and Soviet military measures, Anatoly Chernyaev, a reform-minded staffer employed by the Central Committee, was deeply dismayed. "We're preparing mankind's suicide," he noted in his diary. "It's insane!" But Chernyaev and other critics of the missile buildup made no headway against party conservatives, convinced by the hawkish rhetoric and policies of the Reagan administration that the U.S. government was preparing for the nuclear annihilation of their nation. So terrified did the party leadership become that, in November 1983, during Able Archer—a NATO military training exercise—top Soviet officials concluded that a U.S. nuclear attack was getting under way. Consequently, Soviet command staffs hastily reviewed their strike missions and Soviet nuclear weapons were readied for action. According to a top KGB official, although "the world did not quite reach the edge of the nuclear abyss," it came "frighteningly close."

Thus, as had happened frequently during the Cold War, the hawks on one side bolstered the hawks on the other. "The hostility and militarism of American policy did nothing but create further obstacles on the road to reform," recalled Arbatov. "It posed additional threats to democratic change, justifying both the harsh regime within the country and new Soviet efforts to increase the size of our own military-industrial complex." Dobrynin, too, observed that Reagan's nuclear buildup "strengthened those in the Politburo, the Central Committee, and the security apparatus who had been pressing for a mirror image of Reagan's own policy." In this fashion, the West's nuclear buildup did not encourage peace but, rather, Soviet militarism.

Greater dissent from military orthodoxy emerged elsewhere in Eastern Europe. The East German government, particularly, was dismayed by great power plans to install nuclear missiles in both halves of Germany, thus making its country a target in a future nuclear war and provoking dissent among its citizens. Therefore, it pressed the Soviet government for a "first step" toward resolving the missile impasse and emphasized the importance of continued arms control negotiations. The Czech government, too, challenged the official Soviet position by urging that INF negotiations be continued. In December 1983, shortly after the Soviet government announced a plan for the installation of the new nuclear missiles in East Germany and Czechoslovakia, a meeting of Warsaw Pact defense ministers failed to endorse it. The following March, the Hungarian party publication championed "a semi-independent role" for Soviet bloc nations, "especially . . . when the two major protagonists . . . argued themselves into deadlock."

Outside the military alliance systems, official pressures for nuclear disarmament grew particularly intense. Speaking at the U.N. conference on disarmament in June 1983, Maj Britt Theorin, who handled disarmament affairs for Sweden's social democratic government, presented a plan for a comprehensive test ban treaty. In the following months, Sweden called for a halt to nuclear testing, a Nuclear Freeze, a Nordic nuclear-free zone, and for no first use of nuclear weapons. Lauding the millions of Europeans who had demonstrated against the cruise, Pershing, and SS-20 missiles, Theorin condemned the militarist "dogma" that had "brought the world to the verge of destruction." On May 22, 1984, the heads of state of six nations—Raul Alfonsin of Argentina, Miguel de la Madrid of Mexico, Julius Nyerere of Tanzania, Olof Palme of Sweden, Indira Gandhi of India, and Andreas Papandreou of Greece—formally launched the Five Continent Peace Initiative, calling on the nuclear states "to halt all testing, production, and deployment of nuclear weapons and their delivery systems, to be immediately followed by substantial reductions in nuclear forces." Meeting again in January 1985, they reiterated their 1984 appeal, after which Alfonsin, Nyerere, and Palme flew on to Athens, where Papandreou hosted a meeting of national officials and representatives of the Nuclear Freeze campaign, IPPNW, Greenpeace, CND, and other disarmament groups. "The battle of the streets," insisted the Greek prime minister, "has become the battle of the governments." With nations around the world calling for action, the U.N. General Assembly passed a variety of Nuclear Freeze resolutions by overwhelming margins.

In these circumstances, the Reagan administration's hard line on nuclear policy began to soften. Responding to fierce pressure from its allies, the U.S. government agreed to resume INF negotiations at an early date. But what was there to negotiate? After all, the administration wanted to place the new nuclear missiles in Western Europe. The ingenious answer was provided by the Penatagon's Richard Perle: support the zero option—the removal of all Soviet intermediate range nuclear missiles from Europe and Asia in exchange for a U.S. promise not to deploy the cruise and Pershing II missiles. This seemed certain to trigger Soviet rejection and, thus, provide the justification for U.S. missile deployment. As Thomas Graham of ACDA recalled, the zero option "was adopted because it was believed the Soviets would never accept it." The "real reason that we proposed it" was "to make sure that those negotiations did not succeed, and the deployments would go ahead." Furthermore, at this time of antinuclear upheaval, the zero option had great propaganda value. The "zero option sprang out of the realities of nuclear politics," Reagan admitted. "Now that . . . the American-made INF missiles were being scheduled for shipment to Europe, some European leaders were having doubts about the policy. . . . Thousands of Europeans were taking to the streets and protesting." Or, as McFarlane put it: "The zero option was key to dealing with that popular, street-level criticism."

But this maneuver failed to resolve the hot political controversy. When, as expected, the Russians rejected the zero option, the anti-missile protests heightened and America's NATO allies pressed Washington to drop its non-negotiable

stance. "We have a political problem in Europe," the chief U.S. missile negotiator, Paul Nitze, reported to the State Department. "A considerable percentage of
European public opinion is not satisfied with our zero-zero position." Consequently, he advised "exploring an equitable solution above zero." In December
1982, the new secretary of state, George Shultz, adopted this position, telling
Reagan that, as he recalled, "our allies could not withstand the heat of political
pressure against the installation of our INF missiles unless we . . . were advanc-
ing reasonable and stabilizing positions at the negotiating table." Following up
in January, Shultz told Reagan that the U.S. government must "win the battle
for public opinion by making it clear that it is the USSR, not the U.S., that is
impeding progress toward agreements." Thus, over the furious objections of
administration hawks, Reagan announced a compromise position, the "interim
solution," in March 1983.

Nevertheless, the missile controversy continued to escalate, and Reagan
grew increasingly rattled. In October 1983, as millions of demonstrators poured
into the streets, Reagan told his startled secretary of state: "If things get hotter
and hotter and arms control remains an issue, maybe I should go see Andropov
and propose eliminating all nuclear weapons." Although Shultz retorted that
this would be a terrible idea, he agreed that "we could not leave matters as
they stood." In the ensuing weeks, Reagan—convinced that, "from a propaganda point of view, we were on the defensive"—gravitated toward delivering
a major "peace" address, emphasizing the building of a nuclear-free world. His
only compromise was to postpone its delivery to January, a month when his
wife's astrologer expected more auspicious results. Consequently, on January
16, 1984, Reagan delivered a remarkably dovish speech. In it, he maintained
that the United States and the Soviet Union had "common interests and the
foremost among them is to avoid war and reduce the level of arms." Indeed,
he added, "my dream is to see the day when nuclear weapons will be banished
from the face of the earth." Although it is possible to view this address as no
more that the latest stage in the administration's rhetorical makeover, it was, in
fact, sincere and meant to be taken seriously by an anxious public and by Soviet
leaders.

Additional olive branches followed. With the approach of the 1984 presidential election, Reagan's pollster, Richard Wirthlin, warned him that his hawkish
foreign policy had become his most serious political liability. Accordingly, to
burnish Reagan's peaceful image, the administration sought to schedule a summit conference with Soviet leaders. When this could not be arranged, Reagan

held a White House meeting with Soviet Foreign Minister Gromyko amid great fanfare. Even after the President's re-election, Shultz warned him that Congress "will not support key weapons systems without meaningful negotiations," and "allied support will be problematic if arms control efforts unravel." To cope with these continuing difficulties, Reagan reined in administration hard-liners, pressed for the resumption of serious INF negotiations, and persisted with his talk of a nuclear-free world. Addressing a meeting of top U.S. national security officials in early 1985, Shultz told them that, however improbable it seemed, nuclear abolition had become Reagan's position, and urged them to "think more about the theme of elimination of nuclear weapons."

External pressures also modified the administration's strategic nuclear weapons policy. Although Reagan came to office championing a major strategic nuclear buildup, Congress refused to go along with it. Symptomatically, with peace groups leading the charge against the MX missile program, this centerpiece of the administration's plan received a very tough time in Congress. By 1985, it barely survived, with only 50 missiles authorized—25 percent of the original request. Meanwhile, the Soviet government turned out substantial numbers of new ICBMs. Shultz lamented: "Given the political climate in the United States, we could not keep pace in modernization, production, and deployment of these deadly weapons." Falling behind, of course, meant that limiting Soviet strategic nuclear weapons through an arms control agreement became essential. Furthermore, to attain even a truncated U.S. nuclear buildup, the administration was forced to undertake serious nuclear arms control negotiations. As McFarlane put it, in order to build strategic weapons, "you had to have appropriations, and to get them you needed political support, and that meant you had to have an arms control policy worthy of the name."

These political difficulties provided the backdrop for the emergence of Reagan's Strategic Defense Initiative (SDI). From the outset, this missile defense system was perceived by opponents as a hawkish, isolationist, and risky program. Dubbed "Star Wars" by its many critics, it certainly seemed thoroughly compatible with the traditional national drive toward military supremacy. But, from the administration's standpoint, SDI would also counter the flourishing Nuclear Freeze movement. Indeed, in his March 22, 1983, television address announcing the program, Reagan devoted a full paragraph to assailing the Freeze and contrasting it with SDI, which he claimed would render nuclear weapons "impotent and obsolete." Furthermore, as McFarlane acknowledged, the stalemate on MX efforts in Congress "brought us back, in 1983, to exploring a defensive possibility" in the Soviet-American nuclear arms race. Boxed in by nuclear critics, Reagan had adopted what he considered a popular alternative to both a nuclear buildup *and* the Freeze. Even so, SDI proved less popular than the President hoped. Spurred on by furious opposition to it on the part of peace groups, Congress provided relatively small appropriations for SDI—less than half the amount Reagan requested.

The Reaganites also reversed course on the SALT II treaty. Although the administration's top ranks were filled with people who, during the Carter years, had denounced SALT II as the ultimate betrayal of U.S. national security, this treaty, though unratified, remained sacrosanct after they were in power. Recognizing the symbolic significance of this nuclear arms control agreement to the public, to Congress, and to U.S. allies, the administration continued to abide by its limits—even though it believed that the Russians did not.

Perhaps most significant, the administration shied away from using nuclear weapons. Indeed, given the Reaganites' earlier loose talk about waging and winning a nuclear war, it is striking that they not only dropped such rhetoric, but did not come close to employing nuclear weapons in combat. Although the administration sponsored wars in Central America, the Caribbean, and the Near and Middle East, it does not appear to have factored nuclear weapons into its battle plans. Adelman, who succeeded Rostow as director of ACDA, claimed that he "never heard anyone broach the topic of using nuclear weapons. Ever. In any setting, in any way."

In this fashion, then, the Reagan administration gradually modified its nuclear hard line. These changes in U.S. policy did not occur because of Soviet compromise or capitulation. Indeed, the Reaganites perceived no alteration in Soviet policy during these years. Rather, U.S. policy shifted because of pressure generated by the antinuclear campaign and effectively transmitted by Congress, U.S. allies, and other nations. Peace was beginning to break out in the U.S. Cold War camp. But it was not based on "strength"—unless, of course, one means the strength of the antinuclear movement.

8   Disarmament Triumphant, 1985–1992

Under enormous pressure from the antinuclear movement, a dramatic turn-about in public policy occurred from 1985 to 1992. Before that, of course, there had been important shifts in government programs. But the rise to power of Mikhail Gorbachev in 1985 provided the final ingredient necessary for major advances in nuclear disarmament. Deeply influenced by the antinuclear movement, Gorbachev waged an unremitting campaign against nuclear weapons and nuclear war that, eventually, convinced Reagan to join him in breaking with the Old Thinking and routing their conservative foes. Moreover, even after the departure of Reagan and Gorbachev from power, the collapse of Communist regimes, and the end of the Cold War, the movement constituted a significant force in world politics—strong enough to foster new and important disarmament measures.

The Movement Continues, 1985–1988

Although the antinuclear movement in non-Communist Europe declined somewhat after the great upsurge of the early 1980s, it remained a formidable force in the latter part of the decade. In late 1988, the Dutch IKV still maintained 300 active local branches, while the British CND had 70,000 national members and perhaps another 130,000 local members. Demonstrations, though smaller than a few years before, remained impressive. As late as 1987, antinuclear rallies in Britain and West Germany each drew 100,000 participants. Moreover, other kinds of activism were widespread. In Norway, No to Nuclear Weapons published two newspapers, protested the presence of nuclear weapons in local waters and harbors, assailed plans for SDI, and continued to promote a Nordic nuclear-free zone. The antinuclear campaign could also count on strong support from mainstream political parties, especially those of a social democratic persuasion. In Britain, the Labour Party gamely carried its support of Britain's unilateral nuclear disarmament into the nationwide elections of 1987. And public opinion was clear. A 1986 poll found that the signing of a U.S.-Soviet arms control treaty was rated as either important or very important by 72 percent of the population in Portugal, 73 percent in Belgium, 82 percent in Denmark and Ireland, 84 percent in Britain, 85 percent in France, 89 percent in Norway, 90 percent in the Netherlands, and 92 percent in Finland.

Although the movement lost some momentum in the United States, there, too, it remained a major political force. By 1986, SANE had grown to 150,000 members and the Freeze (which did not have formal membership) to an estimated 1,824 chapters. The following year, when they merged to form SANE/Freeze, it constituted the largest peace organization in U.S. history. Other groups with an antinuclear emphasis were also growing, including Greenpeace (with 650,000 members) and PSR (with 37,000 members and another 32,000 contributors). Drawing upon this strength, leading movement organizations turned increasingly to promoting a nuclear test ban. With a Freeze blocked by conservative resistance in the Senate and the White House, a test ban seemed more politically feasible and, at the same time, an effective way to halt the development of nuclear weapons. In November 1985, when antinuclear activists attended the Geneva summit conference, they brought with them test ban petitions signed by 1.2 million Americans. Meanwhile, large demonstrations began at U.S. nuclear test sites, with thousands arrested each year for nonviolent civil disobedience. In addition, the movement sharply attacked SDI, exposed the dangers of local nuclear weapons production facilities, campaigned for the creation of nuclear-free zones, and protested the persecution of dissidents in Eastern Europe. Major religious bodies and unions continued to speak out against nuclear weapons, as did the Democrats. Polls showed strong public support for cutting U.S. military spending and for securing nuclear disarmament measures. In 1988, 85 percent of Americans favored a test ban treaty and 71 percent favored working with the Soviet Union to eliminate most nuclear weapons.

The movement also retained a powerful presence in Asia and the Pacific. In Australia, the 1986 Palm Sunday antinuclear rallies drew 250,000 people. Two years later, Australian protest flotillas blockaded the arrival of foreign nuclear warships. In Melbourne, the seamen's union boycotted the warships and even the prostitutes went on strike, announcing that the nuclear behemoths could "take their money, ships, bombs, and diseases and go home." In New Zealand, the renamed national movement, Peace Movement Aotearoa, served as the umbrella organization for about 300 peace groups working on projects that ranged from halting French nuclear testing to getting their town or city councils to declare their jurisdictions nuclear-free. The hottest issue, however, remained the Labour government's ban on nuclear warships. In August 1987, the warship ban provided the central issue in nationwide elections, which Labour won handily—its first re-election victory since 1938. At the same time, antinuclear protest raged in Palau, Fiji, the Marshall Islands, and India. Despite a police state atmosphere in South Korea, antinuclear ferment grew among student, women's, and religious groups. In 1986, the National Council of Churches called for the removal of all nuclear weapons from the Korean peninsula or aimed in its direction. Protest even emerged in China. Enraged by the government's nuclear weapons tests at Lop Nur, in Xinjiang province, the local Uighur people staged antinuclear demonstrations in Beijing and other Chinese cities. Polls throughout Asia and the Pacific found strong support for nuclear disarmament.

Activism also persisted in Latin America, Africa, and the Middle East, albeit on a much smaller scale. Brazilian scientists took an important antinuclear step in 1987, when more than 60,000 of them signed a statement calling for a ban on the "construction, storage, and transport of nuclear weapons" in their country. In Africa, branches of the tiny Zimbabwe Organization for Nuclear Education sponsored small marches, a seminar on "South Africa and the Bomb," and a "die-in" to commemorate the Hiroshima bombing. Moreover, the revelation by Mordechai Vanunu, an Israeli nuclear technician, of his country's secret nuclear weapons project helped to make nuclear weapons a political issue in the Middle East. In early 1987, activists organized an Israeli Committee for the Prevention of Nuclear War, and it sponsored a large public meeting in Tel Aviv on the theme of nuclear war in the region.

In the Soviet Union, the movement was thriving. Against all odds, the Trust Groups continued to grow, even producing a monthly magazine and staging an exhibit of antimilitarist art in Red Square. Not at all pleased by this behavior, Soviet authorities responded with harassment, arrests, and imprisonment. But publicity and protests by Western activists helped shield Trust Group members, sometimes securing their release from detention. Moreover, as Soviet authorities, in line with Gorbachev's reform leadership, loosened their authoritarian reins, thousands of small, independent citizens' organizations appeared. Composed primarily of young people, they turned eagerly to discussing a broad range of popular issues, from democratization to disarmament. In June 1987, pacifists from cities around the country staged a demonstration in Moscow. Meanwhile, the CSS, working closely with the FAS and the Natural Resources

Defense Council, played a key role in emerging efforts to secure a nuclear test ban and, in February 1987, organized an International Scientists' Forum on Drastic Reductions and Final Elimination of Nuclear Weapons. Sakharov, freed in 1987 after seven years of house arrest, plunged into meetings with Western nuclear disarmament leaders and established a working relationship with the leaders of the CSS. Addressing the February 1987 forum, the Soviet physicist argued that human rights and disarmament were inseparable.

The movement also showed remarkable vigor in Czechoslovakia. Spontaneous protests against Soviet deployment of nuclear missiles, amplified by the work of Charter 77, continued well into 1985. Moreover, Charter 77 and the Jazz Section of the Prague Musicians Union maintained close contacts with END. But the "Lennonists" proved the most rambunctious. Ever since the murder of John Lennon in December 1980, young Czechs had made yearly pilgrimages to an island in the center of Prague, adorning its "Lennon Wall" with peace symbols and slogans. During the 1985 anniversary celebration, when police ordered the mourners to disperse, about 600 of them broke loose and staged an unauthorized peace march through downtown Prague. Along the way, they chanted subversive slogans, including "No missiles are peaceful!" "Flowers, not weapons!" and "Down with the Red bourgeoisie!" Despite subsequent interrogations and other harassment by the police, their peace and antinuclear actions continued in subsequent years. Finally, in April 1988, Czech activists organized the country's first unofficial peace group since the creation of the Communist regime: the Independent Peace Association. Together with Charter 77, it invited 35 activists representing independent peace and human rights groups from East and West to an international peace seminar in Prague.

Protest against nuclear weapons swept through other East European nations, as well. Although government intimidations, arrests, and expulsions of leading activists undermined the movement in East Germany, the nuclear disarmament struggle there continued, led by a new organization: the Initiative for Peace and Human Rights. In Yugoslavia, some official student and Communist youth organizations, as well as citizens' initiatives, inspired by the West European campaign, began independent antinuclear activities. From Poland, the Committee for Social Resistance sent greetings to the July 1985 END convention, as did Solidarity's Lech Walesa, who declared that he was "watching your work toward peace" with "great interest and approval." Poland acquired a full-fledged peace organization that same year, when young people established Freedom and Peace. Although focused primarily on securing the rights of conscientious objectors, the new organization also assailed "the threat of nuclear war." Defying arrests and other harassment by the authorities, Freedom and Peace activists staged public meetings, marches, sit-ins, and petition campaigns that spread to more than twenty cities. In 1987, despite fierce resistance from the government, Freedom and Peace organized an international peace conference in Warsaw that mixed together representatives from Solidarity, the Green Party of West Germany, END, CODENE, Charter 77, Pax Christi of the Netherlands, the War Resisters League, and other groups.

Naturally, in this atmosphere of ferment, international organizations flourished. In late 1987, Greenpeace claimed three million members in seventeen nations, and was growing by 40 percent a year. Seeking a solid institutional framework, many nonaligned nuclear disarmament groups began to affiliate with the venerable International Peace Bureau.

But the nuclear disarmament international most in the limelight was IPPNW. In October 1985, the announcement that this global physicians' movement had been awarded the Nobel Peace Prize sent its reputation soaring. Although conservative political parties and portions of the Western communications media launched a blistering attack on IPPNW and the Nobel committee, charging that Soviet doctors were Kremlin stooges and that Western doctors were useful idiots, a dramatic rebuttal occurred at the Nobel ceremonies that December. While Lown and Chazov were doing their best to respond to hostile questions at a crowded press conference, a Soviet journalist tumbled to the floor, felled by a cardiac arrest. Lown, Chazov, and other anxious doctors raced to the stricken man's side, taking turns pounding on his chest and giving him mouth-to-mouth resuscitation. Ultimately, they saved his life. When the press conference resumed, Lown, shaken but quick-witted, said: "What you have just seen is a parable of our movement. When a crisis comes, when life is in danger, Soviet and American physicians cooperate." And "the big issue confronting humankind today is sudden nuclear death." This dramatic incident rallied support for IPPNW. By late 1988, it had grown to a federation of physicians' groups in 61 countries, with over 200,000 members.

Indeed, one of the most extraordinary characteristics of the antinuclear campaign was how genuinely international it had become. At peace camps, activists from diverse lands met, lived with each other, and swapped ideas. "Détente from below" flourished. Across the barriers separating East and West, activists appealed for nuclear disarmament and political freedom. Greenpeace blockaded nuclear ships off Canada's west coast, fostered civil disobedience in New

Zealand and Australia, and used radiation symbols to "tag" Soviet warships off
the coasts of Denmark and Tunisia. The Socialist International issued eloquent
appeals for disarmament, while Parliamentarians for Global Action, comprised
of legislators from 35 countries, began a campaign to secure a comprehensive
test ban treaty. END drew mass turnouts (including growing numbers of independent activists from the East) to its annual meetings, with 42 countries represented in 1987. According to Mary Kaldor, at the 1988 convention "there was
a real sense of progress . . . in East-West relations." E. P. Thompson "said that at
last . . . we have put peace and freedom together," whereupon Solidarity's Jacek
Kuron "hugged him, to huge applause."

Government Resistance Begins to Collapse, 1985–1986

With the movement flourishing, government resistance began to collapse—
particularly after March 1985, when young Mikhail Gorbachev became Soviet
party secretary. Scrapping the anti-American assumptions, diatribes, and policies of his predecessors, Gorbachev brought with him a host of party reformers
and their ideas on the imperatives of peace and nuclear disarmament. The Soviet Union would embark upon "a course of peace," he told a meeting of overseas social democratic leaders, for "the peace-loving public of the entire world
calls for an end to the dangerous arms race." Addressing the French parliament
that October, Gorbachev declared that, in an age of nuclear weapons, "Europe's
security cannot be ensured by military means." Faced with the "self-destruction
of the human race," national leaders had no choice but to "burn the black book
of nuclear alchemy" and make the twenty-first century one "of life without fear
of universal death."

This was what Gorbachev meant by the "new thinking," the phrase he first
used publicly in December 1984 and trumpeted thereafter. Speaking with Mitterrand in 1986, he insisted that "the nuclear era requires new thinking from everybody. We all depend on each other. . . . We have no alternative other than to
learn to live in the real world." Gorbachev made the same point in *Perestroika*,
a book he took great pains writing later that year. "The arms race, just like nuclear war, is unwinnable," he insisted. "All of us face the need to learn to live at
peace in this world, to work out a new mode of thinking." And "the backbone
of the new way of thinking is the recognition of the priority of human values,
or, to be more precise, of humankind's survival."

The movement flavor of Gorbachev's rhetoric reflected the fact that, either directly or filtered through his reformist advisors, Gorbachev imbibed the key ideas of the "new thinking" from the antinuclear campaign. As the first Soviet leader since Lenin to have a university education and as a frequent traveler to Western countries, Gorbachev was a far better informed, more intellectually sophisticated individual than his predecessors. In 1955, he was studying at Moscow State University when the Russell-Einstein Appeal—calling for "a new way of thinking" if humanity were to survive—burst onto the world scene. Gorbachev's use of the term "new thinking" to reflect this same concept clearly drew its inspiration from this movement landmark. Indeed, his choice for Soviet foreign secretary, his friend and party reformer Eduard Shevardnadze, recalled that "the Russell-Einstein Manifesto offered politicians the key to the most troublesome and complex riddles of the age." According to Arbatov, who became another of Gorbachev's top foreign policy advisors, major ideas for the new thinking "originated . . . with people such as Albert Einstein, Bertrand Russell, and Olof Palme."

Other components of the antinuclear campaign also affected the new Soviet leadership. Antinuclear scientists from abroad had a particularly strong impact upon Gorbachev, and some of his key foreign policy advisors—including Arbatov, Yakovlev, and Velikhov—had attended Pugwash meetings. After Gorbachev became party secretary, numerous antinuclear intellectuals from abroad met with him and, according to Chernyaev, their "influence on him was huge." Gorbachev himself declared: "The new thinking took into account and absorbed the conclusions and demands of the nonaligned movement, of the public and the scientific community, of the movements of physicians, scientists and ecologists, and of various antiwar organizations."

Upon taking office, Gorbachev began putting the "new thinking" into practice. In April 1985, he announced a reduction in the number of SS-20 missiles in Europe. Responding to the pleas of antinuclear scientists, he refused to order the development of a Soviet SDI program. That July, he proclaimed a moratorium on Soviet nuclear testing and implored the U.S. government to join it while the two powers negotiated a comprehensive test ban treaty. On January 15, 1986, Gorbachev announced a Soviet blueprint for a nuclear-free world. Consisting of three stages, it would eliminate all nuclear weapons around the globe by the year 2000. According to the Soviet leader, this was a sincere effort "dictated by a sense of responsibility about preventing nuclear war and preserving peace." The Soviet stance "accorded with world public opinion" and was "a response" to the Five Continent Peace Initiative.

In fact, though, the proposal had a complex origin. Worried that Gorbachev and his reformist advisors were getting ready to offer serious concessions on the Euromissiles, Soviet military officials sought to head them off by championing nuclear abolition, which they thought would be a good combination of a non-negotiable proposal and useful propaganda—rather like the Reagan administration's zero option. But Gorbachev outmaneuvered them, using the military's stance to legitimize the proposal and, then, to make it official party policy.

Meanwhile, Gorbachev developed an alliance with the nonaligned antinuclear movement. At the Geneva summit conference of November 1985, he met with leaders of SANE and the Nuclear Freeze campaign, assuring them of his belief that government leaders "should heed the voice of all the people of the world. We not only heed that voice," he insisted, "we make our policy from that voice." On a variety of occasions, he spoke directly with other leading antinuclear campaigners, corresponded with them, and encouraged their visits to the Soviet Union. Pushing a proposal through the Politburo to free Sakharov from house arrest, Gorbachev personally phoned the dissident physicist and invited him to return to Moscow. When conservatives on the Central Committee objected, Gorbachev retorted in irritation: "The public should participate in the struggle for peace." This courtship of activists, however, did not extend to the WPC and its affiliates. As the leaders of these groups were usually party conservatives, rather than proponents of the "new thinking," Gorbachev marginalized them—leaving them out of his conferences, his speeches, his writings, and his considerations.

Not all government officials, of course, were as fond of the nonaligned campaign. To head off anticipated protest activities against French nuclear testing in the Pacific, the French government had its agents blow up the Greenpeace flagship, the *Rainbow Warrior*, killing a Greenpeace photographer in the process. In Czechoslovakia, the government prosecuted leading activists in the Independent Peace Association, Charter 77, and the Jazz Section on charges of "incitement." In Britain, the Thatcher government and its allies used the parliamentary elections of 1987 to launch another campaign of defamation against nuclear critics, claiming that they favored "surrender" and foreign occupation. In East Germany, the authorities arrested independent peace, human rights, and ecology activists on charges of "treasonable activity." Even in the United States, where the Reagan administration had begun a shift toward arms control and disarmament, the government continued to regard antinuclear groups with animosity. Repeatedly, White House officials rebuffed requests by delegations from antinuclear groups to meet with Reagan. During a "Children's Summit," organized by antinuclear activists in December 1987, the children offered armfuls of long-stemmed roses to representatives of each superpower. At the Soviet embassy, officials invited them in for cookies and hot chocolate; at the White House, guards turned the children away and dumped their roses in the trash.

Nevertheless, the "nuclear allergy" was spreading. The new Treaty of Rarotonga, adopted in August 1985 by the thirteen members of the South Pacific Forum, established the South Pacific as a nuclear-free zone. Scuttling arrangements for the testing and development of India's nuclear weapons, Indian Prime Minister Rajiv Gandhi offered his nation's "Action Plan for Ushering in a Nuclear-Weapon-Free and Non-Violent World Order." In the Philippines, the government of Corazon Aquino—strongly influenced by growing antinuclear sentiment—adopted a constitution stating that the nation would henceforth be nuclear-free.

Antinuclear policies also advanced within the NATO alliance. In September 1985, the Canadian government announced that it would abstain from government-to-government cooperation in connection with SDI. In April 1988, the Danish parliament passed a resolution requiring foreign warships to proclaim that they were nuclear-free before being allowed to enter Danish ports. The Spanish government, vowing to keep Spain free of nuclear weapons, insisted successfully upon the withdrawal of nuclear-equipped fighter planes from a U.S. military base near Madrid. In Greece, the government rejected a U.S. proposal for the installation of new nuclear weapons and pledged the ultimate withdrawal of all such weapons from its soil.

But major progress in disarmament continued to hinge on the U.S.-Soviet relationship and, initially, Reagan seemed incapable of responding positively to the dramatic changes in the Soviet Union. Deeply suspicious of Communists, he did not think, as he wrote in his memoirs, "that Mikhail Gorbachev was going to be a *different* sort of Soviet leader." Thus, when Gorbachev—in response to proposals by antinuclear organizations—began the Soviet moratorium on nuclear testing, and then extended it, and the U.S. House of Representatives passed a resolution calling on the Reagan administration to reopen test ban negotiations, the administration gave these actions a very chilly response. Discouraged by Washington's rebuff, Gorbachev asked Lown and Chazov: "What is the value of our engaging in unilateral activity when the Americans are not going to honor it?" Even so, noting that "we cannot disregard the huge wave of support that our steps have brought from so many sections of the world community," Gorbachev persisted with the Soviet moratorium on nuclear testing well into 1987.

Despite his failure to respond to the testing moratorium, Reagan—sensitive to the spirit of the time—remained anxious to display some progress toward nuclear disarmament, and accordingly pressed for a summit conference with Gorbachev. Eventually, the meeting was scheduled for November 1985, at Geneva. By this point, Reagan was 74 years old, nearing the end of his career, and with little to show for his years of bitter confrontation with the Soviet Union. Now, it seemed, as he met for the first time with a top Soviet leader, he finally had a chance to put his mark on history. As McFarlane recalled, Reagan badly wanted the summit: "He couldn't wait. . . . He was eager." According to the National Security Advisor, the President had come to see himself as a heroic figure, taking the lead in rescuing humanity from the threat of nuclear weapons and nuclear war. His wife, Nancy, encouraged this vision and also pressed for progress at the conference. According to Michael Deaver, a top White House aide: "She felt strongly that it was not only in the interest of world peace but the correct move politically."

Despite these good intentions, the Geneva summit met with only modest success. In line with his soaring hopes, Reagan assured Gorbachev that "we can create history and do some things that the world will remember in a positive way." Even so, the President's fervent anti-Communism led him to give lectures to Gorbachev on "the long history of Soviet aggression." He also launched into a passionate defense of SDI as "a way to end the world's nightmare about nuclear weapons." For his part, Gorbachev viewed Reagan as "a political 'dinosaur'"—one "so loaded with stereotypes that it was difficult for him to accept reason"—and considered SDI as facilitating a U.S. nuclear first strike capability. Even so, the two national leaders were eager to show some results from the conference. Consequently, they announced an agreement on the desirability of nuclear cutbacks and adopted a joint communiqué repeating Reagan's now-famous antinuclear statement: "A nuclear war cannot be won and must never be fought." According to Jack Matlock, the U.S. ambassador to the Soviet Union, Reagan—under fire for warmongering—was "eager to put his commitment to peace on the record."

Nor was this the end of the issue. As the demand for nuclear disarmament heightened and as Gorbachev issued his January 1986 call for a nuclear-free world, most U.S. officials were horrified. According to Shultz, Perle told him that "the worst thing in the world would be to eliminate nuclear weapons." Shultz considered the idea "utopian." Nevertheless, the secretary of state warned a group of U.S. officials that Reagan "thinks it's a hell of a good idea. And it's a political hot button." Meanwhile, Gorbachev attempted to open up the stalled negotiating process by proposing another conference—this one in Reykjavik, Iceland, in October 1986. Although some of Reagan's advisors opposed holding another summit, Reagan wanted one, at least in part because he assumed it would give the Republicans a political boost in the midterm congressional elections. Furthermore, according to Donald Regan, the White House Chief of Staff: "The President had been speaking out vigorously on disarmament ever since Geneva, and to temporize when he had been offered the chance to negotiate could have incalculable consequences in terms of world opinion."

Although the two leaders came closer to meeting their goals at Reykjavik than at Geneva, they once again fell short of an agreement. For days, the political climate swept them forward. Appealing to Gorbachev, the President told him: "Our people would cheer if we got rid of the missiles." In turn, Gorbachev insisted that Reagan was "just one step away from going down in history as the 'peacemaker President.'" They even spoke breezily, if vaguely, about eliminating all nuclear weapons. Although the experts were aghast, recalled Shultz, the two national leaders "felt what people wanted in a profound way." Nevertheless, Gorbachev, viewing SDI as a threat to Soviet national security, demanded that research on it be confined to the laboratory. By contrast, Reagan, viewing SDI as a guarantor against nuclear attack, rejected any curbs on its development. As both men dug in around this issue, the discussion grew heated and, ultimately, both left the conference in anger, without coming to any agreement on nuclear disarmament.

Over the Top, 1986–1988

Even so, the momentum toward an agreement had become overwhelming. Although upper level U.S. and British national security officials were dismayed by how close the United States and the Soviet Union had come to eliminating their nuclear arsenals, the public responded with intense frustration to the failure of the great powers to make progress along these lines. Nancy Reagan recalled ruefully, that her husband "would have received a great deal of praise for reaching a dramatic agreement with Gorbachev, and as I expected, he took a lot of heat for not signing it." Furthermore, after the Iran-Contra scandal erupted in November 1986, the President's political standing plummeted, reaching a low point in March 1987. Moreover, thanks to victories by Democrats in the November 1986 elections, they had retaken the Senate, giving them control of both houses of Congress. Within the inner circle of the administration, it became clear that the best way to reverse the political slide was through a disarmament agreement. The CIA's Robert Gates recalled that a "major effect of Iran-Contra on U.S.-Soviet relations was to convince Reagan, his wife, and his closest White House advisers that the terrible stain of the scandal could only be removed, or at least diminished, by the President becoming a peacemaker, by his achievement of a historic breakthrough with the Soviet Union."

Popular sentiment abroad pointed in the same direction. Confronted by Gorbachev's dramatic nuclear disarmament proposals, the U.S. government's overseas image was sinking fast, much to the dismay of U.S. officials. According to a panicky USIA report, in the aftermath of the Reykjavik summit most of the public in the large West European countries saw the Soviet Union as making a greater effort than the United States to achieve a nuclear arms control agreement. By May 1987, Gorbachev outpolled Reagan on arms controls by 72 to 9 percent in West Germany, 63 to 13 percent in Britain, and 45 to 16 percent in France. The USIA noted that, in February 1987, the British public had more confidence in Soviet than in U.S. leadership.

In fact, it was Gorbachev who cut through the remaining obstacles to a disarmament agreement. At Reykjavik, the Soviet leader had included a treaty for removal of all the Euromissiles (the zero option) as part of the Soviet negotiating package. Thus, when Reagan insisted upon retaining the right to proceed with SDI, no agreement was possible. But, on February 28, 1987, Gorbachev suddenly announced Soviet willingness to separate the INF issue from the issue of SDI. This decision reflected the influence upon Gorbachev of Western antinuclear scientists, who argued that, with an arms control agreement signed, SDI might never be built. Also, Sakharov assured Gorbachev that, if it were built, the Soviet Union could always take countermeasures. Moreover, public pressures for nuclear disarmament played an important role in this key Soviet decision. At a Politburo meeting shortly before his announcement, Gorbachev summarized the gathering's consensus by remarking that "untying the package on the medium-range missiles" would "be our response to the state of public opinion in the world."

With a Euromissile agreement no longer weighted down by SDI, the two nations made rapid progress toward an INF treaty during the following months.

The real opposition now began coming from conservative West European officials—particularly in Britain and West Germany—uneasy about the emergence
of a non-nuclear Europe. They had supported the elimination of intermediate
range nuclear weapons for propaganda reasons, and now, to their dismay, it was
about to become a reality. But, as Adelman recalled, the "trump card was always
that the zero option was *our* proposal, NATO's proposal. All of our elected leaders had been touting it for six years. . . . We had to take yes for an answer."

Elsewhere, too, conservatives found themselves in a similar bind. In the
Soviet Union, the main threat to Gorbachev's disarmament policy came from
party conservatives and, in fact, numerous military-industrial leaders privately
despised the emerging INF treaty. But they were constrained from opposing
it thanks to their earlier support for the idea of a nuclear-free world. In the
United States, as Shultz recalled, "the Republican right in Congress and some
important former officials" began to line up against the prospective treaty. But
"if the United States reversed its stand now on our willingness to eliminate INF
missiles, after maintaining this position throughout the volatile predeployment
period, such a reversal would be political dynamite."

Ultimately, then, Gorbachev's offer could not be refused. In December 1987,
the Soviet leader met with Reagan in Washington for the signing of the INF
treaty—the first to eliminate an entire class of nuclear weapons. Both men
were upbeat about the event, especially Gorbachev, who was clearly in his element. Vice President Bush recalled that, while driving through the city streets
in Gorbachev's heavily armored car, surrounded by enthusiastic crowds, he
remarked casually to the Soviet leader that "it's too bad you can't stop . . . because I think you'd find warm greetings from the American people." Suddenly
Gorbachev ordered the motorcade to a screeching halt, and the beaming Soviet
leader plunged into the crowds, surrounded by apprehensive security agents
and surging mobs of Washingtonians, screaming with delight. Addressing the
assemblage, Gorbachev told it—as his interpreter recalled—that "the people already understood that our countries should be friends and now the politicians
seemed to understand that too." The crowd "roared back its approval."

As the Washington summit unfolded, the President received his expected
political boost, but Gorbachev was clearly the man of the hour. "'Gorby-mania'
. . . seized the capital," Gates recalled. "Senior officers of government, members
of Congress, top media stars, and celebrities of every stripe fell all over themselves to get close to Gorbachev . . . to see this unique man who was . . . changing so much at home and around the world. In my two decades in Washington,

I had never seen anything like it." At the treaty-signing ceremony, both men gave brief addresses. In line with his hopes, Reagan called the INF agreement "history-making." Gorbachev declared: "Urging us on is the will of hundreds of millions of people.... We ... must build a safer and more democratic world, free from the trappings and the psychology of militarism." Returning to the Soviet Union, Gorbachev told the Politburo: "The world was waiting for that, the world demanded that."

For die-hard conservatives in the United States, the INF treaty was the Great Betrayal. Denouncing it as "appeasement," comparable to Neville Chamberlain's Munich agreement with Adolf Hitler, the Conservative Caucus called upon Americans to oppose Senate ratification. Leading Republicans, including Kissinger, Nixon, and Kirkpatrick, launched attacks upon it. Robert Dole, the Senate Republican leader, declared that "I don't trust Gorbachev," and accused Reagan of "stuffing this treaty down the throats of our allies." In March 1988, during hearings before the Senate Foreign Relations Committee, Senator Jesse Helms, the ranking Republican, led off by accusing the administration of "confusion, misstatements and ... misrepresentation" in its testimony. Bristling with anger, Shultz engaged in a heated exchange with Helms, from which he was rescued by the Democrats. "The real opposition," Shultz lamented, "was all from the GOP side." In this context, Reagan's support for the treaty was crucial, for he carried with him enough Republicans so that, when their numbers were added to the solid ranks of the Democrats, it had the votes necessary for ratification.

The signing of the treaty also dismayed conservatives in other nations. In Britain, conservatives denounced it as a nuclear Munich, while in West Germany they insisted that it decoupled their nation from the United States and subjected the Federal Republic to increased risk of nuclear attack by the Soviet Union. Ironically, within the Soviet Union, as Gorbachev recalled, their counterparts began "claiming that the agreement had undermined the Soviet Union's security and upset the balance of weaponry between the superpowers." Retired Soviet military officers, particularly, bombarded government ministries with statements contending that the treaty was an act of unilateral disarmament.

By contrast, nuclear disarmament activists were absolutely delighted with the INF treaty, for which they claimed considerable credit. Pointing to END's long and vigorous campaign to rid Europe of cruise, Pershing II, and SS-20 missiles, Mary Kaldor declared that "the real responsibility for the agreement belongs to the peace movement." In Britain, CND leaders gathered outside the American and Soviet embassies, cracking open bottles of champagne and celebrating. Meanwhile, in the United States, as SANE/Freeze's newsletter reported, "peace activists publicly toasted the movement's role in bringing about the treaty," and treaty celebrations were held "in almost every major city in the country." In the nation's capital, disarmament groups sponsored a rally and "Bridge to Peace," at which Margaret Papandreou, wife of the Greek prime minister, compared the INF treaty to a baby produced by the "strangest marriage in history," that of Reagan and Gorbachev. "The baby will be baptized by the peace movement because we, after all, arranged the marriage," she told the crowd of thousands, which linked arms to form a human bridge from the Soviet embassy to the White House.

With the agreement on the INF treaty, the character of Soviet-American relations changed significantly. Just as the antinuclear scientists had predicted, the Democratic Congress responded to the disarmament accord by slashing Reagan's budget request for SDI and mandating that SDI testing remain within the limits of the ABM treaty. Gorbachev, particularly, was energized by the Soviet-American agreement. Back in Moscow, he dramatically reined in the military, challenging their pet weapons projects. Meeting with Shultz and National Security Advisor Colin Powell in April 1988, Gorbachev told them, as Powell recalled, that "he was going to change the USSR in ways we never imagined. He was saying in effect, that he was ending the Cold War." Looking directly at Powell, he remarked, with a twinkle in his eye: "What are you going to do now that you've lost your best enemy?" Actually, thanks to growing resistance by conservatives and military officials, negotiations for a strategic arms agreement went much more slowly than either Gorbachev or Reagan would have liked. Even so, they made some progress on this front, as well.

The atmosphere grew even warmer as 1988 progressed. In May, Reagan journeyed to Moscow for yet another meeting with Gorbachev. As the two former enemies strolled pleasantly through Red Square, Gorbachev took a small child from a woman's arms and, cradling him in the crook of his own arm, said: "Shake hands with Grandfather Reagan." Addressing a knot of people that had gathered, Reagan said: "We decided to talk to each other instead of about each other. It's working just fine." When they returned to the Kremlin grounds, a reporter questioned the American President about the "evil empire" he had denounced five years before. "I was talking about another time, another era," he replied. Later that year, Gorbachev acted to implement ideas of "reasonable sufficiency" and "non-provocative defense" in Soviet military doctrine, laying plans for major, unilateral cutbacks in the Soviet armed forces. These were announced on December 7, 1988, in a remarkable address Gorbachev delivered at the United Nations. It had become "obvious," he said, "that the use or threat of force no longer can . . . be an instrument of foreign policy." In their place, the world needed the establishment of a strong international security system, under the direction of a revitalized United Nations, as well as a new spirit of Soviet-American cooperation. He called for a "joint effort to put an end to an era of wars, confrontation, and regional conflicts, to aggressions against nature, to the terror of hunger and poverty. . . . This is our common goal and we can only reach it together."

The Responsibility for the Breakthrough

In retrospect, it is clear that both Reagan and Gorbachev played important roles in bringing about the INF nuclear disarmament agreement that opened the floodgates for other antinuclear measures and for an end of the Cold War. As Powell observed, Reagan "had the vision and flexibility, lacking in many knee-jerk Cold Warriors, to recognize that Gorbachev was a new man in a new age offering new opportunities for peace." Indeed, Reagan eagerly grasped at the chance for securing nuclear disarmament agreements, thereby—in Adelman's words—"giving the kiss of life to the very process he had once deplored." But Gorbachev deserves the lion's share of the credit for this turnabout in Soviet-American relations, for he was the more dynamic actor, overcoming Reagan's virulent anti-Communism and effectively playing upon his newfound desire to lead the way toward a nuclear-free world. As Chernyaev later wrote: "If not for Gorbachev's persistence, his dogged determination to prove to all that nuclear weapons were an absolute evil and unacceptable foundation for world politics, the process would not have started and we would not have had the subsequent historical reversal in the arms race."

Yet the bulk of the credit for the new course—or, as Gorbachev liked to call it, the "new thinking"—lay with the nuclear disarmament campaign and the tidal wave of antinuclear sentiment that it generated. So powerful was the antinuclear pressure that it began transforming Reagan's approach to nuclear weapons even *before* the advent of Gorbachev, thus setting the stage for their later agreements. Once Gorbachev—a movement convert—appeared on the international scene, the nuclear disarmament campaign became irresistible.

A Declining But Persistent Movement, 1989–1993

Nuclear disarmament agreements, the collapse of East European Communist regimes, and, above all, the end of the Cold War—though welcomed by the nuclear disarmament movement—created serious problems for it, as well. After the "Reagan-Gorbachev love-in," lamented William Sloane Coffin, Jr., the first president of SANE/Freeze, public concern about nuclear weapons dwindled. Even many activists, exhausted by their long struggle, breathed a sigh of relief and began to relax a little. A cartoon on the cover of the Italian Peace Association's magazine joked: "I'm taking a nap for peace." Furthermore, many activists who persisted found the issues somewhat different than those of the past. The end of the Cold War *did* lessen nuclear dangers, just as it opened the door to bloody ethnic and national conflicts, especially in Eastern Europe, and conventional wars, as in the Persian Gulf.

The results were hard to miss. In Canada, Project Ploughshares dropped from 47 to 35 local groups. In Britain, CND lost members and financial resources, as well as the support of the Labour Party. In France, CODENE closed its doors in 1989, in Denmark No to Nuclear Weapons dissolved in 1992, in Sweden the Swedish Peace and Arbitration Society lost a third of its members, and in the United States SANE/Freeze, PSR, and WAND experienced declines in membership, volunteers, and income. On the international front, IPPNW survived, but suffered from losses in membership and activism.

Despite these setbacks, however, the nonaligned movement remained an active force in many nations. In Belgium, CNAPD and VAKA conducted a major campaign against modernization of NATO's short-range nuclear forces, including a demonstration in Brussels in April 1989 that the police claimed drew 21,000 people and organizers 75,000. In Norway, the Norwegian Peace Council formed an alliance for a comprehensive nuclear test ban that lobbied embassies, members of parliament, and governments. In the Philippines, powerful nationalist forces—including the press, the lawyers group, and the peasant group—citing the nuclear-free provision in the new constitution, grew increasingly vocal in their demand for the closure of the Subic and Clark Field military bases. Meanwhile, Indian activists continued a three-year effort to block the opening of a nuclear missile testing range in the state of Orissa. Although China remained as repressive as ever, the largest Uighur protest yet against Chinese nuclear testing occurred in May 1992, when some 10,000 people reportedly demonstrated at Kashgar. In Palau, the population—responding once more to pleas by activists—voted down the latest attempt by the U.S. government to override that island nation's nuclear-free constitution.

In the United States, as well, the movement retained some vigor. The nuclear-free zone campaign continued to grow, while peace and environmental groups united behind the Plutonium Challenge, which attacked the nuclear weapons complex on health, safety, and environmental grounds. Joined by the Military Production Network (a coalition of local citizens' groups), as well as by Greenpeace, the campaign against the nuclear weapons complex utilized informational work, nonviolent civil disobedience, and lawsuits to tangle it up in a maze of bad publicity and legal challenges. SANE/Freeze, the largest of the U.S. peace groups, was active in this campaign, and remained a powerful organization, with about 130,000 members in the fall of 1990. At the organization's August 1991 national convention, delegates set its priorities for the following year as working to foster nuclear disarmament, cut military spending, and end the international arms trade.

Thanks to the gradual growth of political freedom in Communist Eastern Europe, the movement there grew substantially. In the Soviet Union, new antimilitarist organizations appeared, most notably the Coalition for Civic Peace and the Russian Peace Society. They usually supported the Gorbachev-Shevardnadze foreign and military policy, just as party conservatives fulminated against it. In Poland, Freedom and Peace continued to promote demilitarization, and worked closely with the Solidarity movement. Its representatives served on Lech Walesa's Citizens' Committee, a quasi-parliament for the opposition. In Czechoslovakia, the Independent Peace Association continued its peace and antinuclear ventures.

Furthermore, as the struggle heightened against the Communist Old Order in East Germany, Czechoslovakia, Hungary, and Poland, independent peace activists emerged among the top leaders of the insurgency. In East Germany, Bärbel Bohley and Ulrike Poppe, two prominent antinuclear campaigners in East Berlin, founded New Forum and Democracy Now, organizations primarily responsible for the peaceful overthrow of the Communist government in the fall of 1989. In Czechoslovakia, Charter 77 provided a crucial ingredient in the "velvet revolution" that overcame the Communist regime. The prominence of peace activists in the upheavals of 1989 reflected not only their unusual courage but their relatively unique experience in fostering nonviolent opposition movements and nonviolent techniques of resisting militarized, repressive governments: peaceful protest rallies, human chains, mass leafleting, and civil disobedience. Many of these techniques were imparted to them by their West European allies, whose tumultuous agitation in the preceding years helped to shatter Eastern Europe's climate of fear and cynicism by demonstrating the possibilities for an aroused civil society.

Against this backdrop, it was hardly surprising that movement activists emerged as important leaders in the new, democratic governments. In East Germany, after the free elections of 1990, Pastor Eppelmann became the minister for defense and disarmament. In Czechoslovakia, the democratic revolution elevated two top Charter 77 activists—Václav Havel and Jiri Dienstbier—to the posts of president and foreign minister. Sakharov was elected to the new Soviet parliament, as was Roy Medvedev, the only Soviet signer of the original END Appeal. In Poland, Jacek Kuron became the minister of labor. Although these former activists were often preoccupied with their new governmental responsibilities, on occasion they did implement their antimilitary views. Eppelmann negotiated the withdrawal of all Soviet military forces from East-Central Europe. Sakharov became a leading critic of Soviet military intervention in Afghanistan and a prominent official spokesperson for nuclear disarmament.

Both during and after these dramatic events, nuclear disarmament campaigners from East and West worked closely together. In 1989, antinuclear scientists in the United States and the Soviet Union joined forces to demonstrate the feasibility of verifying the presence of nuclear weapons on board ship, thus undermining the conservative case that verification of nuclear disarmament on the high seas was impossible. As END's East European constituency grew, Tair Tairov, the organizer of the Civic Peace Coalition, arranged to host END's 1991 conference in Moscow—much to the dismay of the official Soviet Peace Committee. When, almost immediately after the event, Communist Party conservatives launched a coup to oust Gorbachev and restore themselves to power, Soviet peace activists played an important role in the popular resistance that halted the coup attempt. Delighted by the resistance, END's coordinating committee congratulated the Soviet activists, declaring that, "more than ever, we look forward to working closely with you . . . in all of Europe and beyond."

The most significant East-West antinuclear project was probably the struggle to end nuclear testing. As the anti-testing movement heightened in the United States, a parallel campaign began in the Soviet Union. Organized by Olzhas Suleimenov, a renowned Kazakh poet, it focused on halting nuclear tests at the Soviet test site, in Semipalatinsk. Initially, in recognition of protests by American activists at the Nevada weapons testing site, Soviet activists called the new movement Nevada, but it later came to be known as the Nevada-Semipalatinsk movement. Soon the movement was holding demonstrations throughout Kazakhstan. On August 6, 1989, to commemorate the Hiroshima bombing, 50,000 people attended one of its antinuclear rallies—the largest independent demonstration ever held in the Soviet Union. Following the ancient Kazakh custom of flinging stones into the face of evil, thousands of Kazakh citizens hurled rocks toward the test site.

Within a short time, this grassroots antinuclear campaign took on national and international dimensions. The Nevada-Semipalatinsk movement staged demonstrations throughout the Soviet Union, and eventually over a million people signed its antinuclear petition. On August 1, 1989, the Supreme Soviet adopted a resolution, written by Suleimenov, calling for a moratorium on all nuclear tests by the United States and the Soviet Union. By December, when Suleimenov visited the United States to confer with U.S. antinuclear leaders, the Soviet government admitted that, to appease the growing movement, it had canceled eleven out of eighteen underground nuclear tests. The movement, however, was not placated, and continued to grow. In April 1990, activists in the Soviet far north began a campaign to shut down the Soviet Union's other nuclear test site, located on a pair of islands called Novaya Zemlya. Meanwhile, Greenpeace joined the fray. That September, as a Greenpeace protest vessel sailed from one Soviet port to another, it was welcomed by local Soviet citizens—at least until it entered the Novaya Zemlya testing zone, where it was fired upon, boarded, and put under tow by far less appreciative Soviet border guards.

In the following months, the alliance against nuclear testing grew warmer. Enthusiastic delegations of activists from the United States and the Soviet Union swapped assignments by demonstrating at the testing sites in one another's countries. In addition, IPPNW and the Nevada-Semipalatinsk movement teamed up in May 1990 for an even more diverse event—an International Citizens Congress that convened in Alma Ata, Kazakhstan. The congress brought together some 300 delegates from dozens of antinuclear, peace, and environmental groups from 25 countries. In addition, it gathered a substantial number of "downwinders" and atomic bomb survivors from the Soviet Union, the United States, Japan, and the South Pacific, who shared stories of the cancer, genetic deformities, and leukemia that nuclear weapons had brought to their communities. Large crowds of local residents greeted the conference participants, including one of 20,000 cheering people carrying signs, flags, and placards.

Additional Victories, 1989–1992

Initially, the U.S. government resisted these priorities. Coming to office in January 1989, the new administration of George H. W. Bush was deeply skeptical of Reagan's turn toward peace and determined to keep it from going any further. Bush, himself, was appalled by Reagan's antinuclear talk at Reykjavik and by his "sentimental" attitude toward Gorbachev. Meeting with Roz Ridgway, one of Shultz's top aides at the State Department, the new Secretary of State, James Baker, asked her: "Don't you think you all went too far?" In the view of Bush's National Security Advisor, Brent Scowcroft, Reagan had "rushed to judgment" about the direction of the Soviet Union, and Gorbachev was "potentially more dangerous than his predecessors." Thus, immediately upon taking office, Bush ordered a halt to the U.S. government's nuclear arms control and disarmament program while his administration reconsidered its national security options. That February, as a "national security review" got under way, Bush told Scowcroft: "My own sense is that the Soviet challenge may be even greater than before." Month followed month without any plans for a resumption of U.S.-Soviet meetings. Gorbachev recalled that the situation became "quite alarming."

However, that spring, the Bush administration began to recognize the difficulties in obstructing arms control and disarmament. To counter Gorbachev's sweeping calls for disarmament, Bush and Baker put references into their speeches and press statements declaring that the U.S. government wanted to see "deeds, not words" from the Soviet Union. But, as White House press secretary Marlin Fitzwater complained, "the rest of America was rushing headlong into its infatuation with Gorbachev, and the press wasn't even printing our admonitions to demand more than promises." Fitzwater implored the President to "put the ball back in Gorbachev's court." At a White House meeting, a reporter asked the President about the "widespread impression" that he had "no foreign policy." Growing angry, Bush replied that "I've never heard such outrageous hypotheses!" A ripple of laughter went through the room. Clearly irked, the President continued: "I don't worry about that. And we *have* a foreign policy." In April, when George Kennan told the Senate Foreign Relations Committee that Bush had been "unresponsive" to recent "encouraging initiatives" from the Soviet Union, legislators, the audience, and even the committee stenographer responded with a standing ovation. Meanwhile, pressures for bold U.S. action mounted among allied leaders, who worried about adverse public reaction to the Bush administration's faltering commitment to nuclear disarmament. Geoffrey Howe, the British foreign secretary, urged the U.S. government to "get back in the game."

At the time, a key issue in "the game" was the future of short-range nuclear forces (SNF). Having reluctantly agreed to the elimination of all medium-range nuclear forces in Western Europe, the U.S. and British governments wanted to significantly upgrade and expand SNF missiles in that region. Meeting with his staff in February 1989, Baker told them that "any concession" on SNF modernization would provide "a classic slippery slope" toward a nuclear-free Europe. Defense Secretary Dick Cheney warned that the United States "must not fall into this dangerous trap" of SNF negotiations. But a number of West European governments, frightened at the prospect of a revival of public protest, resisted. Kohl told Thatcher bluntly that modernization and a refusal to negotiate on SNF missile reductions were "simply not sustainable politically in Germany." When Gorbachev heightened popular demands for nuclear disarmament by removing SNF missiles from Eastern Europe, Baker was horrified. The Secretary of State recalled: "We were losing the battle for public opinion. We had to do something. . . . NATO could not afford another crisis over deploying nuclear weapons." Thus, the Bush administration retreated, and agreed to negotiate missile reductions. In late 1989 and early 1990, with most NATO nations refusing to accept upgraded missiles, plans for SNF modernization were scrapped.

NATO's retreat on SNF marked the beginning of the end for the Bush administration's hard-line stance toward the Soviet Union. Pressed to respond to Gorbachev's initiatives, the administration agreed to hold a summit conference on Malta in December 1989. As late as October, Bush insisted that the summit would provide no more than a get-acquainted meeting. But, that fall, as Gorbachev and Shevardnadze (pressed by Soviet antinuclear scientists) agreed to separate SDI from a START agreement and as the dramatic events in Eastern Europe unfolded, including the opening of the Berlin Wall, it became impossible to hold to this minimalist position. Robert Blackwill, the NSC official responsible for Europe and the Soviet Union, told his colleagues: "The question now is how to satisfy the wild beast of public opinion." Baker, particularly, was determined not to be "outpropositioned" again by Gorbachev, and made the case for developing nuclear disarmament proposals that would put the U.S. government on the side of public opinion. At the conference, Bush told Gorbachev that he was committed to "reducing strategic offensive weapons" and fostering other disarmament measures, while Gorbachev assured Bush that his government was "devoted to continuation of the process of disarmament in all directions." The Soviet leader added, sympathetically, that "people simply meddle in policymaking," a fact that was "completely understandable since we are essentially talking about the issue of survival. And this kind of public sentiment is strongly affecting us, the politicians."

As a result, the START I treaty was ready for signing in July 1991. As the first treaty in history to reduce the numbers of strategic nuclear weapons, START I required both the United States and the Soviet Union to cut their strategic nuclear forces to 6,000 warheads, a reduction of nearly half of the deployed strategic weapons on each side. It also laid out an ambitious program for the dismantling of the missile launchers under extensive verification. For hawks in both nations, dedicated to maintaining or expanding their nuclear arsenals, the treaty represented a disaster. The following month, convinced that Gorbachev had betrayed the Soviet Union, Soviet hard-liners staged their coup in an attempt to remove him from power. But the presidents of the two nations considered the START treaty a triumph. As Gorbachev put it, the treaty's signing was "a moment of glory for the new thinking."

The START I treaty proved only the prelude to one of the most daring and far-reaching antinuclear actions ever taken by the great powers. On September 27, 1991, Bush announced that all U.S. ground-based tactical nuclear weapons would be destroyed, all seaborne tactical nuclear weapons would be removed from U.S. warships, and the number of air-delivered tactical nuclear weapons in Europe would be cut by 50 percent. In addition, he said, he was going to take all U.S. strategic bombers, as well as some land-based strategic missiles, off alert and was canceling plans for mobile ICBMs and short-range attack missiles. Although Gorbachev, in response, announced sweeping nuclear reductions of his own on October 5, Bush's measures were taken unilaterally, and neither nation bothered with verification.

Although Bush's extraordinary action largely reflected his desire to move quickly and dramatically enough to avoid the dispersion of tens of thousands of nuclear warheads located in the rapidly disintegrating Soviet Union, he had movement-driven motives as well. According to Scowcroft, the weapons withdrawals also resulted from the "undesirable" nature of SNF weapons in Germany and pressures from South Korea to remove U.S. nuclear weapons from that nation. In addition, "a number of countries were reluctant to allow our warships carrying nuclear weapons into their ports," especially Japan and New Zealand. Finally, as peace activists had maintained, Congress was less willing to fund weapons programs when the Soviet Union was less threatening. And Congress, recognizing the evaporating Cold War and public demands, did slash or eliminate U.S. weapons programs, thereby making disarmament an increasingly attractive option.

The movement also played an important role in shutting down nuclear weapons production facilities. Responding to a plea from SANE/Freeze's William Sloane Coffin, Jr. to suspend production of fissile material, Soviet officials summoned him to a meeting in Washington in late March 1989 to tell him that their government was giving the proposal "serious consideration." Two weeks later, Gorbachev announced a Soviet decision to halt the production of highly enriched uranium for military purposes—what he called a "major step toward the complete cessation of the production of fissionable materials for use in nuclear weapons." Meanwhile, in the United States, the campaign to close down the nuclear weapons complex neared success. In June 1989, responding to devastating revelations about the Rocky Flats nuclear weapons facility, federal agents raided it, seizing incriminating records and, in one plant alone, 59 pounds of radioactive dust. In addition, Congress slashed or eliminated funding for new nuclear facilities, while the administration abandoned plans to fund new nuclear facilities at Rocky Flats and Los Alamos and to reopen the plutonium-uranium extraction plant in Washington. Facing popular and legal challenges to the environmental and health hazards at nuclear weapons facilities all over the country, the Bush administration shut them down. By mid-1992, U.S. production and development of nuclear weapons had come to a halt.

The dramatic actions taken in the fall of 1991 were the last major nuclear disarmament ventures in which Gorbachev participated. Following the coup attempt of August 1991, Boris Yeltsin, president of the Russian Republic—a bitter opponent of Communist Party conservatives, but also a personal rival of Gorbachev's—elbowed him aside politically, arranged for the breakup of the nation that December, and left Gorbachev with little choice but to resign from his position as president of a Soviet Union that no longer existed. The longer-term cause of Gorbachev's downfall, however, was the inability of the Soviet Communist Party leadership to follow his path of reform. As one of his aides recalled: "He wanted to reform the party, to help it transform itself into something similar to a social-democratic party of a Western type. . . . But its leaders preferred suicide." Of course, they did not view their coup attempt in this light, but as a promising route toward the restoration of their power and the military might of the Soviet Union. But they failed—disgracing their party, destroying their nation, and ending the political careers of the remarkable reform leaders who had done so much to end the Cold War and the nuclear arms race.

Even so, for a time the antinuclear momentum continued. In response to the Nevada-Semipalatinsk movement, Soviet nuclear tests dropped to one in 1990. The following year, the Soviet minister responsible for the environment pointed out that the Semipalatinsk site "is for all practical purposes not working any more because of a huge grass-roots movement." After the August 1991 coup attempt, Kazakhstan's president officially closed it down. The Soviet government conducted its one nuclear test of 1990 at Novaya Zemlya, but this, too, provoked widespread protest, particularly among officials of the Russian Republic, where the site was located. In November 1991, responding to these protests, Yeltsin announced that Novaya Zemlya would no longer be used as a test site. Thus, Soviet nuclear testing, as well as testing in the nations that emerged from the disintegration of the Soviet Union, came to an end.

Although the Bush administration firmly opposed any limits on the U.S. nuclear testing program, antinuclear activists prevailed on this front, too. The first step came in 1990, with the election of Mike Kopetski, an Oregon Democrat, to the House of Representatives. Indebted to Oregon Peaceworks (the state affiliate of SANE/Freeze) for its political support and deeply affected by a demonstration in which he had participated at the Nevada nuclear testing site, Kopetski agreed to sponsor a Congressional measure to terminate funding for U.S. nuclear tests. The final legislation, promoted by peace groups and by the Democratic leadership, passed in the summer of 1992. It halted underground nuclear testing for nine months, placed strict conditions on further U.S. testing, and required test ban negotiations and an end to U.S. testing by late 1996. The Bush administration was dismayed, but did not dare to veto the legislation, for the measure's clever floor managers had attached it to the energy and water appropriations bill, which provided funding for the construction of the super-conducting super-collider, a $500 million project to be built in Texas. Securing this lucrative project for his home state, with its large bloc of electoral votes, was vital to Bush, who was engaged in an uphill battle for re-election. Thus, in October 1992, the President reluctantly signed the bill, noting that the section on nuclear testing was "highly objectionable" and that he would press for new legislation to reverse it. But Bush never had the opportunity, for that November he was defeated for re-election. Thus, years of efforts by the antinuclear movement came to fruition, and U.S. nuclear testing came to a halt.

Naturally, in this antinuclear atmosphere, it grew ever more difficult to employ nuclear weapons. In 1990, Adelman complained that "officials have come to consider their use totally out of the question, except when the nation's very survival would be at stake." That April, when NATO leaders were planning a joint communiqué, American officials insisted on inserting a phrase stating that nuclear arms were "weapons of last resort." Deeply disturbed, Thatcher felt that "we were slipping towards" the "fatal position" of "no first use of nuclear weapons." In fact, the U.S. government ruled out their use in the 1991 war against Iraq and the Soviet Union did not employ them in its war in Afghanistan—though neither country faced any danger of nuclear retaliation.

The progress made in Soviet-American nuclear disarmament did not show any signs of abating, for the new Russian and American leaders seemed eager to continue the policies of their predecessors. Although Russia's Yeltsin had little interest in the "new thinking" or in international relations, he did desire to improve his image among Russian citizens and among those of the West. Thus, he negotiated a further landmark nuclear disarmament agreement, the START II treaty. Signed by Bush and Yeltsin in January 1993, it made additional deep cuts in the two nations' strategic nuclear arsenals. Similarly, during his successful 1992 presidential campaign, Bill Clinton called for cutbacks in spending on nuclear production and testing and on the SDI program. In their place, Clinton urged preservation of the ABM treaty, ratification of the START treaties, and negotiation of a comprehensive test ban treaty. The United States, he maintained, should have "smaller nuclear arsenals" and had "no need to develop new nuclear weapons designs."

Elsewhere, too, antinuclear policies prevailed. Three of the new republics formed out of the Soviet Union—the Ukraine, Belarus, and Kazakhstan—agreed to divest themselves of all nuclear weapons. China announced that it would sign the nuclear nonproliferation treaty (NPT), as did North Korea. Brazil and Argentina, two longtime holdouts from the nonproliferation regime, formally renounced the manufacture or acquisition of nuclear weapons in late 1990. South Africa, which had produced its first nuclear weapons in 1980, began to dismantle and destroy them in 1990, and signed the NPT in 1991. Although Iraq worked to develop a nuclear weapons capability, India and Pakistan, which probably did have the capability, decided—at least temporarily—not to assemble, test, or deploy nuclear weapons. Even the British and

French governments, long hostile to any constraints on their own nuclear options, were caught up in the antinuclear tide. Both of them publicly renounced the use of nuclear weapons during the Gulf War, with Mitterrand calling it "a recourse to barbarian methods." The French government also announced its decision to adhere to the NPT and to reduce spending on its nuclear forces. In addition, the British and French governments responded to Bush's unilateral withdrawal of non-strategic nuclear weapons by reducing their own. Consequently, a large portion of the world's non-strategic nuclear weapons were removed from service.

Many of these and other antinuclear policies resulted from popular pressure. The South African apartheid regime, desperate to bolster its international image, decided in late 1988 to divest itself of its nuclear arsenal. As South African President F. W. de Klerk told his parliament, nuclear weapons were "an obstacle to the development of South Africa's international relations." In the Philippines, the popular clamor over nuclear weapons at U.S. military bases became so great that the Philippine legislature voted to close them down, thus ending nearly a century of American military presence in that nation. In New Zealand, popular support for the government's nuclear-free policy was so overwhelming that, when the opposition National Party won the 1990 elections, it retained the existing ban on admitting nuclear warships. As Labour's outgoing prime minister, David Lange, observed: "In the end, it was the ordinary people in New Zealand who made their country nuclear-free."

In France, the government announced in April 1992 that it was halting nuclear testing at Moruroa and was urging other nuclear powers to halt testing as well. Although French motives for this policy reversal remain unclear, two suggested at the time were to stop the embarrassing Greenpeace protests and to win favor with the 15 percent of French voters who, in nationwide elections, had just startled political pundits by voting for antinuclear parties.

Ironically, although government leaders adopted disarmament policies, they showed little respect for the antinuclear activists who had generated them. Gorbachev, of course, was an exception. Maintaining close contacts with leaders of the nuclear disarmament campaign, he invited Suleimenov to join him on an official trip to Britain. On one afternoon in June 1990, he spent four hours accepting awards from Western groups, mostly peace and disarmament organizations. By contrast, French officials responded to a new *Rainbow Warrior*'s crew members, who appeared at France's South Pacific test site to study radiation effects, by arresting and deporting them. In Czechoslovakia, the Communist regime worked until its demise to prosecute and imprison members of Charter 77, the Independent Peace Association, and the John Lennon Peace Club.

In the United States, the attitude of the Bush administration toward antinuclear campaigners was thoroughly contemptuous. Bernard Lown of IPPNW recalled that he had ready entrée to the prime ministers of Scandinavian countries, West Germany, and the Soviet Union, but could not meet with his own nation's President. When, at the request of Semipalatinsk disarmament activists, Lown sought to deliver to Bush a piece of sculpture from Kazakhstan—a mammoth's ivory tusk with "Long live peace without violence" carved on it— the President refused to receive him. On three occasions during the televised presidential and vice presidential campaign debates of October 1992, Bush and his running mate, Dan Quayle, denounced the Nuclear Freeze movement. Praising his administration for "winning the cold war," the President insisted that "we never would have got there if we'd gone for the Nuclear Freeze crowd." In January 1992, when Bush delivered his State of the Union address to Congress, even Gorbachev had been airbrushed out of the picture, with Bush proclaiming simply that the U.S. government had "won the Cold War." This self-serving triumphalism drew a standing ovation from the legislators—though, of course, it had little connection with reality.

The reality was that, despite the belittling of the movement by many government leaders, it had secured a remarkable string of victories. From 1985 to 1992 the antinuclear campaign mobilized enough public pressure to play a key role in halting the testing, production, and deployment of nuclear weapons by the United States and the Soviet Union. It also helped to secure the removal (and usually the destruction) of short-range, medium-range, and long-range nuclear weapons from nations where they had been deployed. Moreover, the movement and the antinuclear climate it generated influenced other nations to reduce their nuclear weaponry, to become nuclear-free, or to remain nuclear-free. As a result, the number of nuclear weapons in world arsenals declined very substantially and, perhaps most significant, nuclear powers resisted the temptation to use them. Thanks in large part to the efforts of the antinuclear movement, a safer world was emerging, increasingly free of the menace of nuclear annihilation.

9 Waning Movement, Reviving Arms Race, 1993–Present

The end of the Cold War, the widespread popular distaste for nuclear weapons, and the continued (although lessening) agitation of the antinuclear movement enhanced the possibilities for further strides toward a nuclear-free world. And there were some additional advances through 1996. But these proved to be the last major victories for the antinuclear campaign. As the nuclear disarmament movement faded and hawkish forces began to reassert themselves, the antinuclear momentum slowed and, then, disappeared. Freed from the constraints once placed upon them by a powerful nuclear disarmament movement, the governments of the great powers and their imitators gradually returned to their traditional practices.

A Waning Movement, 1993–1996

The popular mood of the early to mid-1990s provided a difficult terrain for the maintenance of antinuclear activism. "In these post–Cold War days," wrote a British CND leader, "one of the biggest problems for CND is that there is no longer a perception of danger amongst the general public with regard to nuclear weapons." Certainly, the antinuclear movement continued to decline. By the summer of 1993, the membership of SANE/Freeze had dropped to 53,000 and that of PSR to 21,000. In Britain, CND membership also shrank significantly. Some groups adopted different priorities. In Russia, peace activists threw themselves into opposition to the war in Chechnya. The Swedish Peace and Arbitration Society campaigned against landmines and the arms trade. Other groups disappeared entirely. END, once the great powerhouse of European protest against nuclear weapons, expired in late 1993.

Even so, a small but vigorous movement persisted. In Britain, CND campaigned against the Trident nuclear submarine and nuclear proliferation, as well as for a comprehensive test ban treaty. In the United States, SANE/Freeze (renamed Peace Action in 1993) continued its efforts for nuclear abolition and, during 1996, distributed more than a million voter guides on peace and disarmament issues. In India, the Committee for a Sane Nuclear Policy joined with other concerned groups to urge the five declared nuclear powers to halt nuclear testing and move toward complete nuclear disarmament. As in previous years, resistance to nuclear weapons was particularly widespread in Japan. Antinuclear activists in that nation circulated a new Appeal from Hiroshima and Nagasaki, drawing nearly 50 million signatures by 1995. Out of 3,300 Japanese municipalities, 1,964 proclaimed themselves nuclear-free zones by the end of that year. Meanwhile, Uighur protests against Chinese nuclear testing continued to erupt. In March 1993, when Chinese troops opened fire on a crowd of a thousand demonstrators outside the test site at Lop Nor, the enraged protesters stormed the complex—damaging equipment, setting fire to military vehicles and airplanes, and tearing down miles of electronic fencing.

On the international level, as well, the movement retained some strength. Drawing together many of the nonaligned groups, the International Peace Bureau grew into a substantial organization, with its own publications, projects, and headquarters in Geneva. By late 1994, it claimed affiliates in 41 countries, with a combined membership of between 3 and 4 million people. Furthermore, many activist groups, angered by the failure of the 1995 NPT review conference to secure a commitment to nuclear abolition by the nuclear powers, formed their own global network, Abolition 2000, dedicated to securing a treaty for the abolition of nuclear weapons by that year. According to polls in September 1995, 74 percent of the West European public considered nuclear weapons unnecessary. In the United States, a 1994 opinion survey found that 80 percent of the public backed a nuclear test ban treaty, and a 1995 poll reported that 60 percent favored eliminating "all nuclear arms in the world."

Indecision and Some Further Progress, 1993–1996

In the context of declining organizational pressure for nuclear disarmament, a number of major powers exhibited a new resistance to nuclear constraints. In Russia, where the Communists and right-wing nationalists did very well in the December 1995 elections, they helped block ratification of the START II treaty. In Britain, the government plunged ahead with the Trident submarine program and refused to join the U.S.-Russian-French moratorium on nuclear testing. Although China remained committed to a no first-use policy, it, too, resisted joining the testing moratorium. In France, the latest government military planning study reasserted the centrality of nuclear weapons in that nation's defense strategy.

Many other nations, however, retained a commitment to antinuclear priorities. In 1994, Brazil and Argentina finally ratified the 1967 Treaty of Tlatelolco, the South American nuclear-free zone treaty. Two years later, African nations signed the Treaty of Pelindaba, which turned Africa into a nuclear weapons-free zone. That same year, Southeast Asian nations signed the Treaty of Bangkok, which made their region a nuclear-free zone as well. These treaties, together with the 1959 Antarctic Treaty and the Treaty of Raratonga, had the effect of banning nuclear weapons from most of the Southern Hemisphere.

Another indication of the antinuclear stance of most nations was the outcome of the movement's World Court Project, designed to have the world body rule on the legality of nuclear weapons. Spearheaded by the International Peace Bureau, IPPNW, and the International Association of Lawyers Against Nuclear Arms, this proposal secured the backing of an overwhelming vote in the U.N. General Assembly, despite a fierce lobbying campaign against it by the nuclear powers. Taking up the case, the World Court ruled in July 1996 that "the threat or use of nuclear weapons" would "generally be contrary to the rules of international law applicable in armed conflict, and particularly the principles and rules of humanitarian law." Furthermore, the Court declared that "there exists an obligation to pursue in good faith and bring to a conclusion negotiations leading to nuclear disarmament in all its aspects."

In fact, the U.S. government, like the governments of the other nuclear powers, did not seem to feel this obligation very keenly. Although the Clinton team brought to Washington a number of figures with a more antinuclear orientation than their predecessors, cutting back on nuclear weapons did not have a high priority within the new administration. After all, domestic issues had provided the focus of Clinton's presidential campaign. Furthermore, Clinton was wary of challenging U.S. military officials, both because he had sidestepped military service during the Vietnam War and because they responded angrily to his early attempt to alter the Pentagon's opposition to gays in the armed forces. Also, Clinton and the new Vice President, Al Gore, were "New Democrats," eager to distance themselves from Democratic Party liberalism, and had fared poorly in the 1992 election, when they secured only 43 percent of the vote. Thus, the administration's early Nuclear Posture Review ended up reaffirming the status quo. It provided that U.S. strategic forces would drop no lower than START II levels, that nuclear weapons would be maintained in Europe at their current level, and that there would be no significant changes in operational policies, including the first use of nuclear weapons. The administration did implement the START I reductions, press the U.S. Senate to ratify the START II treaty, and propose a treaty to end production of fissile material for nuclear weapons. But the administration let further strategic arms negotiations lapse and, within the realm of nuclear arms controls, accorded the highest priority to non-proliferation, a policy that would restrict the nuclear advances of *other* nations.

The Clinton administration did make some progress on non-proliferation. In 1991, Congress had passed the Nunn-Lugar legislation to provide financial assistance to the states of the former Soviet Union in dismantling their nuclear weapons. But implementing this program did not proceed smoothly. The Ukraine, Kazakhstan, and Belarus began to hesitate about such disarmament, while congressional Republicans—egged on by their friends at the Heritage Foundation—preferred building new U.S. nuclear weapons to eliminating those threatening the United States. Eventually, though, the Clinton administration prevailed, and the three former Soviet republics were denuclearized.

An even trickier situation confronted U.S. officials in North Korea, which was discovered to be separating plutonium in violation of its NPT commitments. Although U.S. Secretary of State Warren Christopher called upon the North Korean government to abandon its nuclear aspirations, threatening sanctions if it did not, little progress was made until June 1994, when ex-President Jimmy Carter came to the rescue. Visiting North Korea, Carter reported that the Pyongyang government had agreed to halt its nuclear program as a prelude to negotiations. After months of tough bargaining, an "Agreed Framework" was reached in October. It provided that North Korea would adhere to the NPT, permit IAEA inspections, and take specific steps to freeze and later dismantle its nuclear weapons program. In return, the United States promised that it would not threaten North Korea with nuclear weapons and that it would provide that nation with heavy fuel oil shipments and light water nuclear reactors, which would supply nuclear power but not the plutonium that could be used for nuclear weapons.

Given the declining strength of the organized antinuclear campaign, it had little impact on these policies. In the preparation of the Clinton administration's Nuclear Posture Review, which peace groups derided as "Cold War Lite," they were completely outmaneuvered by military officials. The movement also lacked significant influence over nonproliferation policy. But one small victory occurred when the movement inhibited official suggestions for wider use of nuclear weapons. When press reports in March 1994 hinted that the Pentagon was changing U.S. policy that forbade targeting non-nuclear states, the Clinton administration issued a public denial. "The NGOs went ballistic," an NSC official recalled, "and we were forced to kick the can." Eventually, buffeted by conflicting pressures, the administration settled for ambiguity on this score.

Much of the movement's remaining strength went into the fight for a Comprehensive Test Ban Treaty (CTBT), and on this issue its efforts came none too soon. Despite the 1992 legislation halting U.S. nuclear testing and calling for the negotiation of a CTBT, in early 1993 the Clinton administration was getting ready for test resumption. The governments of the other nuclear powers, too, though temporarily abiding by the testing moratorium, indicated their interest in resuming nuclear tests—especially the British and French. Aware of the deteriorating situation, the movement sprang into action. In Britain, CND spearheaded the formation of a Nuclear Test Ban Coalition comprising peace, environmental, and development groups. It picketed, demonstrated, and circulated an anti-testing petition throughout the nation. Similar campaigns emerged in France and other European countries. In the United States, a broad range of antinuclear organizations—including Peace Action, PSR, the AFSC, and the Council for a Livable World—waged a concerted campaign to push the Clinton administration back on track. In late April, having pieced together the details of the emerging administration policy, they alerted knowledgeable reporters and key CTBT advocates in Congress. Together with fierce lobbying by antinuclear groups, this led to what the White House congressional liaison called "a firestorm" in the Democratic-controlled Congress. Senator Tom Harkin of Iowa dispatched a protest letter to the White House, signed by 38 senators. Congressman Kopetski sent another, signed by 159 representatives. Activist meetings with newspaper editorial boards helped produce a flood of anti-testing editorials. Meanwhile, a paper on nuclear testing, written by Frank von Hippel of the FAS and circulated by antinuclear activists, brought him to the attention of Hazel O'Leary, the new secretary of the Department of Energy. She invited him to two special meetings that she convened in mid-May to discuss the issue.

As a result, the tide turned in an antinuclear direction. "We got a pretty strong message from the Hill and from editorial pages not to test," a senior administration official admitted to the press. White House political and legislative affairs operatives added their voices against further testing. At a Cabinet meeting, O'Leary—convinced by von Hippel and other movement consultants that further testing was unnecessary—sided with ACDA's Thomas Graham in arguing for an extension of the moratorium and work for a CTBT. Deferring to O'Leary's authority over the weapons labs, Colin Powell, the JCS chair, dropped his opposition to that approach. Thus, in July 1993, the President announced that he would extend the U.S. testing moratorium and would strive to secure a CTBT by September 1996. In turn, Clinton's decision had the effect of boxing in other nuclear nations, which expressed varying degrees of irritation at the new policy—particularly Britain, which needed to use U.S. facilities if it were to conduct further tests.

But the victory was far from won, for almost immediately the nuclear powers began to renege on their commitments. On October 5, the Chinese government resumed nuclear testing. Meanwhile, the U.S. administration began to toy with the possibilities of limiting the treaty to ten years and exempting small-scale nuclear explosions from its provisions. In addition, in June 1995, France's new president, the conservative Jacques Chirac, announced that, although France would sign a CTBT in the future, it was resuming nuclear testing in the Pacific that September.

These actions produced another wave of popular protest. The movement condemned the Chinese nuclear tests and assailed the U.S. backsliding on treaty provisions. But it was the French plan that unleashed what the *Washington Post* called a "Typhoon of Anger." Antinuclear rallies and protests sprang up around the world. Responding to appeals by disarmament groups, consumers boycotted French goods, irate citizens poured French wine into the gutters, and Australian unions refused to handle French cargo or French postal and telecommunication services. Sales of French wines and champagne plummeted in Australia and New Zealand, and polls in the latter nation found that public opposition to the resumption of French nuclear tests hit an astonishing 98 percent. In Papeete, the capital of Tahiti, 15,000 people turned out to welcome the arrival of Greenpeace's *Rainbow Warrior II*, then en route to another protest in Moruroa, and to call upon the French not to test. In Sweden, French wine sales dropped by 50 percent. In France, thousands of Parisians demonstrated against their government's policy. In the United States, a coalition of 40 disarmament, religious, and environmental groups sparked a consumer boycott, while the U.S. Senate unanimously adopted a resolution condemning French and Chinese nuclear testing.

Confronted by this revival of the antinuclear movement, the nuclear powers retreated. The French government abruptly cut short its test series and, abandoning its earlier insistence upon exempting low-yield nuclear tests from a CTBT, suddenly announced that the future treaty should provide for "the banning of any nuclear weapon test." And this put the U.S. government on the spot. Impressed by the upsurge of public protest and no longer able to hide its own appetite for low-yield tests behind the stubbornness of the French, the Clinton administration announced that, henceforth, it would work to secure a total cutoff of nuclear testing.

Things remained largely on track thereafter. Making the test ban its top priority in 1996, Greenpeace organized demonstrations, confrontations, and even a protest voyage to China, whose government, in response to international pressure, announced in July 1996 that it was joining the worldwide moratorium. Activism accelerated in Britain and the United States. True to its promises, the Clinton administration did bring the other declared nuclear powers into line behind a CTBT. When India and Iran refused to cooperate, the Geneva negotiations broke down. But the Australian government brought the test ban treaty directly to the United Nations for endorsement. Pro-test ban groups around the world feverishly pressed their governments to back the Australian resolution. And at a U.N. General Assembly session of September 10, 1996, the representatives approved it by a vote of 158 to 3, opening the way for the CTBT's signature and ratification. Addressing the world body shortly after the vote, Madeleine Albright, the U.S. ambassador to the United Nations, declared: "This was a treaty sought by ordinary people everywhere, and today the power of that universal wish could not be denied."

The Downhill Slide, 1997–2000

Securing the test ban treaty proved to be the movement's last major victory for, beginning in 1997, nuclear arms control and disarmament policy began to unravel. The preconditions for this reverse course were set in previous years, and to a great extent reflected the movement's dwindling strength. But it also resulted from the rise of hawkish forces in Russia, France, India, and other nations, the low priority Clinton administration officials accorded to nuclear disarmament, and the conservative Republican dominance of the U.S. Congress that began with the 1994 elections. In addition, the sex scandals that engulfed Clinton and his administration distracted Americans from issues of greater magnitude and, furthermore, destroyed his ability to govern effectively. The stage was set for policy reversals.

Despite the previous great power talk of moving toward a nuclear-free world, there was little sign of it in the late 1990s. In November 1997, Clinton issued a Presidential Decision Directive reaffirming that the United States would rely on nuclear weapons for the "indefinite future." Indeed, responding to pressure from Jesse Helms, now chair of the Senate Foreign Relations Committee, the administration agreed to congressional legislation that abolished the Arms Control and Disarmament Agency. Meanwhile, the nuclear disarmament process ground to a halt. The Russian Duma—controlled by a hawkish bloc of Communists and right-wing nationalists—repeatedly refused to ratify START II, which led the U.S. government to block the opening of negotiations on a START III treaty. Although Russia's new president, Vladimir Putin, did manage to secure positive action on START II by the Duma in 2000, it voted on a different version of the treaty, thus leaving implementation up in the air. Consequently, at the end of Clinton's term of office, the two nations possessed a total of some 34,000 nuclear weapons, many of them on hair-trigger alert.

The crumbling of antinuclear policies was exemplified by the fate of the test ban treaty. Signed by more than 150 nations—the first of them the United States—the treaty was submitted by Clinton to the U.S. Senate for ratification in September 1997. "Out greatest asset," reported National Security Advisor Sandy Berger, "is the overwhelming support of the American people for the test ban," which the latest polls showed at 70 percent, with only 12.5 percent opposed. Nevertheless, Helms refused to allow the Senate Foreign Relations Committee to hold hearings on the CTBT, thus preventing it from reaching the Senate floor. And the Clinton administration, preoccupied with other matters, backed away from the issue.

Determined to rescue the CTBT, the major U.S. antinuclear organizations, united in the Coalition to Reduce Nuclear Dangers, vigorously promoted its Senate ratification. Coalition leaders pressed Clinton to lead a fight for the treaty, conferred on the issue with administration officials, and strategized with sympathetic senators. They also worked hard to ignite popular support—producing large quantities of pro-test ban literature, generating pro-CTBT editorials in most of the nation's major newspapers, and mobilizing assorted constituencies. By September 1998, they had lined up CTBT endorsements from hundreds of organizations, from the African Methodist Episcopal Church to the American Physical Society.

As a result, the test ban issue reached a climax in 1999. That January, the administration announced that it would make the treaty a priority, and Clinton used his State of the Union address to champion treaty ratification. Meanwhile, Democrats in the Senate, backing the CTBT, concluded that the time had come to force a vote on what they knew was a popular measure. By raising it in the context of a forthcoming election, they hoped to put enough pressure upon Republicans to split their ranks and secure treaty ratification. As bottling up the treaty in a Senate committee was causing embarrassment to the Republicans, Helms and GOP Senate Majority Leader Trent Lott agreed upon a new strategy to kill it. They would bring the CTBT to the Senate floor for a quick vote, thereby giving its supporters insufficient time to mobilize its broad but latent popular backing. Although test ban supporters, caught off guard by this maneuver, worked desperately to mobilize popular pressure, Helms, Lott, and other opponents had more than enough votes in the Senate, with its Republican majority, to deny the treaty the necessary two-thirds ratification vote that October. Thus, the United States failed to join other major powers in ratifying this landmark measure, which remained a dead letter.

The same downhill slide characterized the battle over National Missile Defense (NMD). By the mid-1990s, Republican support for this refurbished SDI program had hardened into a religious faith, which not even its dubious technological feasibility could shake. By contrast, most congressional Democrats and all disarmament groups viewed NMD as scientifically unsound, immensely costly, and likely to revive the nuclear arms race. The issue remained unresolved until shortly after Clinton's 1999 impeachment trial, when he agreed to stop battling against GOP plans for NMD and signed legislation that would permit the deployment of an NMD system "as soon as technologically possible." But when would that be? Disarmament groups waged a ferocious campaign to block NMD by postponing a decision on it to the next administration. Assailing NMD as the dog that "won't hunt," Peace Action attacked it through ads on television and in newspapers. Protest demonstrations erupted around the world. Finally, in September 2000, Clinton announced that he would leave the question of authorizing NMD to his successor. Although this victory was largely attributable to the movement, it boiled down to little more than a holding action.

The direction of nuclear arms control and disarmament policy was more positive in some other nations, particularly in Europe. In the spring of 1997, election victories in Britain by the Labour Party and in France by the Socialist Party produced governments with a greater interest in reducing their nations' reliance on nuclear weapons. In Britain, the new prime minister, Tony Blair, and a majority of his Cabinet were either former or current members of CND, while the new foreign secretary, Robin Cook, had also been a leader of END. Not surprisingly, both the British and French governments cut back their nuclear arsenals and quickly ratified the CTBT. Similarly, the victory of the Social Democratic and Green parties in the September 1998 German elections produced a more antinuclear government in that nation, as well. The new foreign secretary, Joschka Fischer of the Greens, floated the idea of dropping NATO's first-use policy. Leaders from all three governments spoke out against deployment of a missile defense system. Former antinuclear activists also became the foreign secretaries of the Czech Republic, Greece, and Albania, thereby strengthening the ranks of policymakers calling for nuclear restraint.

In a number of other nations, however, nuclear constraints were eroding. Despite some progress in implementing the Agreed Framework with North Korea, that country tested a new long-range ballistic missile in 1998. Meanwhile, with the assistance of outside suppliers, Iran and Iraq pursued efforts to develop nuclear weapons. Moreover, in Russia, where conventional military forces markedly declined, the government relied more heavily than in the past on nuclear weapons for its national defense. Symptomatically, during the war in Chechnya, Russian government officials threatened to use nuclear weapons, as did the Chechens. In addition, as Russia's economy and government controls crumbled, its fissile materials, nuclear expertise, and tactical nuclear weapons constituted an increasingly likely source of nuclear proliferation.

The most dramatic evidence of continued nuclear ambitions came in May 1998, when the governments of India and Pakistan conducted nuclear weapons tests, thus creating two additional nuclear nations. Since 1964, the BJP, a right-wing, Hindu nationalist party, had favored making India a nuclear power. And, with the BJP's victory in India's March 1998 elections, the new prime minister, Atal Bihari Vajpayee, gave an immediate order for test preparations. After the first nuclear explosions rocked the test site at Pokhran on May 11, Indian crowds danced and sang in the streets. Vajpayee proclaimed that the tests would "silence India's enemies and show India's strength," for "we have a big bomb now." Pakistanis, however, who viewed themselves as the targets for India's new weapons, were not silenced, and demands immediately arose to stand up to India by testing Pakistan's nuclear weapons. Vowing to prevent India's "nuclear domination," Pakistan's prime minister, Nawaz Sharif, ordered the beginning of his own country's nuclear test explosions.

Despite the nationalist appeal of "going nuclear," many Indians and Pakistanis expressed their dismay. An October 1998 poll in India—taken after the public had a chance to reflect upon the fact that it was now threatened by Pakistan's nuclear weapons—revealed that support for India's nuclear status had sagged to 44 percent. In November, the BJP suffered serious election defeats. Small antinuclear demonstrations occurred in Indian cities, assailing the nuclear tests as a moral calamity and as a scandalous diversion of resources in an impoverished nation. Demonstrations erupted in Pakistan, as well, and new antinuclear coalitions formed in both nations. The Pakistan Action Committee Against the Nuclear Arms Race excoriated the "jingoistic rhetoric of the nuclear lobbies," proclaiming that "it is high time the peoples of South Asia ... forced their governments to publicly announce the renunciation of nuclear tests and production of nuclear weapons and missiles." The Movement in India for Nuclear Disarmament declared that "the club of nuclear weapons-states has always been a collection of hypocrites," and "India has now put in its application for joining this club." It was "imperative that India return ... to the nuclear disarmament agenda. Our real security lies in a world free of nuclear weapons."

Appalled by the growth of the nuclear club, as well as by the overall lack of progress in disarmament, the foreign ministers of Brazil, Egypt, Ireland, Mexico, New Zealand, Slovenia, South Africa, and Sweden issued a joint declaration, "Toward a Nuclear Weapon-Free World," on June 9, 1998. Known as the New Agenda Coalition, this group of countries called on the nuclear nations "to commit themselves unequivocally to the elimination of their respective nuclear weapons and nuclear weapons capability and to agree to start work immediately on the practical steps and negotiations required for its achievement." That October, the coalition introduced a resolution at the U.N. General Assembly incorporating its nuclear abolition program. Though strongly opposed by the nuclear powers, the resolution carried that December by a vote of 114 to 18, with 38 abstentions. The General Assembly passed a similar resolution in December 1999.

The gathering revolt by non-nuclear nations fed into unusually firm antinuclear rhetoric by the world's governments at the NPT review conference of April-May 2000. Under strong pressure from the non-nuclear countries, the conferees agreed to take thirteen "practical steps" to implement the provisions of the treaty. Among them was an "unequivocal undertaking by the nuclear weapons states to accomplish the total elimination of their nuclear arsenals." Hailing the agreement, Kofi Annan, U.N. secretary general, called it "a significant step forward in humanity's pursuit of a world free of nuclear dangers." By contrast, nuclear disarmament groups were skeptical. And, in fact, nuclear abolition made little headway in subsequent years.

Despite these setbacks, the antinuclear movement persisted. A Canadian Network to Abolish Nuclear Weapons grew to seventeen national member groups and over ninety endorsing organizations. In Japan, both Gensuikyo and Gensuikin continued their antinuclear agitation, and protests erupted against Indian nuclear testing. In Sweden, Women for Peace organized a seminar on disarmament and promoted the work of the Abolition 2000 campaign. In Britain, CND provided media briefings, produced educational materials, erected billboards, placed advertisements, lobbied members of parliament, and worked with sympathetic groups. In the United States, Peace Action protested the Indian and Pakistani nuclear tests, demanded ratification of the CTBT, held demonstrations at the home offices of U.S. senators, and organized two rallies in Washington, highlighted by the appearance of eight giant missiles staging a futile "arms race" down Massachusetts Avenue. The FAS called for pressing ahead to START III and continued to churn out proposals for defusing nuclear confrontation. Dozens of cities and towns passed resolutions in favor of nuclear abolition.

Moreover, the movement maintained its international presence. The IPB, working with three other international organizations—IPPNW, the International Association of Lawyers Against Nuclear Arms, and the World Federalist Movement—convened an international gathering in May 1999 at the Hague. This Hague Appeal for Peace conference was an extraordinary event, for it drew ten thousand people from over a hundred countries, including Nobel Prize winners, the secretary general of the United Nations, and even some national government officials. Meanwhile, the Abolition 2000 movement continued to grow. By the year 2000, it had spread around the world, with more than 2,000 member groups. That April, it presented the president of the NPT review conference with an abolition petition signed by more than 13.4 million people.

Public opinion, too, remained strikingly antinuclear. A poll released in March 1998 showed that 92 percent of Canadians wanted their country to play a leadership role in promoting an international ban on nuclear weapons. Other polls indicated that 72 percent of Belgians, 87 percent of Britons, 87 percent of Germans, 87 percent of Americans, and 92 percent of Norwegians favored such a ban. Asked by pollsters in the fall of 1998 whether countries that possessed nuclear weapons should completely destroy them or keep them to protect themselves, 61 percent of Russians and 78 percent of Japanese favored destroying them.

But there was no hiding the fact that the movement was declining. Although the memberships of a few organizations grew slightly, for the most part they continued to fall during the late 1990s. Young people, particularly, failed to join nuclear disarmament groups, and there was a noticeable graying of their membership. CND, which once had mobilized many thousands of the restless young, no longer had a youth section by 1998. Furthermore, even among the members, there was markedly less participation. Mass demonstrations became relics of the past, while meetings grew smaller. In June 1998, when Maine Peace Action kicked off its "Town Meeting" campaign toward nuclear abolition with a public gathering in Portland, featuring a speech by Jonathan Schell, only ninety people attended the event. Symptomatically, Abolition 2000 lacked a strong central organization and drew only marginal support from its constituent groups. Even public opinion, though certainly antinuclear, was largely unfocused and uninformed. A Gallup poll taken a week after the U.S. Senate defeated ratification of the CTBT found that, although most Americans supported the treaty, 34 percent had never heard of it and only 26 percent knew that the Senate had rejected it.

Reviving the Nuclear Arms Race, 2001–2008

Movement weakness, political regression, and public ignorance were all evident as the world entered the twenty-first century. Thanks to a Republican sweep in the U.S. presidential and congressional elections of 2000, the new administration of President George W. Bush set about scrapping nuclear constraints. Jettisoning the CTBT, it pressed forward instead with plans for national missile defense, the system it believed would guarantee U.S. security and, thus, make arms controls unnecessary—at least for the United States. With the nation swept up in a patriotic frenzy after the terrorist attacks of September 11, 2001, Bush found it remarkably easy to sharply increase the Pentagon budget and cast aside arms control treaties. On December 13, he gave Russia notice that the United States was withdrawing from the ABM treaty to clear the way for U.S. tests of missile defense plans. Playing upon national fears, the President insisted that this withdrawal was necessary because the ABM treaty "hinders our government's ability to develop ways to protect our people from future terrorist or rogue-state missile attacks." Abandoning the ABM treaty also destroyed

START II, as the version of that treaty ratified by the Duma was based on ABM treaty protocols.

The Bush administration's heavy reliance upon nuclear weapons was illustrated by its Nuclear Posture Review. Submitted to Congress in January 2002, this Pentagon-prepared document ignored the U.S. commitment, at the NPT review conference of 2000, to eliminate nuclear weapons. Instead, based on the assumption that nuclear weapons would be part of U.S. military forces for at least the next half-century, it outlined an extensive range of programs to sustain and modernize America's existing nuclear arsenal. New U.S. nuclear weapons would "assure allies and friends," "dissuade competitors," "deter aggressors," and "defeat enemies." Furthermore, the posture review called for drafting contingency plans for nuclear attacks upon China, Iran, Iraq, Libya, North Korea, Russia, and Syria. As most of these countries did not possess nuclear weapons, the review provided a further indication of the growing willingness of U.S. officials to initiate nuclear war against non-nuclear nations.

In this context, nuclear disarmament was largely abandoned. During 2007, the U.S. government resumed production of nuclear weapons for the first time since 1992 and, also, voted against all of the fifteen nuclear disarmament measures that came before the U.N. General Assembly. Although, in May 2002, the U.S. and Russian governments signed a Strategic Offensive Reductions Treaty that provided for cutting the number of deployed strategic nuclear warheads by almost two-thirds by 2012, the treaty allowed the warheads to be placed in storage, thus enabling the two nations to quickly reassemble their previous nuclear arsenals. Furthermore, the warheads that remained deployed could be upgraded and improved, and there were no treaty provisions concerning verification or dealing with the large number of tactical nuclear weapons.

Nor did the picture look brighter elsewhere. As tensions heightened between India and Pakistan, with both countries preparing for a military showdown, they worked feverishly to develop their nuclear weaponry. The Indian government not only expanded the number of nuclear warheads it possessed, but worked to develop new missiles and—like the United States—a complete triad of nuclear delivery systems. Pakistan's government upgraded its nuclear arsenal, as well, while one of its top nuclear officials, A. Q. Khan, sold nuclear secrets and technology to Libya, Iran, and North Korea. For its part, the Iraqi government proved reluctant to give U.N. weapons inspectors complete information and access to alleged nuclear sites—largely, as was later learned, because it feared showing military weakness before neighboring Iran. In fact,

Iraq had no nuclear weapons or production facilities—although the Bush administration, claiming that it did, launched a bloody military invasion and occupation of that country. Iraq's destruction apparently convinced the North Korean government that it was next on Washington's hit list and, accordingly, it scrapped its agreement with the United States and produced its own nuclear weapons. Despite denials of similar plans by the Iranian government, U.N. inspections did raise suspicions that Iran was using its nuclear power program as the launching pad for a nuclear weapons capability. Meanwhile, in Britain and France, the governments brought forth proposals for the development of new nuclear weapons systems.

Of course, the remnants of the antinuclear movement continued to resist. Although opposing the Iraq War preoccupied the U.S. peace movement, the Council for a Livable World, Peace Action, PSR, and other antinuclear groups did vigorously challenge the Bush administration's nuclear weapons program. During the U.N.'s NPT review conference of 2005, thousands of Americans turned out for a nuclear abolition march and rally in New York City, making it the largest antinuclear demonstration in the United States for decades. In 2007, spirited protests took place at U.S. nuclear weapons development sites and at the University of California, where students staged hunger strikes to protest that institution's complicity in the ongoing U.S. nuclear weapons program. Peace Action roughly doubled in size, growing to 100,000 members. In June 2008, the U.S. Conference of Mayors unanimously voted to support the abolition of nuclear weapons.

Opposition to nuclear weapons also persisted around the world. CND led a tumultuous campaign in 2007 against the British government's development of a new nuclear weapons system, with one rally drawing 100,000 participants. After years of decline, CND's membership increased to 35,000. On the global level, IPPNW launched an International Campaign to Abolish Nuclear Weapons, which brought together the World Federation of United Nations Associations, Mayors for Peace, Abolition 2000, the WILPF, CND, and other organizations. The IPB, the world's largest peace and disarmament network, reinforced that antinuclear pressure, for by 2008 it had 282 member groups in 70 countries. And public opinion remained antinuclear. A poll taken in July 2007 found that eliminating all the world's nuclear weapons through an enforceable agreement drew the support of 74 percent of Americans, 78 percent of Israelis, 85 percent of Britons, 87 percent of the French, 95 percent of Germans, and 95 percent of Italians.

These and other antinuclear pressures continued to have some impact on policymakers. In Britain, the opposition to Trident's replacement proved so widespread that the government agreed to bring the issue back to parliament before final action was taken. Visiting India in early 2008, Prime Minister Gordon Brown pledged that Britain "will be at the forefront of the international campaign to accelerate disarmament ... and to ultimately achieve a world that is free from nuclear weapons." In the United States, both Republican- and Democratic-led congresses defeated every new nuclear weapons program proposed by the Bush administration. This included appropriations for the nuclear "bunker buster," "mini-nukes," and the "reliable replacement warhead." In 2008, rejecting the administration's latest plea for new nuclear weapons, Congress called instead for a far-reaching review of U.S. nuclear policy. Former top national security officials in both the United States and Britain repeatedly spoke out for nuclear abolition, as did the victorious U.S. presidential candidate, Barack Obama.

And yet, at the end of 2008, there were disturbing signs that the nuclear situation was deteriorating. Although, thanks to reductions in their nuclear weapons stockpiles by Russia, the United States, and some other nuclear powers, the number of nuclear weapons around the globe actually shrank, some 27,000 still existed—more than enough to destroy the world. Furthermore, some countries (such as India, Pakistan, and China) were increasing the size of their nuclear arsenals, others were "improving" them, and still others were interested in developing them. Tracking this situation, the editors of the *Bulletin of the Atomic Scientists* set the hands of their famous "doomsday clock" at five minutes to midnight—two minutes closer than at the clock's inception, in 1947.

Overall, then, the unraveling of nuclear arms control and disarmament policies in the years after 1993—despite the absence of the Cold War or other major conflicts among the great powers—underscored the degree to which progress in controlling nuclear weapons was dependent upon mobilizing public opposition to them. With this mobilization, nations made headway toward a nuclear-free world. Without it, national governments reverted to their traditional policies of seeking national security through military might. And the result was a nuclear arms race, with the ever-present danger of nuclear war.

Conclusion: Reflections on the Past and the Future

This study indicates that nuclear arms control and disarmament measures have resulted primarily from the efforts of a worldwide nuclear disarmament campaign, the biggest mass movement of modern history. Admittedly, this citizens' crusade was uneven—stronger in some countries than in others, addressing a variety of national circumstances, and waxing and waning over time. But, in the context of the nuclear arms race and threats of nuclear war, it had enough strength and cohesion to mobilize key institutions within civil society, including professional associations, unions, religious bodies, and political parties. Even within Communist-ruled Eastern Europe, where civil society barely existed, the movement gradually emerged as a force to be reckoned with—challenging dictatorial regimes and, ultimately, helping to sweep them away. At the core of the movement lay the educated middle class, particularly the liberal intelligentsia. At its periphery stood the general public, which, by and large, agreed with the movement's critique of the arms race and its demand for nuclear disarmament. Thus, at an exceptionally dangerous juncture in history, when numerous governments scrambled to build nuclear weapons and threatened to employ them for purposes of annihilation, concerned citizens played a central role in curbing the nuclear arms race and preventing nuclear war.

Furthermore, this book suggests that most government officials—particularly those of the major powers—had no intention of adopting nuclear arms control and disarmament policies. Instead, they grudgingly accepted such policies thanks to emergence of popular pressure. To be sure, a small group of government officials—among them Jawaharlal Nehru, Olof Palme, and Mikhail Gorbachev—did not need pressuring. They welcomed the antinuclear movement, either because they already shared its perspective or found its arguments convincing. But most officials had a more negative view of the nuclear disarmament campaign, for it challenged their reliance upon nuclear weapons to safeguard national security. And yet they could not ignore the movement, either, particularly when it reached high tide. Confronted by a vast wave of popular resistance, they concluded, reluctantly, that compromise had become the price of political survival. Consequently, they began to adapt their rhetoric and policies to the movement's program. They replaced ambitious plans to build, deploy, and use nuclear weapons with policies of nuclear disarmament and nuclear restraint.

Overall, this story of citizen activism for nuclear disarmament is a heartening one. Of course, most government leaders find it embarrassing, for it reveals them not as steely-eyed, self-confident shapers of national destiny, but as beleaguered, apprehensive officials, giving way to the demands of a restive public. This is not their preferred image of themselves. And it is certainly not the image they wish to convey to "enemy" nations—nations, they remain convinced, that are eagerly awaiting signs of "weakness" before commencing assaults upon the national ramparts. Nevertheless, persons farther from the centers of national power should take some satisfaction that, even within the closely guarded realm of national security, citizen activism—which might be considered the highest form of democracy—has some impact. More broadly, there is good news in the fact that, when it comes to nuclear weapons and nuclear war, the human race has shown the good sense, intelligence, and ability to avoid destroying itself.

Unfortunately, there is also some bad news: the nuclear arms race continues, with no sign that the Bomb is about to be banned. Despite the Herculean efforts of its critics and the popularity of their critique, tens of thousands of nuclear weapons remain in existence. Thousands remain on alert, ready to massacre hundreds of millions of men, women, and children and turn what is left of the earth into a radioactive wasteland. In the midst of worldwide recognition that nuclear war means planetary doom, this is a remarkable anomaly. It raises the question: Why have nations not taken the logical step of abolishing these weapons of global annihilation?

The answer lies in the pathology of the nation-state system. With no higher authority to set guidelines for national behavior or to resolve international disputes, nations traditionally have resorted to wars to secure the "national interest." To enhance the prospect of victory or merely to intimidate rival nations, national officials have drawn upon the most lethal weapons available to them. Since the 1940s, these have been nuclear weapons. Although antinuclear groups have argued that nuclear weapons are not weapons at all, but simply instruments of suicide, most national leaders *do* consider them weapons of war. And war is what they are preparing for in a world of rival nation-states. In this context, most national officials view disarmament, and especially nuclear disarmament, as an unnatural act. As U.N. Secretary General Kofi Annan put it: "In a world where states continue to compete for power, disarmament does not get proper scrutiny."

Given the tension between the widespread desire for nuclear disarmament and the national security priorities of the nation-state, nuclear policy usually has proved a rough compromise, unsatisfactory to either the nuclear enthusiast or critic. Often it takes the form of arms control, which regulates or stabilizes the arms race rather than bringing it to an end. The same tension often produces an ambiguous policy, with officials claiming that they favor nuclear disarmament while fostering the development of nuclear weapons or tacitly condoning the nuclear arsenals of their allies. Sometimes, of course, the balance of forces tips decisively and—based on which side has gained the upper hand—there will be either a surge in the nuclear arms race or a tilt toward nuclear disarmament. But, from the standpoint of abolishing nuclear weapons, the crucial fact remains that the location of the Bomb within the nation-state system—a system that throughout its history has produced arms races and wars—has set limits on progress toward a nuclear-free world.

What, then, will it take to abolish nuclear weapons? As this study suggests, it will certainly require a vigilant citizenry, supportive of peace and disarmament groups, that will settle for nothing less than banning the Bomb. But, in the context of war-making nations, it seems likely that it will take something more, something "deeper" than an attack upon specific weapons. What is that? Humanity's greatest prophets and ethical leaders have implored people to cast aside hatred and embrace love. If they did, they surely would cease murdering one another in wars or threatening one another with nuclear weapons. Unfortunately, however, we seem very far from this state of affairs and faced, instead, with a world in which fanatical nationalism and other forms of tribalism persist. Thus, although replacing hatred with love is desirable and certainly would lead to a nuclear-free world, it does not provide us with a timely solution to the problem of the nuclear arms race and its motor-force, the nation-state system.

Fortunately, however, the abolition of nuclear weapons does not require this profound a change in human behavior. If the roots of the nuclear problem lie in a pathological nation-state system, then we need to do no more (and should do no less) than change that system. Some of the necessary changes have been recognized for a century or more. Foremost among them is strengthening international authority so that it can provide an effective system of security for all nations. This process was begun with the creation of the League of Nations and the United Nations. It has been strengthened by the growth of international law and by the emergence of international peacekeeping operations. But many nations—and especially the great powers—though grudgingly supportive of this approach during World Wars I and II, when the nation-state system collapsed into anarchy, reneged on their commitment to international security in subsequent years. Rather than transfer some of their sovereignty to a world peacekeeping organization, they clung greedily to their traditional prerogatives. This betrayal of their commitment to an international security approach left the League of Nations and the United Nations too weak to handle many of the international crises that emerged. But if peace movements can force nations to follow through on creating an effective international security organization, they can pull the deadly fangs of the nation-state system. Working together, these citizens' movements (on the grassroots level) and a strengthened United Nations (on the global level) could rein in war-making states until, like New Jersey and New York, these semi-sovereign jurisdictions would never think of resolving their disputes through war, much less nuclear war.

Adopting a long-term strategy of taming the war-making nation-state through the creation of an effective international security system does not eliminate the need for pursuing a short-term strategy of fostering nuclear arms control and disarmament. Indeed, the two are complementary. Without a program that goes "deeper" than the weapons, we seem likely to be left, at best, with the present kinds of unsatisfactory, unstable compromises between arms races and disarmament. Conversely, without an arms control and disarmament strategy, we are likely to be obliterated in a nuclear holocaust long before our arrival in that new world of international peace and security. But by pursuing both strategies simultaneously, we have the possibility of turning back the threat of nuclear annihilation and, along the way, transcending the disgraceful international violence that has accompanied so much of the human experience.

We live at a potential turning point in human history, for the latest advances in the "art" of war—nuclear weapons—have forced upon us a momentous choice. If nations continue to follow the traditional "national security" paradigm, then—sooner or later—their leaders will resort to nuclear war, thus unleashing unspeakable horror upon the world. Conversely, this unprecedented danger could be overcome through arms control, disarmament, and transformation of the nation-state system. Are the people of the world capable of altering their traditional institutions of governance to meet this challenge? Are they ready for the new thinking about international relations necessitated by the nuclear age? If one looked solely at their long record of war, plunder, and other human folly, one might conclude that they are not. But an examination of the history of the nuclear disarmament movement inspires a greater respect for human potential. Indeed, defying the national barriers and the murderous traditions of the past, millions of people have joined hands to build a safer, saner world. Perhaps, after all, they will reach it.

Index

Libya, 218
Lilienthal, David, 30, 31, 33, 35. *See also* Acheson-Lilienthal Plan
Lis, Ladislav, 169
Live Without Armaments (West Germany), 119
Lodge, Henry Cabot, Jr., 79
London, antinuclear demonstrations, 82–83, 84, 119, 166
Los Alamos, 6–7, 13, 41, 200. *See also* Manhattan Project
Lott, Trent, 213
Lown, Bernard, 127–28, 131, 168, 181, 185, 204
Lucky Dragon, 52, 57–58, 75, 79

Macmillan, Harold, 72, 76, 102, 106, 107
Maine Peace Action, 217
Malenkov, Georgi, 43, 54
Manhattan Project: Chicago Metallurgical Laboratory (Met Lab), 3, 4, 5, 7, 13; conflict between scientists and officials, 3–8; expenditures, 5; scientists' opposition to atomic bomb use, 3–8, 13
Mao Zedong, 54, 76, 78
Marcos, Ferdinand, 125
Markey, Edward, 155
Marshall Islands: antinuclear protests, 179; health effects of nuclear tests, 126; occupation of islands, 125–26, 160–61; U.S. hydrogen bomb tests, 52–53, 58, 72–73, 78, 160–61
Maruki, Iri and Toshi, 10–11, 65
Massey, H. S. W., 35
Matlock, Jack, 186
MAUM, *see* Movement Against Uranium Mining
May 8 Movement (Belgium), 87–88
Mayors for Peace, 219
MCAA, *see* Movement Against Atomic Armament
McCarthy, Joseph, 35
McCartney, Paul, 84
McCloy, John, 6
McFarlane, Robert, 166, 173, 175–76, 186
McGovern, George, 94
McTaggart, David, 116
Medvedev, Roy, 126, 195
Melman, Seymour, 122
Mexico: government support of disarmament, 215; pacifists, 23; public opinion, 23, 95; world federalists, 23
Middle East, public opinion, 95. *See also individual countries*
Military Production Network, 194
Mitterrand, François, 150, 182, 203
Mobilization for Survival (U.S.), 121–22, 123
Moch, Jules, 88
Molander, Roger, 152
Mondale, Walter, 156
Moore, Eleanor, 17
Moruroa, French nuclear tests, 115, 116, 203, 210
Moscow: antinuclear demonstrations by foreigners, 91, 92, 97, 120–21; San Francisco to Moscow Walk, 92, 96–98, 101, 107; World Peace Council conferences, 99
Moscow Group to Establish Trust Between the USSR and the USA, 163, 165, 168, 179
Movement Against Atomic Armament (MCAA; France), 88–89
Movement against Further Testing, Manufacture, and Use of Nuclear Weapons (New Zealand), 65
Movement Against Uranium Mining (MAUM; Australia), 124
Movement for Disarmament, Peace, and Liberty (France), 120
Movement in India for Nuclear Disarmament, 215
Movement for Life and Peace (Argentina), 161
Movement for Peace (France), 26
Movement of Religion (Italy), 20
Muller, Hermann, 73
Murrow, Edward R., 12
Muste, A. J., 14, 68, 92, 94
MX missiles, 117, 122–23, 133, 142, 153, 175

Nagasaki bombing, 8; commemorations, 122; *hibakusha* (atomic-bomb affected

Protestant Churches: in Canada, 158; in East Germany, 127, 162; in France, 150; in Italy, 151; in Netherlands, 146; in United States, 155, 156, 167; in West Germany, 19, 148
Provance, Terry, 131
PSAC, *see* President's Science Advisory Committee
PSR, *see* Physicians for Social Responsibility
Psychological Strategy Board (U.S.), 37
PTBT, *see* Partial Test Ban Treaty
Public opinion: on British nuclear weapons program, 50, 59, 71, 145; on Euromissiles, 133–34, 145, 147, 149, 151; government attempts to manage, 72–73, 75; support of world federalism, 16, 17, 24, 28
Public opinion, antinuclear: in Australia, 17, 65, 85–86, 159; in Belgium, 178, 216; in Britain, 16, 39–40, 59, 60, 71, 76, 84, 102–3, 118, 145, 178, 216, 219; in Canada, 16, 85, 101, 106, 124, 157, 216; in Denmark, 61–62, 106, 178; in Finland, 150, 178; in France, 19, 89, 150–51, 178, 203, 219; in Germany, 216, 219; in Greece, 151; impact of nonaligned movement, 28; in India, 66; influence on governments, 70, 101, 106, 204, 220, 221–22; in Ireland, 178; in Israel, 219; in Italy, 20, 89, 151, 219; in Japan, 58, 91, 158, 216–17; in Latin America, 66; in Mexico, 23; in Middle East, 95; in Netherlands, 22, 61, 118, 147, 178; in New Zealand, 160, 210; in Norway, 70, 77, 106, 150, 178, 216; in Poland, 97–98; in Portugal, 178; in Russia, 216–17; in South Korea, 160, 199–200; in Soviet Union, 97; in Spain, 152; support for test ban treaty, 110, 123, 212–13, 217; in Sweden, 62, 86–87; in Third World, 66, 95; in United States, 15, 65, 93–94, 123, 157, 178, 187–88, 206, 216, 219; in Western Europe, 70, 152, 206; in West Germany, 19–20, 60, 61, 70, 87, 149. *See also* Arms control, public support
Pugwash Conferences on Science and

World Affairs, 98, 128; Austrian participants, 88; British government views, 71–72, 102; cancelled, 71; first, 56; Japanese participants, 90; Soviet participants, 67, 70, 95, 183; Soviet support, 100; Tito's approval, 68–69; U.S. government view of, 105; in Vienna, 69
Putin, Vladimir, 212

Quakers, 96. *See also* American Friends Service Committee; Friends Peace Committee
Quayle, Dan, 204

Rabinowitch, Eugene, 4, 5, 6, 7, 12–13, 72
Rainbow Warrior, 184, 203
Rainbow Warrior II, 210
Rakosi, Matyas, 46
Randle, Michael, 94, 116
Rarotanga, Treaty of, 170, 185, 207
Reagan, Nancy, 141, 186, 187
Reagan, Ronald: arms control views, 138, 139, 142, 174, 175; CPD membership, 142; criticism of antinuclear campaign, 165, 166; effects of pressure from disarmament movement, 173–76, 192; on Euromissiles, 170; European trips, 150, 167; "evil empire" speech, 142, 143, 167, 191; Geneva summit (1985), 178, 184, 186; INF treaty and, 189–90; on limited nuclear war, 143; Moscow summit (1988), 191–92; on nuclear war, 167–68, 174; presidential campaign (1980), 138, 139–40; presidential campaign (1984), 174–75; relations with Soviet Union, 142, 143, 174–75, 185, 186, 191–92, 197; Reykjavik summit (1986), 187, 188, 197; rhetorical changes, 167–68, 174–75; vision of nuclear-free world, 175, 197
Reagan administration: arms control policies, 142, 175, 176, 186–92; Euromissile issue, 167, 170, 173–74, 175; hawkish policies, 141–43, 152–53, 171, 172, 174; Iran-Contra scandal, 187–88; military buildup, 137–38, 139–40, 142–43, 153, 172; nuclear war policies, 167–68, 174, 176, 186, 192; responses to antinuclear

Wilson, Charles, 75
Wilson, Dagmar, 93
Winpisinger, William, 122
Wirthlin, Richard, 138, 139, 174
WMWFG, *see* World Movement for
World Federal Government
Women for Peace organizations, 120, 128,
145–46, 149, 164, 216
Women's Action for Nuclear Disarmament (WAND; U.S.), 153, 156, 193
Women's International League for Peace
and Freedom (WILPF): campaign
to abolish nuclear weapons, 219;
conferences, 20; in Eastern Europe,
47; effects of World War II, 9; FBI
surveillance, 74, 103; membership,
49; relations with Communist-led
movement, 27; Scandinavian branches,
21, 49, 50; Soviet views of, 43; support
of disarmament, 23; Swiss branch,
49; U.S. branch, 14, 153; West German
branch, 19
Women's peace activism: in Australia,
158–59; in Britain, 144–45, 169; in
Canada, 85, 101, 111, 114–15, 123–24; in
Denmark, 120, 149; international links,
98, 128; in Italy, 151; in Netherlands,
128, 145–46; in New Zealand, 86, 159;
in Norway, 120; peace camps, 144–45,
151, 153, 158–59, 164, 169; in Sweden,
120, 216; in Switzerland, 128; in United
States, 92–93, 103, 153; in West Germany, 128
Women Strike for Peace (WSP; U.S.):
activities, 92–93, 120; Carter and, 129–
30; FBI investigations of, 103; international meetings, 98; Kennedy administration and, 104, 105, 110; period of
decline, 112; test ban support, 110
Woodward, Mary, 86
Workers Defense Committee (KOR;
Poland), 163
World Association of Parliamentarians
for World Government, 55
World Citizens movement, 18, 19, 24, 49
World Congress of Intellectuals for Peace,
25

World Council of Churches, 55, 98, 164
World Court Project, 207
World Disarmament Campaign, 128
World Federalist Movement, 216
World Federalists of Canada, 16
World Federation of United Nations
Associations, 219
World government movement: atomic
energy control and, 31; in Australia,
17; in Belgium, 22; in Britain, 15–16;
in Canada, 16; in Denmark, 20; in
Eastern Europe, 22, 46, 47; in France,
18; growth, 24; history, 10; in Italy, 20;
in Japan, 12, 91; in Netherlands, 22;
in New Zealand, 17; in Norway, 21;
public support, 16, 17, 24, 28; relations
with Communist-led movement, 27;
scientists' support, 13; seen as linked
to Communists, 50; Soviet fear of,
44; in Sweden, 21; Third World support, 48; in United States, 13–14, 36;
U.S. government criticism, 36; United
World Federalists, 14, 36, 44; in West
Germany, 19
World Meeting for World Federal Government, 27
World Movement for World Federal Government (WMWFG), 17, 22, 24, 49
World Pacifist Meeting, 23
World Peace Congress, 25, 27
World Peace Council (WPC): in 1950s, 26;
in 1960s, 99; in 1970s, 128–29; in 1980s,
165, 168, 184; American members, 34;
conferences, 68, 99; Gorbachev's policies, 184; nonaligned movement's view
of, 27; organization, 26; pro-Soviet
views, 68, 128–29, 165; Reagan's view
of, 165; Soviet support, 42, 69, 100, 128,
130, 168
World Peace Day, 11, 17, 19, 22, 23
World War II: effects on pacifist organizations, 9; Manhattan Project, 3–8, 13;
Nagasaki bombing, 8, 11, 12–15, 36–37,
58, 122; scientists' opposition to atomic
bomb use, 5–6. *See also* Hiroshima
bombing
WPC, *see* World Peace Council

Stanford Nuclear Age Series

General Editor, Martin Sherwin

Confronting the Bomb: A Short History of the World Nuclear Disarmament Movement. Lawrence S. Wittner. 2009.

Apocalypse Management: Eisenhower and the Discourse of National Insecurity. Ira Chernus. 2008.

Spying on the Nuclear Bear: Anglo-American Intelligence and the Soviet Bomb. Michael S. Goodman. 2007.

The End of the Pacific War: Reappraisals. Edited by Tsuyoshi Hasegawa. 2007.

Eisenhower, Science Advice, and the Nuclear Test-Ban Debate, 1945–1963. Benjamin P. Greene. 2006.

A World Destroyed: Hiroshima and Its Legacies, 3rd edition. Martin Sherwin. 2003.

Averting 'The Final Failure': John F. Kennedy and the Secret Cuban Missile Crisis Meetings. Sheldon M. Stern. 2003.

The Struggle Against the Bomb, volume 3: *Toward Nuclear Abolition, A History of the World Nuclear Disarmament Movement, 1971–Present.* Lawrence S. Wittner. 2003.

Another Such Victory: President Truman and the Cold War, 1945–1953. Arnold A. Offner. 2002.

Einstein and Soviet Ideology. Alexander Vucinich. 2001.

Cardinal Choices: Presidential Science Advising from the Atomic Bomb to SDI. Revised and expanded edition. Gregg Herken. 2000.

'The Fate of the Earth' and 'The Abolition.' Jonathan Schell. With a new introduction by the author. 2000.

The Struggle Against the Bomb, volume 2: *Resisting the Bomb, A History of the World Nuclear Disarmament Movement, 1954–1970.* Lawrence S. Wittner. 1997.

James B. Conant: Harvard to Hiroshima and the Making of the Nuclear Age. James G. Hershberg. 1993.

The Struggle Against the Bomb, volume 1: *One World or None, A History of the World Nuclear Disarmament Movement Through 1953.* Lawrence S. Wittner. 1993.

A Preponderance of Power: National Security, the Truman Administration, and the Cold War. Melvyn P. Leffler. 1992.

The Wizards of Armageddon. Fred Kaplan. New foreword by Martin J. Sherwin. 1983. Reissued 1991.

Robert Oppenheimer: Letters and Recollections. Edited by Alice Kimball Smith and Charles Weiner. New foreword by Martin J. Sherwin. 1980. Reissued 1995.

The Advisors: Oppenheimer, Teller, and the Superbomb. By Herbert F. York. With a new Preface and Epilogue. Historical essay by Hans A. Bethe. 1976. Reissued 1989.

The Voice of the Dolphins and Other Stories. Leo Szilard. 1961. Reissued 1991.

Atomic Energy for Military Purposes. Henry D. Smith. Preface by Philip Morrison. 1945. New foreword 1989.